JOURNAL FOR THE STUDY OF THE OLD TESTAMENT
SUPPLEMENT SERIES
244

Editors
David J.A. Clines
Philip R. Davies

Executive Editor
John Jarick

Editorial Board
Robert P. Carroll, Richard J. Coggins, Alan Cooper, J. Cheryl Exum,
John Goldingay, Robert P. Gordon, Norman K. Gottwald,
Andrew D.H. Mayes, Carol Meyers, Patrick D. Miller

Sheffield Academic Press

Participants of the Lethbridge conference on urbanism from left to right: Front row: M. Fortin, E. Ben Zvi, T. Banning, C. Routledge, M. Tsipopoulou. Second row: R. Sweet, M. Sweet, A. Rosen, W. Dever, B. Routledge, B. MacKay. Third row: D. Redford, M. Daviau, W. Aufrecht, L. Herr, N. Mirau, D. Rupp. Not pictured: S. Rosen.

Urbanism in Antiquity

From Mesopotamia to Crete

edited by
Walter E. Aufrecht, Neil A. Mirau
& Steven W. Gauley

Journal for the Study of the Old Testament
Supplement Series 244

For
Richard J. Scheuer

Copyright © 1997 Sheffield Academic Press

Published by Sheffield Academic Press Ltd
Mansion House
19 Kingfield Road
Sheffield S11 9AS
England

Printed on acid-free paper in Great Britain
by Bookcraft Ltd
Midsomer Norton, Bath

British Library Cataloguing in Publication Data

A catalogue record for this book is available
from the British Library

ISBN 1-85075-666-X

CONTENTS

Foreword   7
Abbreviations   8
List of Contributors   11
Introduction   13

E.B. BANNING
Spatial Perspectives on Early Urban Development in Mesopotamia   17

RONALD F.G. SWEET
Writing as a Factor in the Rise of Urbanism   35

MICHEL FORTIN
Urbanisation et 'redistribution' de surplus agricoles
en Mésopotamie septentrionale (3000–2500 av. J.-C.)   50

STEVEN A. ROSEN
Craft Specialization and the Rise of Secondary Urbanism:
A View from the Southern Levant   82

ARLENE MILLER ROSEN
The Agricultural Base of Urbanism
in the Early Bronze II–III Levant   92

NEIL A. MIRAU
The Social Context of Early Iron Working in the Levant   99

WALTER E. AUFRECHT
Urbanization and Northwest Semitic Inscriptions
of the Late Bronze and Iron Ages   116

BRUCE ROUTLEDGE
Learning to Love the King:
Urbanism and the State in Iron Age Moab   130

LARRY G. HERR
Urbanism at Tell el-'Umeiri
during the Late Bronze IIB–Iron IA Transition   145

P.M. MICHÈLE DAVIAU
Tell Jawa:
A Case Study of Ammonite Urbanism during Iron Age II   156

WILLIAM G. DEVER
Archaeology, Urbanism, and the Rise of the Israelite State   172

EHUD BEN ZVI
The Urban Center of Jerusalem and the Development
of the Literature of the Hebrew Bible   194

DONALD B. REDFORD
The Ancient Egyptian 'City': Figment or Reality?   210

CAROLYN ROUTLEDGE
Temple as the Center in Ancient Egyptian Urbanism   221

DAVID W. RUPP
'Metro' Nea Paphos: Suburban Sprawl in Southwestern Cyprus
in the Hellenistic and Earlier Roman Periods   236

METAXIA TSIPOPOULOU
Palace-Centered Polities in Eastern Crete:
Neopalatial Petras and its Neighbors   263

D. BRUCE MACKAY
A View from the Outskirts: Realignments from Modern
to Postmodern in the Archaeological Study of Urbanism   278

Index of Authors   286

FOREWORD

We at The University of Lethbridge are proud of our emphasis on the Liberal Arts. We feel that an appreciation of the Liberal Arts helps us not only to increase our awareness of who we are, but increases our appreciation and enjoyment of life itself. Archaeology, as I see it, has a strong element of art.

As a scientist, I am aware of and appreciate the contribution of past scientists. We build on the shoulders of scientists of yesterday. Many great past discoveries may seem commonplace to us today, but in their day, they were great advances. Looking back, we realize that these past discoveries have permitted others to make advances that have contributed to our own welfare and enjoyment.

Archaeology is also a science. Archaeologists have the challenging problem of understanding what people in the past did and the advances that they made. The lack of written texts does not lessen the importance of the 'breakthroughs' that resulted in the development of past civilizations. It is the work of archaeologists that enables us to understand these ancient civilizations, to understand ourselves and our civilization.

I am pleased to note that, in addition to the many scholars from across Canada who participated in this conference, there were scholars from Greece, Israel and the United States of America. Their visit enlivened our community and enriched our knowledge.

Dr Robert Hironaka
Chancellor, The University of Lethbridge

ABBREVIATIONS

AA	*American Anthropologist*
AAAS	*Annales archéologiques arabes syriennes*
AASOR	Annual of the American Schools of Oriental Research
ABD	D.N. Freedman (ed.), *Anchor Bible Dictionary*
AcAr	*Acta Archaeologica*
ADAJ	*Annual of the Department of Antiquities of Jordan*
AfO	Archiv für Orientforschung
AJA	*American Journal of Archaeology*
Akk	*Akkadica*
Ant	*Antiquity*
AmAnt	*American Antiquity*
ARA	*Annual Review of Anthropology*
AS	*Anatolian Studies*
ASHL	*The Archaeology of Society in the Holy Land* (ed. T.E. Levy; New York: Facts on File)
ATU	*Archaische Texte aus Uruk* (Berlin: Gebr. Mann)
AUSS	*Andrews University Seminary Studies*
BA	*Biblical Archaeologist*
BAR	*Biblical Archaeology Review*
BASOR	*Bulletin of the American Schools of Oriental Research*
BAT	*Biblical Archaeology Today: Proceedings of the International Congress on Biblical Archaeology, Jerusalem, April 1984* (ed. J. Amitai; Jerusalem: Israel Exploration Society, Israel Academy of Sciences and Humanities, American Schools of Oriental Research, 1985)
BATS	*Biblical Archaeology Today, 1990: Proceedings of the Second International Congress on Biblical Archeology, Pre-Congress Symposium: Population, Production and Power, Jerusalem, June 1990, Supplement* (ed. A. Biran and J. Aviram; Jerusalem: Israel Exploration Society, 1993)
BCH	*Bulletin de Correspondance Hellénique*
BCSMS	*Bulletin of the Canadian Society for Mesopotamian Studies*
BeO	*Bibbia e oriente*
BIFAO	*Bulletin de l'institut français d'archéologie orientale*
BRev	*Bible Review*
BO	*Bibliotheca orientalis*

BSA	Annual of the British School in Athens
CA	*Current Anthropology*
CR:BS	*Currents in Research: Biblical Studies*
CRIPEL	*Cahiers de recherches de l'institut de Papyrologie et d'Egyptologie de Lille*
Er-Is	*Eretz-Israel*
Geo	*Geoarchaeology*
HTR	*Harvard Theological Review*
HUCA	Hebrew University College Annual
IEJ	*Israel Exploration Journal*
JAA	*Journal of Anthropological Archaeology*
JAR	*Journal of Anthropological Research*
JARCE	*Journal of the American Research Center in Egypt*
JBL	*Journal of Biblical Literature*
JEA	*Journal of Egyptian Archeology*
JESHO	*Journal of the Economic and Social History of the Orient*
JFA	*Journal of Field Archaeology*
JMA	*Journal of Mediterranean Archaeology*
JNES	*Journal of Near Eastern Studies*
JNSL	*Journal of the Northwest Semitic Languages*
JR	*Journal of Religion*
JRom	*Journal of Roman Studies*
JRS	*Journal of Religious Studies*
JSOT	*Journal for the Study of the Old Testament*
JSP	*Journal for the Study of the Pseudepigrapha*
LASBF	*Liber Annuus Studii Biblici Franciscani*
LdÄ	*Lexicon der Ägyptologie*
Lev	*Levant*
MARI	*Mari, Annales de recherches interdisciplinaires*
MDAIK	*Mitteilungen des deutschen archäologischen Institut, Kairo*
MDOG	Mitteilungen der deutschen Orient-Gesellschaft
Meso	*Mesopotamia*
MMA	*Monographs in Mediterranean Archaeology*
NABU	*Nouvelles assyriologiques brèves et utilitaires*
NEAEHL	*The New Encyclopedia of the Archaeological Excavations in the Holy Land* (ed. E. Stern *et al.*; New York: Simon & Schuster, 1993)
OLP	Orientalia lovaniensia periodica
Or	*Orientalia*
PAM	*Polish Archaeology in the Mediterranean*
PEFA	Palestine Exploration Fund Annual
PEQ	*Palestine Exploration Quarterly*
PGL	*Phoinikeia Grammata, Lire et écrire en Méditerranée* (ed. C. Baaurain, C. Bonnet and V. Krings; Namur: Sociéte des Etudes Classiques, 1991)

RA	*Revue d'assyriologie et d'archéologie orientale*
RB	*Revue biblique*
RDAC	Department of Antiquities of Cyprus, Annual Report
RevArch	*Revue archéologique*
SciAm	*Scientific American*
Sem	*Semitica*
SJOT	*Scandinavian Journal of the Old Testament*
TA	*Tel Aviv*
TCY	*The Crisis Years: The Twelfth Century BC* (ed. W.A. Ward and M.S. Joukowsky; Dubuque: Kendall Hunt, 1992)
Trans	*Transeuphratène*
UF	*Ugarit-Forschungen*
WA	*World Archaeology*
WO	*Die Welt des Orients*
ZAH	*Zeitschrift für Althebräistic*
ZAW	*Zeitschrift für die alttestamentliche Wissenschaft*
ZDPV	*Zeitschrift für des deutschen Palästina-Vereins*
ZfA	*Zeitschrift für Assyrologie*

LIST OF CONTRIBUTORS

Walter E. Aufrecht, Professor of Archaeology, The University of Lethbridge, Lethbridge, Alberta T1K 3M4, Canada

E.B. Banning, Associate Professor of Anthropology, University of Toronto, Toronto, Ontario M5S 1A1, Canada

Edud Ben Zvi, Associate Professor of Religious Studies, University of Alberta, Edmonton, Alberta T6G 2E6, Canada

P.M. Michèle Daviau, Associate Professor of Archaeology, Wilfrid Laurier University, Walterloo, Ontario N2L 3C5, Canada

William G. Dever, Professor of Near Eastern Archaeology and Anthropology, University of Arizona, Tucson, Arizona 85721, USA

Michel Fortin, Professeur titulaire d'archéologie de l'Université Laval, Québec City, Québec G1K 7P4, Canada

Larry G. Herr, Professor of Religious Studies, Canadian Union College, Lacombe, Alberta T4L 2E5, Canada

D. Bruce MacKay, Assistant Professor of Archaeology, The University of Lethbridge, Lethbridge, Alberta T1K 3M4, Canada

Neil A. Mirau, Assistant Professor of Archaeology, The University of Lethbridge, Lethbridge, Alberta T1K 3M4, Canada

Donald B. Redford, Professor of Egyptology, University of Toronto, Toronto, Ontario M5S 1A1, Canada

Arlene Miller Rosen, Adjunct Professor of Archaeology, Ben Gurion University of the Negev, Beersheba 84105, Israel

Steven A. Rosen, Professor of Archaeology, Ben Gurion University of the Negev, Beersheba 84105, Israel

Bruce Routledge, Assistant Professor of Archaeology, University of Pennsylvania, Philadelphia, Pennsylvania 19104, USA

Carolyn Routledge, Department of Near Eastern Studies, University of Toronto, Toronto M5S 1A1, Ontario

David W. Rupp, Professor of Classics, Brock University, St Catharines, Ontario L2S 3A1, Canada

Ronald F.G. Sweet, Professor of Assyriology, Emeritus, University of Toronto, Toronto, Ontario M5S 1A1, Canada

Metaxia Tsipopoulou, KD' Ephoreia of Prehistoric and Classical Antiquities, Polytechneiou 10, Ayios Nicolaos, Crete 72 100, Greece

INTRODUCTION

In January 1996, two of the editors of this volume, Aufrecht and Mirau, co-chaired a conference entitled 'The Origins and Development of Urbanism in the Ancient Near East' at The University of Lethbridge in Alberta, Canada. The conference was organized to provide a forum to examine what we believe to be fundamental issues in archaeology in general and the archaeology of the ancient Near East in particular. As the title indicates, those issues revolve around the emergence of cities and their role as a primary component of all complex cultures, past and present. The ancient Near East (expanded perhaps a bit for the purposes of the conference to include Crete and Cyprus!) has been called the 'Cradle of Western Civilization'. It was there that the first cities emerged. The subsequent development in the Near East, and elsewhere, of complex societies has fundamentally altered the way in which the majority of humans think and act, and this is due in no small part to ancient cities and the people in those cities.

The city, in fact, has become the dominant form of human settlement in so-called developed countries. Furthermore, as increasing numbers of people in 'developing' and 'underdeveloped' countries of the world move to cities, urban existence has become a necessary, if not always desirable, way of life. Many, especially those in the world's more developed countries, would find survival outside of an urban environment difficult if not impossible. Indeed, most cultures have become the product of developments that mostly take place within cities, and it appears that the city will continue to dominate as a primary element of these cultures for the foreseeable future.

We tend to take cities for granted, to regard them as part of the natural state of affairs for human cultures. That is, we see cities as a logical outcome of the evolution of our cultures. The matter of origin and development of cities is, however, far from a natural outcome of 'cultural evolution'. In fact, our understanding of how cities first developed and the ideological, political, environmental, technological, economic and other pressures which precipitated the emergence of the first urban cultures is still weak.

A fundamental goal of our conference and this volume, is to identify and investigate problems and issues which will help improve our understanding of cities, their origins and paths of development, and how they were affected by technological, political, economic, ideological and environmental problems and issues. This is not to say that we intended to answer all or even many of the questions that can be asked regarding urbanism and its role in the development of complex cultures. Rather we wanted to bring some of the issues into debate and discussion and from there, hopefully, provide some insights into some important elements and outcomes of urbanism in the ancient Near East.

We believe that the conference participants who are the authors of the papers in this volume have indeed identified and investigated some of these fundamental problems and issues of the origins and development of urbanism. They brought with them a variety of experiences, expertise and theoretical approaches that resulted in significant debate as the conference papers were presented and in the informal sessions afterwards. The participants were able to critique the views of others and have their own positions likewise critiqued in an atmosphere that was cordial, candid and academically and intellectually challenging. Despite these debates, we believe the authors are united in their view that the subject of the conference and this volume is central to the archaeology and history of not only the ancient Near East, but to all of us who are heirs of the cultural developments which occurred in the Near East in antiquity.

Lethbridge in January can be a pleasant place to hold a conference such as this. Alas, January of 1996 was not one of those times. As the conference opened, we had a record-setting cold spell of arctic temperatures. But that did not impede our goals. We brought some real (not to say lively!) archaeological debate and exchange to our small but interested and interesting archaeological community at the university and in Southern Alberta. The conference participants came from across Canada and abroad, from places that were warmer than Lethbridge. Despite the cold, they all expressed their enjoyment and enthusiasm at being here and participating in the conference. We know that they sacrificed much time and effort in the preparation of their papers, and in actually getting to Lethbridge. We are extremely grateful to them.

All of the papers of the conference are included here, except one. D. Bruce MacKay lectured on urbanization at Tell Miqne/Ekron, but for reasons beyond his control, his paper could not be published. Despite this disappointment, we are grateful that Bruce agreed to our suggestion that he 'pull together' the results of the conference into a summary paper. To our delight and appreciation, it is included in this volume as the final essay, and it's a humdinger. We suspect that it will generate some talk in its own right.

We would also like to acknowledge and express our gratitude to the many individuals and organizations who assisted with the conference and the preparation of this volume. Within The University of Lethbridge, these are: the Department of Geography (where we archaeologists have our academic home); the Student's Union; the Department of Theatre and Dramatic Arts; and Conferences Services. We are grateful to Dr Robert Hironaka, Chancellor of The University of Lethbridge, whose warm welcome on behalf of the university is printed in this volume. To our colleagues who not only gave us their enthusiastic support, time, and effort, and some of whom also participated in the conference, we are deeply grateful. They are: René Barendregt, James Byrne, Lisa Doolittle, John Dormaar, Dan Johnson, Tom Johnston, Dennis Sheppard, Larry Steinbrenner, Leanne Wehlage, Ian MacLachlan, Rod McNaughton, Heather Mirau, and most especially Geography Department Chairman Robert Rogerson, whose encouragement and advice never ceased—nor ceased to amaze.

We are indebted to and grateful for our students. They helped us with endless details, from running errands and slide projectors to dog sitting. And they too attended the conference! They are: Stephanie Cardinal, Jason Gallespie, Fred Green, Marko Hilgersom, Colin McDonald, Kevin McGeough, Joshua Richholt and Shelly Rouse.

We want to express our sincere thanks and gratitude to those agencies who provided funding, without which the conference could not have been held. They are: the H.R. and Helen Scheuer Foundation of New York, the Social Sciences and Humanities Research Council of Canada, the American Schools of Oriental Research in Canada and the Archaeological Society of Alberta.

We wish to acknowledge and thank Kevin McGeough for catching errors large and small; and Philip Davies, his staff and Sheffield

Academic Press for their efforts, patience and, ultimately, the publication of this volume.

Finally, we offer thanks to Richard J. Scheuer. His generous contribution to our conference really *did* make it possible. Dick Scheuer's generosity is exceeded only by his modesty, a characteristic which all too often hinders the recognition he deserves. To impede that, and to express gratitude, respect and affection, we dedicate this volume to him.

The Editors
Lethbridge, Alberta
November 1996

SPATIAL PERSPECTIVES ON EARLY URBAN DEVELOPMENT IN MESOPOTAMIA

E.B. Banning

When V. Gordon Childe (1950) proposed ten characteristics to define early urbanism, he concentrated on features of social, economic and intellectual institutions that one would expect to find in urban centres, and not on the relationships of these centres with the hinterlands that must have supported those institutions. Although Childe recognized that craft specialists, for example, many of whom produced luxuries for the elite, would depend on a rural surplus, he did not dwell on such issues as how the centre, or its elite, was able to extract this surplus from outlying villages or farms. More recent researchers, including Adams (1965, 1981), Adams and Nissen (1972), Wright (1969, 1977), Johnson (1977, 1980), Kowalewski (1982), Falconer and Savage (1995), have attempted to interpret spatial patterning in site distributions at the regional scale in terms of settlement hierarchy and political and economic control. Nor did Childe specifically explore archaeologically accessible evidence for any changes in social institutions, at the level of household or lineage, that we might expect to accompany the rapid concentration of power in the hands of a few families at the expense of the many. Where there have been reasonably large horizontal exposures of sites followed by reasonably thorough publication of architecture and find-spots, however, patterns in the spatial organization of houses and neighborhoods may reveal hints of changes in social organization (Henrickson 1981; Stone 1981; Stone 1987).

The following will briefly review some of these attempts and present the possible directions of future research in these areas.

Site Hierarchies in the Ancient Near East

The single greatest contribution to the study of early urban systems at the regional scale was the group of surveys conducted in the Diyalah and Uruk regions in the 1950s and 1960s (Jacobsen and Adams 1958; Adams 1965; Adams 1981; Adams and Nissen 1972). These ambitious surveys not only made a large body of data available to other scholars, but also spurred other researchers to carry out similar, and in some cases more sophisticated, surveys in other parts of the Near East.

Adams was able to use data derived from the surveys to draw attention to some interesting changes in the distribution of sites by size that he connected with important changes in political organization. He noted that in the Uruk region, by the Uruk Period, there was a distinctly bimodal site-size distribution, with the single site of Uruk itself absorbing 65–75 per cent of the regional population. The establishment of true urbanism, to some people's surprise, seemed to correspond with the disappearance of many second- and third-rank sites and a concentration of almost the entire population into the highest ranked site in the settlement hierarchy.

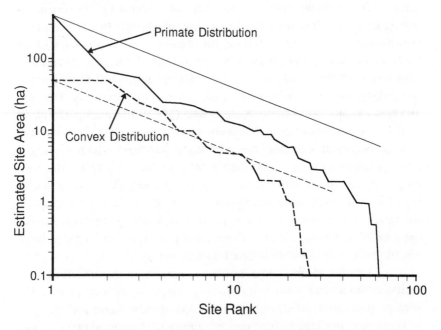

Figure 1. Early Dynastic I rank–size distributions for the Uruk (solid lines) and Adab–Nippur (dashed lines) settlement systems (after Falconer and Savage 1995). The former is a primate and the latter a convex distribution.

Both Adams (1981: 74-75) and Johnson (1977, 1980) investigated this pattern in more detail by employing the rank–size relationship. In large, modern countries, this relationship tends to be log-normal, so that the largest city has double the population of the second largest city, three times the population of the third-ranked city, and so on. In early Mesopotamia, by contrast, this relationship does not always hold. Sometimes 'primate' distributions are found in which the first-ranked settlement is so much bigger than all other settlements that the distribution quickly falls off well below the log-normal line. This is what Adams observed when he noted how population seemed to be concentrated in Uruk. At other times, 'convex' distributions can be seen, in which the several largest sites are of very nearly equal size, or in which there are many sites of intermediate size, so that the distribution is 'flatter' than would be expected when plotted on log-log paper (fig. 1). Some distributions, called 'primo-convex', appear to be primate among the most highly ranked sites, but convex at lower levels of the site hierarchy.

The interpretation of these plots can be difficult. Most researchers assume that primate distributions indicate extreme centralization of political or economic institutions, or both, as appears to have been the case with Uruk. Convex distributions, on the other hand, are usually taken as indicating that there was relatively little regional integration in the settlement system, that is, at least the large and middle-sized sites were relatively autonomous, and particularly that there was less 'vertical' integration between urban and rural communities (Johnson 1980). In addition, convex distributions can result from the operation of a Christalleran 'central place' settlement lattice, in which a hexagonal organization, with six second-order sites for each first-order site, and so on, results in a much flatter, step-like, distribution (Christaller 1933). But some inescapable problems may inhibit an accurate interpretation. The shape of the distribution is highly dependent on the placement of boundaries on the settlement system: including a large site that really does not belong with the other sites, or combining two or three distinct settlement systems, will make the distribution look convex; while data omission, which can result from restricting the data set to a subset of the whole settlement system, can make the plot look primate, because second- and third-rank sites may be missing. But the most serious problems are related to sample size and, particularly, unevenness in the probability of discovering large and small sites.

More recent studies have continued to use the 'rank–size rule' as the jumping-off point for distinguishing primate from convex and primo-convex distributions, but have made their analyses more sophisticated by attempting to control for sample size and by using statistical means of deciding which distributions depart sufficiently, at a given sample size, from log-normal to be classified as either primate or convex (Falconer and Savage 1995).

All of these studies have made important contributions in the identification of variability over time and between regions in the form of the relationship between urban centres and their hinterlands, but some problems remain. In spite of Falconer and Savage's attempts to deal with it, the sampling problem persists. Their optimistic assessments of survey coverage (that is, they often assume that these surveys successfully detected 70–75 per cent of the sites), are not very realistic and, more importantly, fail to account for the fact that the probability of site detection varies with size. Large, high tells may have a probability of detection around 0.9, while small, low tells may have probabilities closer to 0.1, and many of the smallest sites in areas subject to alluviation and colluviation may have detection probabilities close to zero (Banning 1995, 1996a). This results in a shortage of small sites on the rank–size graphs.[1] And this in turn can lead to pronounced primacy in the distribution that researchers typically interpret as evidence for an Uruk-like urbanism. Fortunately the site detection probabilities for large sites are much higher, but there can be problems in that part of the distribution also. Falconer and Savage (1995: 43) recognize that differential discovery probability is a problem and suggest that they could explicitly include a 'sliding scale' of site recovery, but this awaits future research. All of the analyses usually assume, *a priori*, that the highest order site is always included in the sample (although this is not necessary for the method). If detection of the largest site has a probability of 0.9, this is not a totally unreasonable assumption, but it still leaves a 10 per cent chance that the largest site is unknown (probably because it has been destroyed by recent development or buried deeply by later deposits). Since the overall primacy or convexity of the rank–size graph depends considerably on the size of the two or three largest sites, accidentally omitting an unusually large site or one of two sites of nearly equal size could easily change a convex distribution to a concave one or vice versa. No doubt future work on Monte Carlo simulations of rank–size distributions will take these problems into account.

---

1.   Note how they typically fall off dramatically at the right when we would intuitively expect them, following Christaller (1933), to show convexity.

More work is needed also on what exactly these rank–size plots are telling us. If, as Adams and Johnson suggest, second-order central places are being absorbed into first-order ones, why is this happening and how is it accomplished? What implications does it have for the ways in which the centre extracts income from the periphery? Christaller (1933) argued that having several levels of central places organized in a hexagonal lattice was a very efficient way to organize economic exchanges and services, at least within a modern state with a market economy. If cities such as Uruk abandoned such an efficient system, what were the reasons for the change? Does it imply that a redistributive economy, rather than a market one, worked better under extreme centralization? More work is needed on these questions in which study of storage and elite facilities at individual sites (e.g. Schwartz 1994; Fortin, this volume, complements the regional settlement analyses).

The Spatial Organization of Houses and Settlements

A different approach from interpretation of rank–size distribution plots is to focus on individual settlements and to search for patterns in the spatial organization of rooms, houses and streets that might be related to social hierarchies, household organization and other aspects of the social and political landscape. There are many possible methods for this. One is to focus on graphing techniques and statistical summaries of the connections between rooms and houses (Banning 1996b; Banning and Byrd 1989) on the assumption that these reveal structure in the way people, particularly inhabitants and strangers, can encounter one another or inhibit one another's access to particular features or resources. Another approach is to summarize the overall spatial structure of, or even simulate the construction history of, an entire settlement (Hillier *et al.* 1976; Hillier and Hanson 1984; Banning 1996c). A more traditional approach, which can also be used to augment the first two, is to look for spatial patterning across buildings or neighbourhoods in the distribution of artifacts that can reasonably be associated with small social groups, such as lineages or families (cf. Hill 1970; Longacre 1968).

There is insufficient space here to discuss fully the details of the various methods. However, the following will illustrate them with some examples before discussing what they may reveal about the early development of urbanism in the Near East.

Urbanism in Antiquity

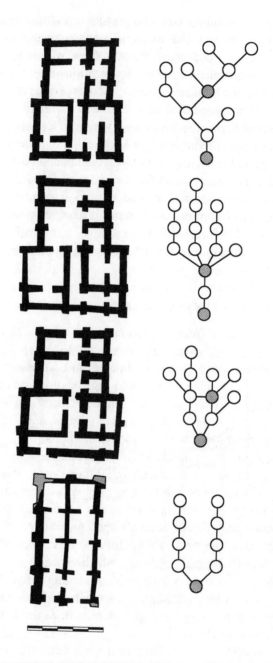

Figure 2. Samarran house plans and their respective graphs. Note that they are tree-like with long branches (after Abu es-Soof and el-Wailly 1965; Abu es-Soof 1968; Abu es-Soof 1971; and Oates 1969).

Graphs are a convenient way to represent spatial relationships in an individual building or a collection of buildings without being distracted by the geometric shapes of buildings, rooms or the features within them. Each space (usually a room) is represented by a circle; and the connections between spaces (usually doorways) by line segments. This facilitates recognition of patterns in 'interconnectedness' that might be overlooked when studying the original site plans. If it is reasonable to assume that these patterns have some significance with respect to, for example, the role of private property (protection of storage areas); the concept of privacy (e.g. access to sleeping areas or women's work areas); separation between domestic and 'business' activities; and the number of people and social roles in the household, we have a foothold in the seemingly intangible realm of social systems.

In fig. 2, for example, a few examples of Samarran house plans with their accompanying graphs can be seen. Note that the plans of houses at Tell as-Sawwan and Choga Mami look fairly different from each other except that they each have nine or ten rooms and buttresses

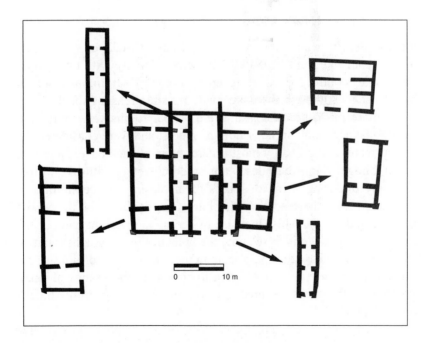

Figure 3. Anatomical parts of a tripartite house at Tell as-Sawwan (cf. Forest 1983; Kubba 1987).

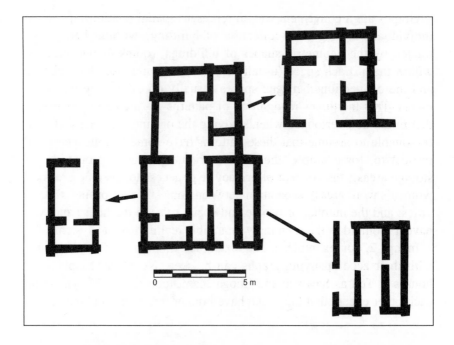

Figure 4.   Anatomical parts of a T-house at Tell as-Sawwan (cf. Margeraud 1989).

in the walls. But when plotted on a graph, they all take on a combination of 'path-like' and 'tree-like' structures, usually with one or two spaces that 'control' access to 'deeper' rooms by serving as a sort of 'bottle-neck'. Although there are many possible reasons for this, one of the more probable ones is that the deeper rooms were only supposed to be accessible to household members, and were considered the more private, and probably most secure, parts of the house. Note also that at Choga Mami the houses are predominantly 'path-like', often with only one long string of rooms of increasing inaccessibility, or contain circuits that increase the interconnectedness of the whole structure and, presumably, the ease of access to different parts of the house. One approach is to see how the branches in the graphs relate to what seem to be structural segments in the morphology of houses: for instance, all Samarran houses seem to combine long strings of small chambers with blocks of three long rooms and megaron-like blocks (figs. 3 and 4).

But such things as interconnectedness and accessibility may also be summarized numerically. Geographers have used some of these measures for decades to do such things as measure how well railway systems are serving a region. But Hillier and Hanson (1984) and their colleagues have offered some novel ways to measure some of these things at the scales of the individual room, the whole house, and the whole village or town. Table 1 illustrates some of these statistics for the spaces in house 8 at Choga Mami.

Space no.	Depth from Carrier	RA	RR of Space	RR from Space
0	0	0.405	0.250	0.153
1	1	0.312	0.250	0.178
2	1	0.405	0.375	0.178
3	1	0.437	0.250	0.153
4	2	0.125	0.250	0.153
5	2	0.375	0.125	0.133
6	3	0.312	0.250	0.133
7	3	0.375	0.125	0.107
8	4	0.437	0.125	0.097
9	4	0.625	—	0.077
Mean	2.33	0.381	0.250	0.151

Table 1.   Spatial statistics for Samarran rooms at Choga Mami, House 8.

Hillier and Hanson (1984) also provide measures of how well houses are integrated into the streetscape as well as a methodology for dividing the open spaces of a settlement into unit spaces. In the neighbourhood of 'Middle Street' at Tell Asmar, for example, it is possible to identify branching in the street system that tends to group certain houses together, impose controls over accessibility, and leave some streets virtually unbroken by doorways while other streets seem much 'friendlier'. Much earlier, at Tell as-Sawwan (Abu es-Soof 1968; Abu es-Soof 1971; Abu es-Soof and el-Wailly 1965; al-'Adami 1968; Breniquet 1991; Forest 1983; Kubba 1987; Wahida 1967) the houses are grouped into two or three distinct (and poorly interconnected) neighborhoods, suggesting the possibility that these belonged to distinct social units, perhaps clans. Houses 8, 10 and 15, in particular, seem to form a distinct unit (fig. 5). Such analyses can be supplemented with Rapoport's (1969: 65) suggestion that we should investigate whether the arrangement of doorways along the street facilitates or eliminates the possibility of looking into houses from outside. At Tell Asmar, doorways tend to alternate along the street, and entrance antechambers have a bent axis (fig. 6). At Tell as-Sawwan, the doorways of houses in the isolated eastern quarter are arranged in such a way as to facilitate inter-house communication; in the western quarter, which is more open to strangers, they are not.

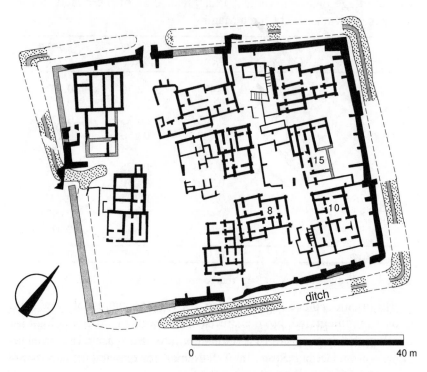

Figure 5.   Map of level III at Tell as-Sawwan (revised from Abu es-Soof 1968; Abu es-Soof 1971; Abu es-Soof and el-Wailly 1965; Breniquet 1991). Note how houses 8, 10 and 15 form a cluster with doorways opening onto a shared yard.

One way to combine the preceding approaches with a more traditional approach is to examine the distribution of certain symbolically loaded artifacts and wealth items across households and over time. Tell Asmar and Tell Khafajeh have provided data for an attempt of this kind that is focused on artifacts that are not only symbolic, but are far more likely to have been included in the final publication than, for example, domestic pottery. These are metal luxuries, probably a reasonable indication of wealth, and cylinder seals, whose iconography may have some symbolic feature that helped to identify the seal's owner or his clan, much as totems and heraldry do in some more recent societies.

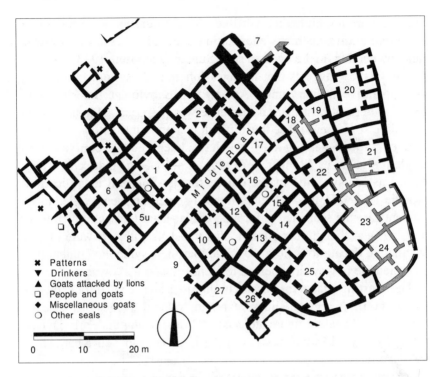

Figure 6. Map of the Middle Road area at Tell Asmar (ancient Eshnunna), with the
approximate provenances of cylinder seals with abstract patterns and
showing people drinking from straws, and various goat themes (modified
from Delougaz *et al.* 1967). Note that doorways along opposite sides of
the Middle Road are usually offset.

Sample size can be a problem with this type of analysis and currently only hints of patterns can be identified in these distributions.
Cylinder seals have nonetheless shown some promise. The working
assumption is, *if the designs on cylinder seals have some connection to
the clan or lineage of their owners,* and *if seal owners practised a pattern of post-marital residence that caused them to prefer residence
close to, or in the same house as, their father* (if patrilineal) *or moth-
er's brother* (if matrilineal), *then one could expect seals found in different levels of the same house* (and in neighbouring houses), *to be
more similar to one another in their iconography than seals found in
spatially distant houses.* Documentary evidence (particularly patro-
nymics and inheritance texts) indicates that patrilineal descent was in
force by Old Babylonian times, and probably by Early Dynastic III
(Diakanoff 1974; Diakanoff 1985; Gelb 1979; Postgate 1992; Powell

1986). There are hints that patrilineal kinship groups were important corporate entities, perhaps constituting clans or tribes with corporate land ownership in Early Dynastic Sumer (Jacobsen 1943). Adams (1966: 81-85) suggests that lineages functioned as work groups and administrative–military units. And by Old Babylonian times the preferred pattern of post-marital residence was patrilocal, although urban crowding sometimes made this difficult or impossible (Stone 1987).

Even though sealing may not have been legally equivalent to modern signatures (Renger 1977: 79), it still seems that seals 'functioned as idiosyncratic markers used for personalized identification' (Rathje 1977: 25), the seal-cutter himself sometimes being called in 'to authenticate the seals he cut for a particular legal transaction' (Renger 1977: 79). Although it is possible that the seals' subjects were merely distinctive decorations, it is plausible that their symbolic content was interpretable in ways that helped to identify the seals' owners.

The starting-place for research should be to concentrate on the major motifs (e.g. goats, lions, stars) and overall themes of the seals' scenes (e.g. kneeling figure attacked by lions), using the Early Dynastic and Early Akkadian seals from Tell Asmar and Tell Khafajeh as the database:

1	None	15	Plant
2	Goat	16	Snake
3	Scorpion	17	Dog
4	Dagger	18	Branch
5	Antelope	19	Crouching human
6	Vase	20	Lion
7	Plow	21	Tortoise
8	Bird	22	Lizard
9	Crescent	23	Goat and ram, tête-beche
10	Reeds	24	Vase with tubes
11	Rectangle with bars	25	Goat head
12	Star	26	Eagle
13	Drill holes	27	Seated figure
14	Fish	28	Human-faced bull

Table 2.   Cylinder seal elements in the Diyala.

Animal motifs, in particular, should be emphasized, in light of their use as totems in many modern tribal societies and following Adams's (1966: 84-85) observation that many Sumerian descent groups 'are named after animals (e.g. snakes and donkeys) or gods (*lu*-^{d}ENKI)'. A text of Gudea inaugurating the E-ninnu temple at Girsu mentions labour groups or clans (*im-ru-a*) each having a standard (*su-nir*), and being named after a patron deity. Themes may be divided into broad categories (e.g. 'man wrestling animals', 'banquet') because there would otherwise be too few cases in each class to recognize patterns.[2]

Very few classes so far show any signs of the clustering within houses in close proximity that would be expected under the hypothesis of patrilocal residence. Those that did appear to cluster to some extent included seals with themes containing goats, lions and banquet scenes. Others were either scattered among widely separated buildings or too few in number to permit comparisons (e.g. only one 'god in boat' seal at Tell Asmar).

Those classes that seemed to cluster by overall theme, along with others that could reasonably be viewed as parallel themes (e.g., bulls and goats are often interchangeable in the scenes, and could represent alternative representations of the same class, or two distinct, but parallel, classes), then formed the basis for partitioning groups of buildings into groups so that all seals found within each spatially restricted group could be compared. Again, if the patrilocal hypothesis is valid, seals within each of these residential groups might be expected to be more similar to each other than they collectively are to the seals of other groups.

Without going into statistical tests (most are violated by having too small sample sizes anyway), a look at the distribution of some of the seal themes and motives suggests that these distributions are probably not random. In Stratum Va of the Middle Road area at Tell Asmar, for example (fig. 7), seals in which goats are prominent seem to cluster in the northwestern periphery; while neighbouring houses I and II share three seals depicting seated figures drinking from tubes; adjacent houses I, II and VI share five examples of seals showing two lions attacking goats; and houses II, V and VI, all on the northwest side of the Middle Road, have seals in which a goat occurs along with a scorpion. In the two levels of the 'North Palace' at Tell Asmar, weak evidence is found for the clustering of seals depicting lions or other cats attacking goats or, more rarely, bulls. At Khafajeh, contiguous houses 31 and 32 shared three seals with 'laurel wreath' themes, two banquet scenes and two scenes with a lion and a man jointly attacking animals;

---

2. Limitations of space preclude detailed discussion of assumptions about how the seals were deposited in the archaeological record.

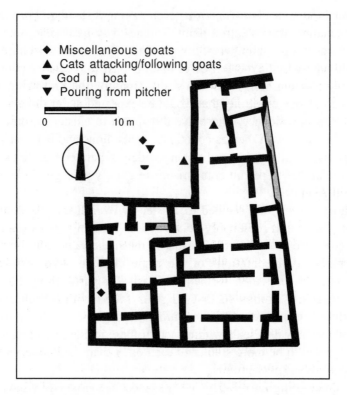

Figure 7.   Map of the North Palace at Tell Asmar, showing the approximate
provenances of cylinder seals (modified from Delougaz *et al.* 1967).

while houses 47, 50 and 52 shared three seals with similar patterns of
lozenges and dots; houses 50, 53 and the street between them shared
three seals with the 'god in boat' theme; and houses 53 and 54 shared
two seals with presentation scenes. With the small sample size available, however, it cannot be shown that these distributions are statisti-
cally significant. For example, goats may be such a popular element
on seals that they do not help to distinguish the groups. Similarly,
bulls and lions are such common elements that they show almost uniform distribution among houses at Tell Asmar and Tell Khafajeh in
which seals are present. In addition, the fact that no seals at all were
found in many of the houses may contribute to the impression of
greater spatial pattern than actually exists, while overlap between the
groupings indicates that the seals in any case do not distinguish groups
of potentially related households as cleanly as one would like. Site formation processes may have blurred the distributions.

Although these results have been somewhat disappointing, more sophisticated analyses, perhaps reducing the seal designs' complexity to extract more subtle patterns with the help of Digard's (1975) very ambitious coding system, might ultimately permit us to identify the role of extended family households in concentrating wealth and political influence in Early Dynastic I, followed by their breakdown in the cities after the state became entrenched.

Conclusions

It is in ancient Sumer that the first steps were made toward the kinds of economic and social inequality and complexity that are associated with early states. There, some sites, perhaps those able to control access to limited water supplies, were elevated in the site hierarchy. Meanwhile, there were also changes in domestic arrangements that seem to have involved increasing differentiation between and within households. In particular, some houses became large, with complex organization of space. Perhaps increases in the size of the labour pool and in the number of social roles within some households helped subsidize pastoralism, imported goods and elites. Although textual evidence provides some hints of the nature of these changes, most of the texts come from Old Babylonian times or later, so archaeological evidence is critical. Research on changes in the composition and organization of Early Dynastic and earlier households (e.g. Stone 1981, 1987), may help us understand how these processes contributed to the appearance of social inequality and city-states.

BIBLIOGRAPHY

Abu es-Soof, B.
    1968   'Tell es-Sawwan: Excavations of the Fourth Season (Spring 1967)',
                Sumer 24: 3-15.
    1971   'Tell es-Sawwan: Fifth Season's Excavations (Winter 1967, 1968)',
                Sumer 27: 3-7.
Abu es-Soof, B., and F. el-Wailly
    1965   'The Excavations at Tell es-Sawwan: First Preliminary Report', *Sumer*
                21: 17-32.
al-'Adami, K.
    1968   'Excavations at Tell es-Sawwan (Second Season)', *Sumer* 24: 57-60.

Adams, R.McC.
  1965   *Land behind Baghdad: A History of Settlement on the Diyala Plains* (Chicago: University of Chicago Press).
  1966   *The Evolution of Urban Society* (Chicago: Aldine).
  1981   *Heartland of Cities: Surveys of Ancient Settlement and Land Use on the Central Floodplain of the Euphrates* (Chicago: University of Chicago Press).

Adams, R.McC., and H.J. Nissen
  1972   *The Uruk Countryside* (Chicago: University of Chicago Press).

Banning, E.B.
  1995   'Review of *Archaeological Views from the Countryside: Village Communities in Early Complex Societies*' (ed. G.M. Schwartz and S.E. Falconer); *BASOR* 299-300: 123-24.
  1996a   'Highlands and Lowlands: Problems and Survey Frameworks for Rural Archaeology in the Near East', *BASOR* 301: 25-45.
  1996b   'Houses, Compounds and Mansions in the Prehistoric Near East', in *People Who Lived in Big Houses: Archaeological Perspectives on Large Domestic Structures* (ed. G. Coupland and E. Banning; Madison: Prehistory Press): 165-85.
  1996c   'Pattern or Chaos? New Ways of Looking at "Town Planning" in the Ancient Near East', in *Debating Complexity: Proceedings of the 26th Chacmool Conference* (ed. P. Dawson *et al.*; Calgary, AB: University of Calgary): 510-18.

Banning, E.B., and B.F. Byrd
  1989   'Alternative Approaches for Exploring Levantine Neolithic Architecture', *Paléorient* 15: 154-60.

Breniquet, C.
  1991   'Tell es-Sawwan—realités et problemes', *Iraq* 53: 75-90.

Childe, V.G.
  1950   'The Urban Revolution', *Town Planning Review* 21.1: 3-17.

Christaller, W.
  1933   *Die zentralen Orte in Süddeutschland: eine ökonomisch-geographische Untersuchung über die Gesetzmässigkeit der Verbreitung und Entwicklung der Siedlungen mit städtischen Funktionen* (Jena: n.p.).

Delougaz, P., H.D. Hill, and S. Lloyd
  1967   *Private Houses and Graves in the Diyala Region* (Oriental Institute Publications, 88; Chicago: University of Chicago Press).

Diakonoff, I.M.
  1974   *Structure of Society and State in Early Dynastic Sumer* (Malibu: Undena).
  1985   'Extended Families in Old Babylonian Ur', *ZfA* 75: 47-65.

Digard, F.
  1975   *Répertoire analytique des cylindres orientaux, établi sur ordinateur* (Paris: CNRS).

Falconer, S.E., and S.H. Savage
  1995   'Heartlands and Hinterlands: Alternative Trajectories of Early Urbanization in Mesopotamia and the Southern Levant', *AmAnt* 60: 37-58.

Forest, J.-D.
    1983   'Aux origines de l'architecture obeidienne: les plans de type Samarra',
                Akk 34: 1-47.

Gelb, I.J.
    1979   'Household and Family in Early Mesopotamia', in *State and Temple
                Economy in the Ancient Near East* (ed. E. Lipiński; Louvain: Peeters):
                1-97.

Henrickson, E.
    1981   'Non-Religious Residential Settlement Patterning in the Late Early
                Dynastic of the Diyala Region', *Meso* 16: 43-133.

Hill, J.N.
    1970   *Broken K: A Prehistoric Society in Eastern Arizona* (Tucson, AZ: Uni-
                versity of Arizona Press).

Hillier, B., and J. Hanson
    1984   *The Social Logic of Space* (Cambridge: Cambridge University Press).

Hillier, B., A. Leaman, P. Stansall, and M. Bedford
    1976   'Space Syntax', *Environment and Planning* 3: 147-85.

Jacobsen, T.
    1943   'Primitive Democracy in Ancient Mesopotamia', *JNES* 2: 159-72.

Jacobsen, T., and R. McC. Adams
    1958   'Salt and Silt in Ancient Mesopotamian Agriculture', *Science* 128:
                1251-58.

Johnson, G.A.
    1977   'Aspects of Regional Analysis in Archaeology', *ARA* 6: 479-508.
    1980   'Rank–Size Convexity and System Integration: A View from Archae-
                ology', *Economic Geography* 56: 234-47.

Kowalewski, S.
    1982   'The Evolution of Primate Regional Systems', *Comparative Urban
                Research* 9.1: 60-68.

Kubba, S.A.A.
    1987   *Mesopotamian Architecture and Town Planning* (Oxford: BAR Inter-
                national Series).

Longacre, W.A.
    1968   'Some Aspects of Prehistoric Society in East-central Arizona', in *New
                Perspectives in Archeology* (ed. S. Binford and L.R. Binford; Chicago:
                Aldine): 89-102.

Margeraud, J.-C.
    1989   'Architecture et société à l'époque d'Obeid', in *Upon This Founda-
                tion: The 'Ubaid Reconsidered* (Copenhagen: CNI): 43-76.

Oates, J.
    1969   'Choga Mami 1967–1968. A Preliminary Report', *Iraq* 31: 115-52.

Postgate, J.N.
    1992   *Early Mesopotamia: Society and Economy at the Dawn of History*
                (London: Routledge).

Powell, M.A.
    1986   'The Economy of the Extended Family According to Sumerian
                Sources', *Oikumene* 5: 9-14.

Rapoport, A.
    1969   *House Form and Culture* (Englewood Cliffs, NJ: Prentice–Hall).
Rathje, W.L.
    1977   'New Tricks for Old Seals: A Progress Report', in *Seals and Sealing in the Ancient Near East* (ed. McG. Gibson and D. Biggs; Malibu: Udeana): 25-32.
Renger, J.
    1977   'Legal Aspects of Sealing in Ancient Mesopotamia', in *Seals and Sealing in the Ancient Near East* (ed. McG. Gibson and D. Biggs; Malibu: Undena): 75-88.
Schwartz, G.M.
    1994   'Rural Economic Specialization and Early Urbanization in the Khabur Valley, Syria', in *Archaeological Views from the Countryside: Village Communities in Early Complex Societies* (ed. G. Schwartz and S. Falconer; Washington: Smithsonian): 19-36.
Stone, E.C.
    1981   'Texts, Architecture and Ethnographic Analogy: Patterns of Residence in Old Babylonian Nippur', *Iraq* 43: 19-33.
    1987   *Nippur Neighborhoods* (Studies in Ancient Oriental Civilization, 44; Chicago: University of Chicago Press).
Wahida, G.
    1967   'The Excavations of the Third Season at Tell es-Sawwan, 1966', *Sumer* 23: 167-76.
Wright, H.T.
    1969   *The Administration of Rural Production in an Early Mesopotamian Town* (Ann Arbor: University of Michigan, Museum of Anthropology).
    1977   'Recent Research on the Origin of the State', *ARA* 6: 379-97.

Writing as a Factor in the Rise of Urbanism

Ronald F.G. Sweet

The earliest known instance of fully fledged urbanism appeared in the Near East towards the end of the fourth millennium BCE at Warka, known from texts of the third millennium BCE as the Sumerian city of Uruk. Excavations conducted by the Deutsche Orient Gesellschaft from 1912 to 1989, with interruptions occasioned by the two world wars, revealed a settlement that covered an area of 100 hectares already in the Late Uruk Period (Adams 1981: 71), that is, archaic levels V–IV in the Eanna precinct, to be dated c. 3300–3100 BCE. If one estimates the population 'on the standard of 125 persons per hectare of actual site area, or about 100 persons per hectare as calculated only from measurement of maximum length and width', which Adams (1981: 69) calls 'a reasonable and perhaps conservative estimate', the population of Warka at this time will have been between 10,000 and 12,500.

City life in Warka at this period was marked by a number of well-known cultural innovations: architecture of monumental proportions, art that can be interpreted as commemorative in intention and the use of the cylinder seal. Another innovation that appeared at the very end of the Late Uruk Period, in phase a of archaic level IV, was the earliest known form of writing.

Clay tablets with abstract and pictographic signs that in many cases can be recognized as the forerunners of later cuneiform signs continue to appear in the following archaic level III, which is assigned to the Jemdet Nasr Period (c. 3100–2900 BCE). The tablets also appear in archaic level I, which belongs to the Early Dynastic I Period (the original identification of an archaic level II is now recognized as unjustified). Between 1928 and 1929, when excavation was resumed after the First World War, and 1976, almost 5000 of these proto-cuneiform tablets, including fragments, were found in archaic levels IVa up to I in the Eanna area.

Almost 250 tablets, using the same repertoire of signs at the developmental stage attested in Warka level III, have also been found 180 km to the north-west of Warka at Jemdet Nasr, the original type-site of the period so named. Approximately 80 tablets of the Jemdet Nasr Period were acquired through the antiquities trade for the Swiss Erlenmeyer Collection in Basel. These were auctioned off in 1988 and the majority are now owned by the state (Land) of Berlin; the remainder were purchased by the British Museum, the Louvre and the Metropolitan Museum of New York (Nissen, Damerow and Englund 1993: ix, 21a). Two proto-cuneiform tablets were also excavated in the 1930s at Khafajeh in the Diyalah area, and four were excavated in 1940–41 at Tell Uqair, 15 km north-west of Jemdet Nasr.

The linguistic affiliation of these tablets is unknown. The people who occupied southern Iraq in the middle of the third millennium BCE, and who employed the cuneiform script which developed from the signs used on the archaic tablets, were certainly Sumerians. In the absence of any evidence that a new ethnic group entered southern Iraq earlier in the third millennium BCE, it is a reasonable guess that the Sumerians were already present in the Late Uruk Period. But the proto-cuneiform tablets cannot be read in the sense that one can supply the pronunciation that may have been given to a sequence of signs by the scribes who wrote them. The meaning of many of the signs can nevertheless be determined. This is the case when a proto-cuneiform sign sufficiently resembles a later cuneiform sign with a known ideographic meaning. The former can be identified as the precursor of the latter. The possibility of identifying an archaic sign form with a cuneiform sign known from the middle of the third millennium BCE is facilitated by the presence among the Warka and Jemdet Nasr tablets of lists of groups of signs that can be recognized as forerunners of the so-called lexical lists that were copied and transmitted from generation to generation in the later Sumerian scribal centers. The fixed order of the entries in these word lists permits many an obscure proto-cuneiform sign to be paired with its later form.

About 700 of the 5000 proto-cuneiform tablets found at Warka are of the lexical class. The remainder were clearly written for administrative purposes. In the administrative tablets, signs easily recognized as numerals, because of their similarity to later Sumerian numerals, are followed by groups of, presumably, ideographic signs that express the object enumerated and/or the name or office of someone associated with the object quantified. The numeral signs are easily recognized because they were made by pressing the flat end of a stylus into the clay, with the stylus held either vertically or obliquely relative to the surface of the clay. The styli were circular in section, like a reed (the most likely material from which they were made), and came in two thicknesses. A vertically held stylus made a circular impression, and an obliquely held stylus made a bullet-like impression, in each case large or small depending on the diameter of the stylus. The stylus used for the non-numeral, or ideographic, signs must have had a sharp point, because it was used to draw narrow lines, straight or curved, on the clay. Such a point was used to add short fine strokes to some of the numeral signs; perhaps it was the other end of a stylus used for making circular impressions, suitably sharpened. The signs, both numeral and ideographic, were grouped in cases, and the cases were arranged in one or more columns.[1]

The relevance of these tablets, and in particular those of the Late Uruk Period, to the question of the beginnings of urbanism is that their appearance is commonly believed to have been not merely coincidental with the rise of city life but, in conjunction with other factors, productive of city life. Writing is thought to have contributed to that major mutation in the forms of social organization which we call urbanism. Writing, it has been argued, provided a means for the complex record keeping which is virtually essential for the organization, administration and social control of large numbers of people living cheek by jowl in urban conditions.

If the earliest writing found at Uruk was indeed a tool for the central organization of urban life, the contents of at least some of the documents, if they could be understood, should show that the quantities of the objects enumerated were of a magnitude consistent with a situation of governmental administration. If it should turn out that the contents of a typical archaic administrative tablet are of the nature of 'Farmer A has received two sheep and three bushels of barley from farmer B, to be repaid in four months' time', the grounds for regarding the tablets as instruments of municipal administration would be

1. All the known proto-cuneiform tablets of the Late Uruk and Jemdet Nasr Periods, regardless of their provenance, together with tablets of the immediately following Early Dynastic I and II Periods (c. 2900–2600 BCE), are currently being studied and edited by the Berlin Uruk Project, begun in 1964 under the direction of Hans J. Nissen of the Free University of Berlin (Nissen, Damerow and Englund 1993).

greatly diminished. Many administrative, or at least 'economic', texts of the early second millennium BCE, in the Old Babylonian Period, are in fact of the kind caricatured here.

Whatever may have been the situation in the Late Uruk Period, there can be no question that proto-cuneiform tablets were used for governmental administration in the Jemdet Nasr Period. This is clear from the quantities of objects listed in some of the texts. For example, a Warka tablet of this period shows a broken, and therefore incomplete, sequence of numeral signs that Damerow and Englund understand to express 'an amount of about 550 tons of emmer' (Nissen, Damerow and Englund 1993: 32 fig. 30 caption),[2] which constitutes 'the largest amount of grain known from the entire proto-cuneiform text corpus' (Nissen, Damerow and Englund 1993: 35). It is unlikely that this huge quantity of grain was the property of an individual farmer. One may see here evidence of governmental administration.

But can we assume that the forms of social organization that existed at Warka in the Jemdet Nasr Period were already in place in the Late Uruk Period at that critical point when urbanism and writing first appeared? It is conceivable that social institutions underwent major changes as mastery of the new art of writing developed and the potential of this art as a tool for large-scale central administration came to be realized. The hypothesis that writing was used for governmental administration from the very beginning of its invention could be confirmed only by internal evidence of the earliest proto-cuneiform tablets themselves. Such evidence would be at hand if the numeral signs on at least some of the earliest tablets were of a magnitude to suggest the activities of government administrators and not those of small-scale farmers or merchants. One should not expect to find records of huge quantities of materials in all the tablets. If one entertains the idea that a central authority distributed rations to the families

---

2. The tablet is W 19726a, now at the University of Heidelberg (Nissen, Damerow and Englund 1993: 158). The numeral signs referred to are on the reverse: 3-N46 2N49 # 5-N19 # 2-N04 # 1-N41 (see Englund 1994: databank on diskette, sort no. 3215). These numeral signs are in the Š″ system, described below. Calculated in the manner used in this paper, the notation is equivalent to 23,420.93 Imperial bu. The weight of grain varies with its moisture content, but the weight of wheat is usually reckoned as 60 lbs per Imperial bu. At this reckoning, and assuming that a bushel of emmer wheat weighed the same as a bushel of standard wheat today, the emmer wheat recorded in this text would be 627.34 long tons, or 637.38 metric tons.

of the community, say once a month, and that most of the tablets are records of these transactions, one would expect that the quantities referred to in most of the tablets would be relatively modest. But one might equally expect that the occasional tablet would record the large quantities in, presumably, communal storehouses that the central authority must have had at its disposal in the scenario presented here.[3]

But which of the tablets excavated at Warka belong to the Late Uruk Period? Almost all the tablets and tablet fragments excavated from the archaic levels were found in rubble used as fill and, to make a bad situation worse, the excavators did not record the find spots accurately and precisely. In the first published volume to issue from the Berlin Uruk project (Green and Nissen 1987), Nissen attempted to assign tablets to the strata in which they were discovered on the basis of the archaeological reports and field notes (Nissen 1987). In most cases he found the records quite inadequate for this purpose. Of the approximately 5000 archaic tablets found at Warka, only 26 can be regarded as possibly forming part of the inventory of the buildings in which they were found, namely, 7 found on the floor of Temple C and 19 found on the floor of the White Temple (Nissen 1987: 24).[4] However, of the tablets found in the Eanna precinct, and apart from the seven found on the floor of Temple C, Nissen was able to determine that 892 were from fill that was dumped earlier than level IIIc, that is, earlier than the earliest phase of the level assigned to the Jemdet Nasr Period. More exactly, Nissen established that 53 tablets have as their *terminus ad quem* a layer of fill that lay between levels IVa and IIIc in the area of Temple C and that served as an occupation level before it was sealed by terracing belonging to IIIc.[5] This intervening layer of

3. The means for determining the quantities of materials recorded in the proto-cuneiform tablets of the Late Uruk Period at Warka are now available in the database of the Berlin Uruk project published in the floppy disk included with Englund (1994). The database, which is complete as of August 1994, includes a text catalogue of all known archaic texts to the Early Dynastic II Period, an index of the signs used in the texts and transliterations of all the texts. The text catalogue has about 6,000 entries, and there are about 32,000 lines of text in transliteration.

4. For the 7 tablets from the floor of Temple C, W 21300, 1–7, see Nissen (1987: 39). The 19 tablets from the White Temple are gypsum tablets with seal impressions and numeral signs, but no non-numeral signs (Nissen 1987: 50; Englund 1994: 18).

5. The area in question falls within squares Oc XVI 2, Ob-Od XVI 3, and Ob-Od XVI 4 on the excavation grid (Green and Nissen 1987: 37-39, and for the grid

fill, or *Zwischenschicht*, as Nissen calls it, may also be the *terminus ante quem* of another 17 tablets; but in the case of this group Nissen makes the attribution with a question mark. Level IIIc can be identified as the *terminus ante quem* for the deposition of a further 822 tablets that were found in other areas of the Eanna precinct (Green and Nissen 1987: 50).[6]

As mentioned above, the numeral signs denoting quantities of objects are easily recognized by their distinctive form, circular and bullet-shaped impressions in the clay. That these are numeral signs is not in doubt, because numerals could be written in this way as late as the Ur III Period (c. 2100–2000 BCE), even though most proto-cuneiform signs had developed into the well-understood true cuneiform by this time. The numeral signs pose considerable difficulties, however. Sixty numeral signs have been identified, including those that do not appear before the Jemdet Nasr Period. The value of one numeral sign relative to that of another can sometimes be readily recognized when several discrete numbers are given on the obverse of a tablet and what is clearly the total is given on the reverse. But the complexities of the numeral system, or rather systems, have been clarified only within the last 20 years.[7]

Some of the numeral signs are used in more than one system. For example, the large circle designated N45 by Damerow and Englund (i.e. number sign 45) represents 3600 units of N1 (a horizontal bullet pointing right) in system S, but only 60 units of N1 in system Š. This

Green and Nissen 1987: 23). The grid is also shown in Nissen, Damerow and Englund 1993: 6, fig. 5).

6. The registration numbers of the tablets assigned to these groups are given *passim* in chapter 1 of Green and Nissen (1987).

7. Building on the pioneering work of Vaiman and Friberg, Damerow and Englund of the Berlin Uruk project have identified five basic systems: (1) a sexagesimal system (S); (2) a bisexagesimal system (B), characterized by the use of the number 120 and multiples thereof; (3) a system for measuring grain by volume, especially barley, termed the ŠE system (abbreviated Š; *še* is the Sumerian word for barley); (4) a system for measuring area, which has been termed the GAN$_2$ system (abbreviated G; *gan$_2$* is a Sumerian word for field); and (5) the so-called EN system, which is found on only 26 tablets, all of them from level IVa at Warka. Systems S, B, and Š have one or more derivative systems that show slight graphic modifications of the signs of the parent system. Systems for denoting time and the volume of specific products have also been identified (Nissen, Damerow and Englund 1993: 26, 28-29; Damerow and Englund 1994).

multivalency characteristic of certain signs, which unfortunately include those most commonly used, often makes it difficult to determine which system is employed in a particular instance. The presence of a numeral sign distinctive of one system will sometimes determine the values of otherwise ambiguous signs. In other cases the sequence of the signs, if there are several, can decide the matter. The number of times that a sign shared by more than one system can occur before being replaced by a sign of higher value may vary with the system; this fact can identify the system in some instances. Sometimes one may attempt to resolve an ambiguity by referring to the accompanying ideographic signs that perhaps denote the object enumerated. But since the meaning of so many of these signs is unknown, it is often impossible to establish with certainty the system in which a multivalent sign is used.

In this paper, attention is paid only to numerals in the Š system and its derivatives, that is, the Š′ system ('used to note capacity measures of a certain grain, probably germinated barley [malt] used in beer brewing'), the Š″ system ('used to note capacity measures of a certain grain, probably various kinds of emmer') and the Š* system ('used to note capacity measures of grain, probably barley groats used to make certain grain products') (Nissen, Damerow and Englund 1993: 29). These systems have been chosen because the Mesopotamian economy was based on cereal crops in the historical period, and the same may reasonably be assumed of the Late Uruk Period. Barley and other grains are the commodities most likely to have appeared in records of governmental administration.

The numeral signs in the Š system and its derivatives represent various quantities of a basic unit. What was the basic unit, and what was its absolute value? Damerow and Englund (1987: 153-54 n. 60) have concluded that the N30a sign represents the capacity of the variety of bevel-rimmed bowl called *Glockentopf* in German, namely, about 0.8 of a liter. If they are correct, the measure therefore corresponds to the basic Sumerian measure of capacity in the later third millennium BCE, the sila$_3$. The correctness of their conclusion will be assumed for the purpose of this paper. Table 1 shows the relative values of the numeral signs of the Š system and its derivatives, together with the equivalents of the signs in liters and Imperial bushels (bushels being a standard measure for grain in the English-speaking world).

System Š		N48	10 ← N34	3 ← N45	10 ← N14	6 ← N1	5 ← N39	6 ← N30a
System Š´				N45´	10 ← N18	6 ← N3	5 ← N40	
System Š´´	N46	6? ← N49	10 ← N36	3 ← N46	10 ← N19	6 ← N4	5 ← N41	
System Š*			N37	3 ← N47	10 ← N20	6 ← N5	5 ← N42	
Multiples of N30a	324,000	54,000	5,400	1,800	180	30	6	1
Liters	259,200	43,200	4,320	1,440	144	24	4.8	0.8
Imperial bushel	7,020	1,170	117	39	3.9	0.65	0.13	0.022

Note: Numeral signs that rank below N39 in the Š system are omitted in this table except N30a. Those that rank below N42 in the Š* system are also omitted. The number above a left-pointing arrow to the left of the reference number of a numeral sign indicates the factor which when multiplied by the value expressed by the numeral sign produces the value expressed by the next higher numeral sign to the left.

—1 liter = 0.88 Imperial quart = 0.027 Imperial bushel
—1 Imperial bushel = 36.37 liters
—(1 liter = 0.908 US dry quart = 0.028 US bushel)
—(1 US bushel = 35.242 liters)

Table 1. Numeral signs of the Š, Š´, Š´´ and Š* systems, their relative values, and their values expressed in liters and Imperial bushels.

Before searching through the archaic texts from Warka for notations of large quantities of cereals to test the hypothesis of government administration, one must decide what is to count as a 'large quantity'. The minimum quantity proposed here is the amount of barley that a family received as rations in a year in the Sargonic and Ur III Periods (c. 2350–2000 BCE). This can be estimated, as shown below, as about 1968 liters, or 53 imperial bushels. One cannot be certain that individuals received rations in the Late Uruk Period, but the amount of barley consumed by a family at that time was probably little different from that consumed by a family in the late third millennium BCE. An ordinary citizen of Warka in the Late Uruk Period, if we may conceive of such a person, is unlikely in ordinary circumstances to have been a party to a transaction that involved the total staple food supply of his family for a whole year. The more a quantity exceeds this amount, the greater the probability that a 'private citizen' is not involved.[8]

I.J. Gelb's (1965) study of the barley ration system used in the Sargonic Period (c. 2350–2150 BCE) showed that the normal monthly allowance for a man was 60 $sila_3$, for a woman 30 $sila_3$, for children beyond infancy between 20 and 30 $sila_3$, and for infants 10 $sila_3$. The system was 'very much standardized all through the Sargonic and Ur III Periods, although deviations of different types are found occasionally' (Gelb 1965: 233, cf. chart 232). The following will assume that the system was already in place in Late Uruk times. If it is also assumed that one of the four children in the typical family was an infant, the family's monthly rations would have been 60 + 30 + 30 + 25 + 25 + 25 + 10 = 205 $sila_3$. If the volume of the $sila_3$ is taken as 0.8 liter, the family's barley ration for a month would have been 164

8.   Tablet Ki 1056 of the Old Babylonian Period from the north Babylonian city of Kish (Donbaz and Yoffee 1986: 57-69) gives an idea of the size of a typical family (see also Postgate 1992: 93). The tablet lists various quantities of some unspecified object, presumably barley, against the names of individuals who make up families. The relationship of each individual to the head of the family is specified, for example, 'his wife', 'his son'. Originally, 22 families were listed, but the entries have been preserved intact for only 11. The largest family consists of a man, his wife, a slave woman and four children. The Old Babylonian Period is admittedly more than a thousand years later than the Late Uruk Period. But, in the absence of better evidence closer in time to the period we are interested in, and on the assumption that the size of the family remained fairly stable in Sumerian and early Babylonian society, we may accept a family of one man, two women and four children as not atypical.

liters, and for a year 1968 liters, or about 53 Imperial bushels. For an 'ordinary citizen' this must have been a large quantity.

The transliterations of all the Warka proto-cuneiform tablets that Nissen identified on archaeological grounds as earlier than archaic level IIIc have been searched to find numeral notations in systems Š, Š´, Š´´ and Š* that express quantities as large as, or larger than, 53 Imperial bushels. The results are set out below. The first text presented is the earliest of the eight reproduced. Nissen established that the tablet was deposited in its find spot in the area of Temple C before the *Zwischenschicht* between levels IVa and IIIc was laid. In the case of the other texts (texts 2–7 and W 9393,d), Nissen could not define the *terminus ante quem* more precisely than level IIIc. A reference is given to the page or pages in Green and Nissen (1987) which define a text's stratigraphical location. Texts 2–7 are presented in the order of their excavation numbers (W = Warka), since a chronological ordering is not possible.

The transliterations are reproduced from the database of the Berlin Uruk project as published on the floppy disk that comes with Englund (1994). Lines are defined as being on the obverse (O) or reverse (R), and by case number (01, 02, etc.), followed by line number (01, 02, etc.). A semicolon marks the boundary between numeral signs and ideographic signs. The transliterations of the ideographic signs have been retained for the benefit of readers who may want to see the numeral signs in full context, but they have been ignored as a possible aid in identifying the objects quantified, with the one exception of W 9393,d, as noted below. The abbreviation *ZATU* refers to the sign-list in Green and Nissen (1987), and SZ and H represent Š and Ḫ, respectively. The sign # is placed before a damaged sign, and ' indicates a break in the text.

Each transliteration is followed by a 'translation' in which the number signs are converted into their equivalents in Imperial bushels (the ideographic signs are ignored). The numeral system is identified at the beginning of each line of 'translation'. A + sign after the system identifier Š´´ indicates that the line includes one or more signs from another system, specifically, the Š system; the system identifier for these signs is indicated in square brackets after each of the signs.[9] The # sign in the 'translations' indicates the equivalent of a numeral

9. For the use of signs from the Š system together with signs from the Š´´ system, see Green and Nissen (1987: 140).

notation with one or more damaged signs; the original notation in such cases can be assumed to have been greater than what has been preserved.

(1) W 21060,2. *Terminus ante quem*: *Zwischenschicht* (Green and Nissen 1987: 38, 40)

O0101	1-N47 3-N05 4-N42A ; U4 SZE-A EN-A
O0102	1-N20 ' ; '
O0103	1-N47 ' 1-N05 ; DUG-A '
R0101	2-N47 3-N20 1-N05 4-N42A ; KAB NAM2 GIR3-A+SZE-B SZE-A

O0101	Š*	$(1 \times 39) + (3 \times 0.65) + (4 \times 0.13)$	= 41.47 bu
O0102	Š*	(1×3.9) break	= 3.90 (+ χ ?) bu
O0103	Š*	(1×39) break + (1×0.65)	= 39.65 (+ χ?) bu
R0101	Š*	$(2 \times 39) + (3 \times 3.9) + (1 \times 0.65) + (4 \times 0.13)$	= 90.87 bu[10]

(2) W 9123,v. *Terminus ante quem*: IIIc (Green and Nissen 1987: 34)

O0101	' 1-N36; ' # NESAG2-A # TE
O0102	1-N36; GI AL
R0101	# 3-N36 ' ; # AN '

O0101	Š″	break (1×117)	= 117 (+ χ?) bu
O0102	Š″	(1×117)	= 117 bu
R0101	Š″	$(\#3 \times 117)$ break	= #351 (+ χ ?) bu

(3) W 9335,r. *Terminus ante quem*: IIIc (Green and Nissen 1987: 34)

O0101	' # 1-N25; ZATU621-B '
O0102	1-N42A ; # SZA '
O0103	' ; '
R0101	' # 1-N01 ; U4 # EN-B '
R0102	1-N34 # 8-N14 4-N01 # 3-N39B ; SZA
R0103	# 1-N34 ' ; '

O0101	Š*	break $(\#1 \times 0.065)$	= #0.065 (+ χ ?) bu
O0102	Š*	(1×0.13)	= 0.13 bu
O0103		break	break

10. If 3-NO5 is restored in the break in O0102, and if 1-N20 is restored in the break in O0103, the numeral notation on the reverse gives the total of the notations in the three lines of the obverse. For a simple example of this kind of text, using the S system, see Nissen, Damerow and Englund 1993: 20, fig. 22. Texts 2 (W 9123,v) and 7 (W 20740,6) below may be of the same type, but they have too many breaks and damaged signs for the restorations to be obvious.

R0101   Š?   break (#1 × 0.65)   = #0.65 (+ χ ?) bu
R0102   Š^{11} (1 × 117) + (8 × 3.9) + (4 × 0.65)   = 150.8 bu
R0103   Š?   (#1 × 117) break   = #117 (+ χ ?) bu

(4) W 9579,w. *Terminus ante quem*: IIIc (Green and Nissen 1987: 34)

O0101   # 9-N34 # 1-N45 # 7-N14 # 3-N01 ; X
O0102   # 5-N36 # 1-N46 2-N14 # 3-N01 ; X
O0103   1-N36 2-N46 # 1-N04 ; # DU8-C+HI ?
O0201   # 1-N46 # 1-N19 ' # 2-N01; # GI
O0202   # 2-N36 # 1-N46 # 2-N19 # 2-N01 ?; # GI
O0203   # 2-N36 # 1-N46 ' # 1-N01 ; X '
O0204   # 1-N36 # 8-N14 # 1-N01 ; DA-C # U4 '

O0101   Š^{12} (#9 × 117) + (#1 × 39) + (#7 × 3.9) + (#3 × 0.65)
                                               = #1,121.25 bu
O0102   Š''+ (#5 × 117) + (#1 × 39) + (2 × 3.9) + (#3 × 0.65 [Š])
                                               = #633.75 bu
O0103   Š''   (1 × 117) + (2 × 39) + (#1 × 0.65)   = #195.65 bu
O0201   Š''   (#1 × 39) + (#1 × 3.9) break (#2 × 0.65)
                                               = #44.2 (+ χ?) bu
O0202   Š''+ (#2 × 117) + (#1 × 39) + (#2 × 3.9) + (#2 × 0.65 [Š])
                                               = #282.1 bu
O0203   Š''+ (#2 × 117) + (#1 × 39) break + (#1 × 0.65 [Š])
                                               = #273.65 (+ χ?) bu
O0204   Š''+ (#1 × 117) + (#8 × 3.9) + (#1 × 0.65 [Š])   = #148.85 bu

(5) W 9655,h. *Terminus ante quem*: IIIc (Green and Nissen 1987: 34)

O0101   1-N48 # 7-N34 ' # 6-N14 ' 3-N01 ; # SZE-A

O0101   Š^{13} (1 × 1,170) + (#7 × 117) break + (#6 × 3.9)
         break + (3 × 0.13)   = #2,012.79 (+ χ?) bu

(6) W 9656,k. *Terminus ante quem*: IIIc (Green and Nissen 1987: 34)

O0101   # 3-N34 2-N45 ; # NESAG2-A

O0101   Š^{14} (#3 × 117) + (2 × 39)   = #429 bu

11. The Š system is identified in R0102 by the presence of N39B, which is unique to that system.

12. The sequence of signs in O0101 identifies the system as Š.

13. The sequence of signs is the same as in the S system, but N14 can occur no more than five times in S.

14. The sequence of the signs identifies the system as Š.

(7) W 20740,6. *Terminus ante quem*: IIIc (Green and Nissen 1987: 37, 40)

O0101	1-N49 # 2-N36 # 1-N46 # 3-N19 ' ; '
O0102	# 1-N48 # 4-N34 # 2-N14 # 1-N01 ' ; '
R0101	' # 4-N36 # 1-N45 # 4-N14 # 3-N01 ' ; SZE-A 3-N57 '

O0101 Š″ (1 × 1,170) + (#2 × 117) + (#1 × 39) + (#3 × 3.9) break
$$= \#1,454.7\ (+\ \chi?)\ \text{bu}$$

O0102 Š? (#1 × 1,170) + (#4 × 117) + (#2 × 3.9) + (#1 × 0.13) break
$$= \#1,645.93\ (+\ \chi?)\ \text{bu}$$

R0101 Š″ + break (#4 × 117) + (#1 × 39 [Š]) + (#4 × 3.9 [Š]) + (#3 × 0.65 [Š])
$$= \#524.55\ (+\ \chi?)\ \text{bu}$$

One other text is reproduced here, although it has not been included in the sequence of the preceding seven. This is because it does not meet the search criteria established for the other texts. It is W 9393,d, the text mentioned above as an exception to the rule that the ideographic signs have not been taken into account in establishing the identity of the objects quantified. Only three numeral signs are used in the four-line text (N-14, N-34 and N-48), and each line has only one numeral sign. N-14 is used in the S, B, E, G, and Š systems; N-34 is used in the S, B, and Š systems; and N-48 is used in the S and Š systems. The text nicely illustrates the problem caused by the multivalency of many of the numeral signs. However, the ideographic signs HI.GUNU in the first line denote a kind of grain according to Damerow and Englund (1987: 133-34, 139). This suggests that the numeral signs should be understood as belonging to the Š system, as assumed below.

(8) W 9393, d. *Terminus ante quem*: IIIc (Green and Nissen 1987: 34)

O0101	# 3-N14 ; # HI.GUNU-A?
O0102	1-N48;
O0103	1-N48;
O0104	1-N34;

O0101 Š	(#3 × 3.9)	= #11.7 bu
O0102 Š	(1 × 1,170)	= 1,170 bu
O0103 Š	(1 × 1,170)	= 1,170 bu
O0104 Š	(1 × 117)	= 117 bu

Table 2 shows the quantities of cereals as large as, or larger than, 53 Imperial bushels that are recorded in texts 1–7 in descending order

48 *Urbanism in Antiquity*

of magnitude, rounded off to the nearest whole number. Calculations based on notations with damaged signs, or from lines with breaks, are followed by + to indicate that the amount recorded on the complete tablet was probably larger than what is indicated here.

Imperial bushels	Reference
2,013+	W 9655,h O01101
1,646+	W 20740,6 O0102
1,455+	W 20740,6 O0101
1,121+	W 9579,w O0101
634+	W 9579,w O0102
525+	W 20740,6 R0101
429+	W 9656,k O0101
351+	W 9123,v R0101
274+	W 9579,w O0201
194+	W 9579,w O0103
151	W 9335,r R0102
149+	W 9579,w O0204
117+	W 9335,r R0103
117	W 9123,v O0101, O0102
91	W 21060,2 R0101

Table 2. Quantities of cereals of 53 Imperial bushels or larger that are recorded in texts 1–7.

These quantities are large enough to support the hypothesis that the proto-cuneiform tablets on which they were recorded were used for government administration. And this conclusion strengthens the argument that writing was a contributing factor in the rise of urbanism. Further evidence would undoubtedly be available if the search were extended to tablets that can be dated to the Late Uruk Period only on the basis of palaeography, and if due attention were paid to the ideographic entries on the tablets.

BIBLIOGRAPHY

Adams, R. McC.
1981   *Heartland of Cities* (Chicago and London: University of Chicago Press).

Damerow, P., and R.K. Englund
    1987   'Die Zahlzeichensysteme der Archaischen Texte aus Uruk', in *Zeichen-liste der Archaischen Texte aus Uruk* (ed. M.W. Green, H.J. Nissen, P. Damerow and R.K. Englund; Berlin: Gebr. Mann): 117-66.

Donbaz, V., and N. Yoffee
    1986   *Old Babylonian Texts from Kish Conserved in the Istanbul Archaeological Museum* (Malibu: Undena).

Englund, R.K., with a contribution by R.M. Boehmer
    1994   *Archaic Administrative Texts from Uruk: The Early Campaigns* (Berlin: Gebr. Mann).

Gelb, I.J.
    1965   'The Ancient Mesopotamian Ration System', *JNES* 25: 230-43.

Green, M.W., and H.J. Nissen with assistance of P. Damerow and R.K. Englund
    1987   *Zeichenliste der Archaischen Texte aus Uruk* (Berlin: Gebr. Mann).

Nissen, H.J.
    1987   'Datierung der Archaischen Texte aus Uruk', in *Zeichenliste der Archaischen Texte aus Uruk* (ed. M.W. Green, H.J. Nissen, P. Damerow, and R.K. Englund; Berlin: Gebr. Mann): 21-51.

Nissen, H.J., P. Damerow and R.K. Englund
    1993   *Archaic Bookkeeping* (Chicago: University of Chicago Press).

Postgate, J.N.
    1992   *Early Mesopotamia* (London and New York: Routledge).

URBANISATION ET 'REDISTRIBUTION'* DE SURPLUS AGRICOLES EN MÉSOPOTAMIE SEPTENTRIONALE (3000–2500 AV. J.-C.)

Michel Fortin

Depuis la création du concept de 'Révolution urbaine' par Childe (1936, 1950), l'urbanisation a été un phénomène socio-économique qui a fait l'objet de plusieurs recherches par les anthropologues et les archéologues travaillant dans différentes aires culturelles (Ucko *et al.* 1972; Manzamilla 1987; Huot 1988), mais notamment par ceux oeuvrant au Proche-Orient (Lampl 1968; Huot *et al.* 1990) et en particulier en Mésopotamie (Nissen 1987; Huot 1989: 23-34; 1994) d'autant que cette région du monde antique fut, en particulier avec la ville d'Uruk, une source d'inspiration importante pour Childe (1952: 123-47) dans l'élaboration de son concept révolutionnaire.

L'étude de l'urbanisation en Mésopotamie doit beaucoup aux prospections d'Adams (1966, 1972, 1981; Adams et Nissen 1972). Mais toutes ces recherches pour tenter de définir le processus de mise en place de l'urbanisation en Mésopotamie, dès le IVème millénaire, soit pendant la période d'Uruk, se sont concentrées essentiellement sur le sud de la Mésopotamie.

Les débuts de l'urbanisation en Mésopotamie septentrionale

La Mésopotamie septentrionale a pendant longtemps été négligée à cet égard. Toutefois, en 1965, dans une synthèse sur *The Advent of the Era of Townships in Northern Mesopotamia*, Jawad (1965: 42-76) traita de l'émergence de l'urbanisation en Mésopotamie septentrionale au IIIème millénaire à partir uniquement des maigres données alors disponibles.

---

* L'usage des guillemets s'explique par le fait que ce concept de redistribution, souvent invoqué dans les études portant sur l'évolution culturelle des sociétés pré-étatiques, a été récemment repensé: Bayman 1995: 37-41.

Depuis, de récentes recherches archéologiques menées dans la région dite du 'triangle du Khabour', au nord-est de la Syrie, ont démontré que des sites comme (fig. 1): Chuera (Orthmann 1986, 1990: 11-37), Leilan (Weiss 1983, 1985, 1986, 1990b; Weiss *et al.* 1990), Mozan (Buccellati et Kelly-Buccellati 1988; Kelly-Buccellati 1990b) et Brak (Oates 1985, 1986, 1990: 139-44; Oates et Oates 1994) sont devenues de véritables villes au cours du IIIème millénaire (Schwartz 1985, 1987; Oates 1993a; Wilkinson 1994).

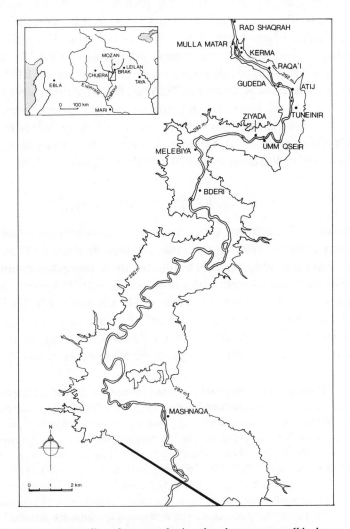

Figure 1.   Carte montrant l'emplacement de sites dans la moyenne vallée du Khabour et en Haute Mésopotamie mentionnés dans le texte.

La fouille de ces sites a révélé que non seulement ce phénomène est-il survenu plus tardivement en Mésopotamie septentrionale qu'en Mésopotamie méridionale, mais encore que la Mésopotamie méridionale aurait exercé, selon certains, une influence déterminante—particulièrement manifeste à Leilan (Weiss 1990a, 1990b)—dans la formation d'états secondaires (Fried 1967: 240-42; Price 1978) dans la plaine du Khabour, en Syrie du nord (Weiss 1992, 1993; Weiss *et al.* 1993).[1]

En effet, s'inspirant des théories de formation des états secondaires axées sur l'acquisition de matières premières et le commerce avec l'extérieur (Posnansky 1973; Adams 1974; Webb 1974, 1975; Haas 1982; Kipp et Schortman 1989), Weiss (1990a) et Kelly-Buccellati (1990a, 1990b: 131), ont récemment argumenté que les Mésopotamiens du sud seraient passés par les plaines du Khabour, au IIIème millénaire, pour accéder aux mines de Turquie (Palmieri 1985: 209; Moorey 1993: 41-42) qui furent très importantes à cette époque (Palmieri *et al.* 1993) notamment pour l'exploitation de l'étain (Yener et Özbal 1987; Yener *et al.* 1991; Yener et Goodway 1992; Yener et Vandiver 1993a, 1993b; Vandiver *et al.* 1993; Muhly 1993; Yener 1995).

La moyenne vallée du Khabour (Syrie)

Dans leurs déplacements vers ces régions septentrionales, les Mésopotamiens devaient, entre autres routes d'accès, remonter le Khabour, le plus important affluent de l'Euphrate, alors navigable comme des extraits de textes provenant des archives de Mari l'attestent (Kupper 1964: 115; Graeve 1981: 17; Finet 1984; Klengel 1984: 27; Durand 1988: 156 note a; Charpin *et al.* 1988: 513 note 32).[2] Ce faisant, ils passaient par la moyenne vallée du Khabour. Or, depuis 1984, les fouilles réalisées sur plusieurs petits établissements ruraux du IIIème

1. Schwartz (1994a) est plutôt d'avis que l'apparition des cités en Mésopotamie septentrionale et en particulier en Syrie du nord est endogène: des chefferies complexes se seraient graduellement transformées en systèmes étatiques. Pour une critique de ce modèle néo-évolutionniste, proposé originellement par Service (1962, 1975), dans lequel la chefferie (Earle 1987, 1991) précède l'apparition de l'état, voir notamment, Yoffee (1979, 1993), McGuire (1983) et Paynter (1989).

2. Contrairement à ce qu'a affirmé Mallowan (1936: 2) dans le bref compte rendu de sa reconnaissance de la vallée. La navigabilité du Khabour semble s'être continuée certainement jusqu'au Moyen Age quand le commerce du coton, dont la région du Haut Khabour est si riche, se faisait par la rivière (Lewy 1952: 2; Stange 1905: 95).

millénaire situés dans cette portion de la vallée du Khabour (Bounni 1990; Fortin 1991a), directement sur les berges de la rivière, nous portent à croire que ces derniers, d'après les indices archéologiques qu'ils ont révélés, ont certainement joué un rôle déterminant dans la mise en place et le développement de l'urbanisation en Mésopotamie du nord (fig. 1).

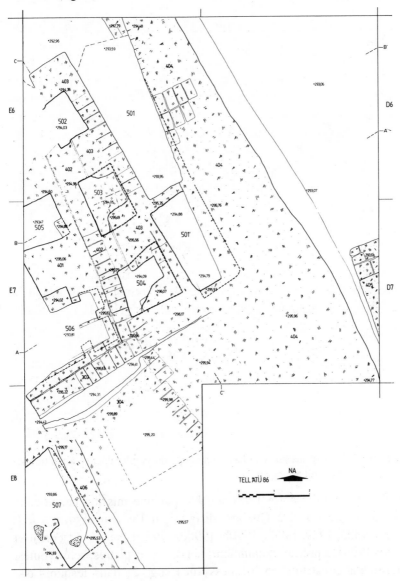

Figure 2a.

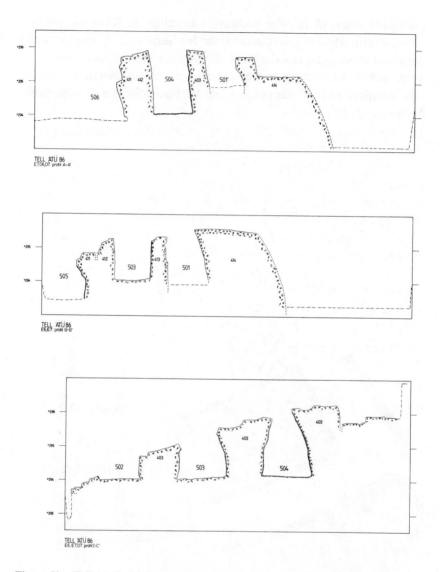

Figure 2b. Tell 'Atij: dessins en plan et en coupe du grenier dégagé à l'extrémité
nord du tell principal.

Tell 'Atij, fouillé entre 1986 et 1993 par une mission canadienne
de l'Université Laval à Québec, dirigée par l'auteur (Fortin 1987,
1988a, 1988b, 1989, 1990a, 1990b, 1990c, 1993, 1994, 1995; Fortin et
Cooper 1994), a produit notamment: (1) des silos plâtrés, semi-voûtés,
entièrement construits en briques crues (fig. 2) dans lesquels des
grains avaient été entreposés et dans lesquels également avaient été

jetées, au moment de leur abandon, quelques jarres de dimensions comparables qui ont probablement servi d'étalons de mesure pour le transvasement des grains, opération qui nécessitait l'usage d'entonnoirs qui furent également retrouvés; (2) des entrepôts rectangulaires aux sols et aux murs plâtrés ainsi qu'aux plafonds voûtés, superposés les uns aux autres dans les 13 niveaux du tell principal (figs. 3 and 4); (3) un édifice au plan en grillage (fig. 4) construit pratiquement sur le sol vierge; (4) un épais mur d'enceinte érigé dès la première phase d'occupation du site (fig. 5); (5) des *calculi* (fig. 6) et une tablette numérale (fig. 7) qui témoignent de l'existence d'un système, bien qu'archaïque pour l'époque, de comptabilité; (6) un sceau-cylindre (fig. 8): indice probant d'activités liées à l'exportation et au commerce; (7) la représentation d'une embarcation à voile tracée sur la face d'une roue de char miniature en terre cuite (fig. 9); (8) des ancres en pierre que devaient posséder ces barques (fig. 10) et des lests pour ralentir leur course lors de leur descente du Khabour en raclant le lit de la rivière (Finet 1984: 93).

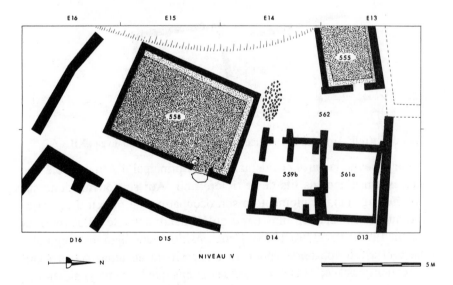

Figure 3.   Tell 'Atij: plan des structures d'entreposage du niveau V.

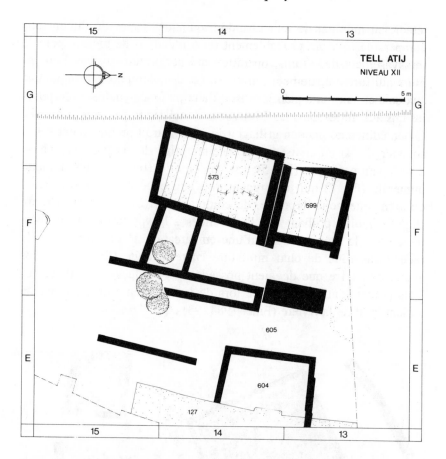

Figure 4.   Tell 'Atij: plan de l'édifice en grillage mis au jour au niveau XII.

Par ailleurs, la paroi occidentale du tell principal d'Atij a révélé une succession d'anciens lits de la rivière; tell 'Atij se trouvait donc sur une île (fig. 11), au moment de son occupation, au milieu d'une rivière qui était beaucoup plus large qu'à l'heure actuelle (Blackburn et Fortin 1994; Blackburn 1995). Cette position géographique singulière est tout à fait appropriée pour un comptoir ou un relais commercial où étaient stockés, dans des silos, des grains que l'on chargeait sur des barques qui naviguaient sur le Khabour en se servant de lests pour ralentir leur course en descendant la rivière.

A tell al-Raqa'i, la présence d'un grand édifice circulaire, préservé jusqu'à une hauteur de trois mètres, comprenant des corridors voûtés, plusieurs plate-formes, des fours et des silos sans porte avec plafonds en encorbellement, des édifices au plan en grillage ainsi que de nombreuses petites pièces agglutinées tout autour, a amené les fouilleurs (Curvers 1987; Curvers et Schwartz 1990; Schwartz et Curvers 1992, 1993–94; Schwartz 1994b: 20-28) à voir en ce site un petit établissement rural spécialisé où des grains étaient entreposés et transformés, sur une échelle 'industrielle' artisanale, en produits alimentaires. La découverte d'une tablette numérale et d'empreintes de sceaux est venue corroborer cette interprétation.

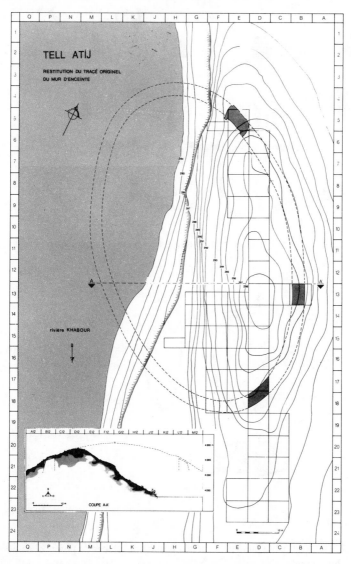

Figure 5. Tell 'Atij: carte reconstituant le tracé originel le mur d'enceinte.

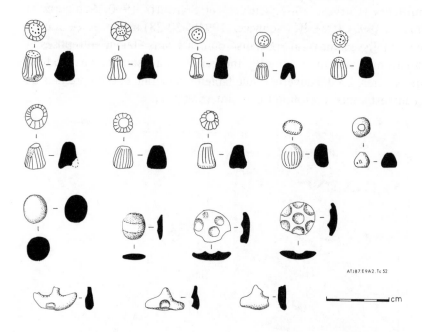

ATJ87.E9A2.Tc 52

cm

Figure 6.   Tell 'Attij: calculi en terre crue retrouvés en association avec un grenier.

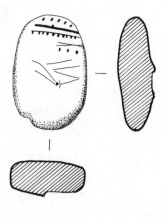

ATJ87. D13A18.Tb1

Figure 7.   Tell 'Atij: petite tablette numérale portant des traces de points et de lignes
            horizontales.

ATJ86.D15A4.L28

Figure 8.   Tell 'Attij: dessin d'un sceau-cylindre trouvé au sommet du tell principal.

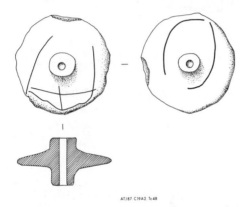

ATJ87.C19A2.Tc48

Figure 9.   Tell 'Atij: silhouette d'une barque tracée sur une roue de char miniature en terre cuite.

Un grand, 5 x 10 m, édifice au plan en grillage, qui aurait été construit au Dynastique Archaïque I, a également été retrouvé à Mashnaqa (Beyer 1993: 7, 1995: 44).

La fouille du petit site de Kerma a révélé une grande pièce rectangulaire, 4 x 6 m, au toit en encorbellement, autour de laquelle étaient accolées des cellules sur deux de ses côtés; tout le complexe était entouré d'un épais et massif mur de défense en briques crues. La découverte sur les sols de ces pièces de très grandes quantités de grains carbonisés, surtout de l'orge et un peu de blé, nous confirme leur fonction d'entreposage (Saghié 1991). Une seconde structure similaire, équipée de banquettes plâtrées, a été dégagée dans un autre secteur du tell ainsi qu'un petit canal en pente douce entièrement construit en briques crues et enduit d'un crépi à l'intérieur qui aurait servi de déversoir pour faciliter le transport des grains depuis les silos jusqu'à une embarcation qui aurait accosté à proximité.

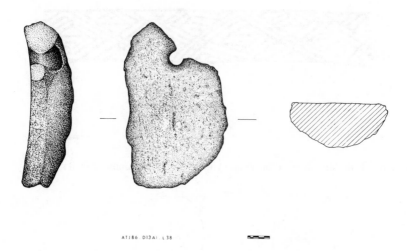

ATJ 86 D13 A1 L 38

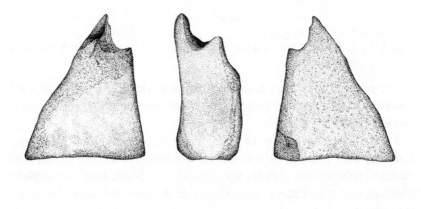

ATJ 86 . E7A6'. L 49

Figure 10. Tell 'Attij: modèles d'ancres en pierre abandonnées dans divers niveaux
            du tell principal.

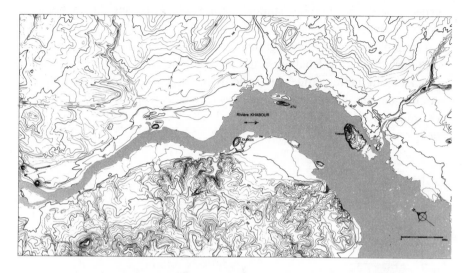

Figure 11. Carte montrant que le tell principal d'Attij était une île au moment de son occupation.

Au milieu du village moderne de Rad Shaqrah, furent exhumées plusieurs grandes pièces aux murs et aux sols plâtrés contenant encore des jarres d'entreposage et des bassins en plâtre de gypse. Ces installations liées à l'entreposage et au traitement des produits qui y étaient stockés étaient accolées à un mur d'enceinte de briques crues épais de quatre mètres, renforcé par un glacis en pierres (Bielinski 1992, 1993, 1994, 1995).

La grande tranchée en escalier pratiquée sur un flanc du tell de Ziyada a permis de mettre au jour quelques silos rectangulaires plâtrés munis de banquettes (Buccellati, Buia et Reimer 1991).

Enfin, tell Gudeda, le second site de la zone de sauvetage fouillé par la mission canadienne placée sous la direction de l'auteur (Fortin 1988b, 1990a, 1990b, 1991b, 1993, 1994, 1995; Fortin, Routledge et Routledge 1994), n'a pas donné de silos mais, dans un secteur, une concentration de fours à cuisson près desquels plus d'une quarantaine de meules en pierre locale furent ramassées et des bassins en plâtre de gypse dégagés (fig. 12). Si des grains n'étaient pas stockés à tell Gudeda, ils y étaient toutefois transformés en produits comestibles.

Donc, tous les dispositifs d'entreposage à caractère public découverts sur ces sites du IIIème millénaire de la moyenne vallée du Khabour, les artefacts qui leur sont associés ainsi que, dans certains cas, les données environnementales, nous autorisent à interpréter ces sites comme des espèces de dépôts à grains, stratégiquement placés le long du Khabour, une voie fluviale utilisée pour les échanges commerciaux.

Qui plus est, ces dépôts à grains furent érigés dans une zone limitée du cours moyen du Khabour à une époque—le IIIème millénaire—où précisément cette vallée fut soudainement et densément peuplée comme en témoignent les résultats des récentes prospections de Kühne (Kühne et Röllig 1974–75, 1977–78, 1978–79, 1983; Kühne 1988) et de Monchambert (1983, 1984a, 1984b).

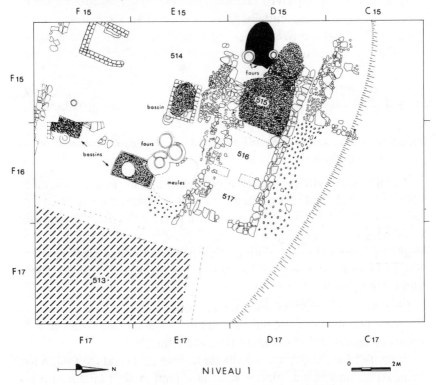

Figure 12. Tell Gudeda: plan du niveau I indiquant la position d'und concentration de fours autour desquelles furent retrouvés plusieurs meules en pierre et des bassins en plâtre de gypse.

Ce peuplement de la vallée, très différent de celui que connaissent les plaines du Haut Khabour à la même époque (Stein et Wattenmaker 1990; Stein 1994), est toutefois insuffisant (Hole 1991: 17-19) pour justifier la présence d'une telle concentration de sites aussi spécialisés. A mon avis, cette dernière devait être reliée, d'une manière quelconque, à une entité politique distincte située en dehors de la moyenne vallée du Khabour.

Urbanisation et entreposage de surplus agricoles

Par ailleurs, comme le lien entre l'entreposage de surplus de produits agricoles et l'urbanisation a été démontré depuis longtemps (Childe 1946: 18; Redman 1978: 216; Adams 1966: 46, 1984: 95), selon moi, ces dépôts à grains auraient été construits et administrés, durant le IIIème millénaire, par une ou des cités-états qui venaient y chercher un complément à leur approvisionnement habituel dans le cadre de cette 'second, managerial, agricultural révolution', comme l'appelle Postgate (1992: 157-58), qui a lieu précisément au début du IIIème millénaire et qui est une conséquence directe du développement urbain en Mésopotamie.

Il est difficile d'imaginer comment des sites de la moyenne vallée du Khabour où étaient stockées et traitées des quantités appréciables de grains (Schwartz 1994b: 25-28) puissent avoir eu un rôle à jouer dans le réseau d'approvisionnement de centres urbains comme Mozan, Leilan et Brak qui étaient entourés de vastes et fertiles plaines dont les riches terres bien arrosées par les pluies annuelles, plus de 300 mm, étaient plus productives que celles de la moyenne vallée et largement suffisantes pour subvenir aux besoins alimentaires des habitants de ces villes du nord (Weiss 1986),[3] d'autant qu'une prospection réalisée autour de Leilan en 1987 semble indiquer que même lorsque Leilan devint une ville, son territoire agricole environnant ne fit pas l'objet d'une exploitation en vue de créer des surplus agricoles (Stein et Wattenmaker 1990; Stein 1994).

Quant à la possibilité que les surplus de production de grains récoltés dans ces fertiles et productives plaines septentrionales aient été stockés dans les greniers de la moyenne vallée du Khabour pour être redistribués ensuite à des entités politiques plus sujettes à des disettes en raison de la faiblesse des précipitations annuelles, moins de 250 mm, ou de leur imprévisible fluctuation d'une année à l'autre, à savoir celles au sud de la moyenne vallée du Khabour soumises aux aléas de la culture irriguée, elle est intenable à mes yeux parce que ces

---

3. Si les fouilleurs de tell Brak sont d'accord avec cette observation (Oates 1993a: 52), l'inventeur de tell Leilan, Harvey Weiss, quant à lui, croit que les greniers d'Atij, de Kerma et de Raqa'i auraient pu *aussi* avoir servi à compléter l'approvisionnement en grains de tell Brak (Weiss 1993: 43) via Aswad situé à mi-chemin entre Brak et les dépôts du Moyen Khabour (Weiss 1992: 93; Weiss et Courty 1993: 137).

dépôts sont antérieurs à l'apparition de villes en Syrie du nord et qu'en plus la paléobotaniste associée à notre mission (McCorriston 1995) nous a appris que les occupants d'Atij ne remplissaient pas leurs silos de grains importés des plaines du triangle du Khabour mais plutôt de grains de plantes qui croissaient dans la vallée même.[4] Du reste, s'explique ainsi la présence de nombreux éléments de faucilles en silex dans tous les niveaux d'occupation du tell principal d'Atij.[5]

Dès le IVème millénaire (période d'Uruk), voire même avant (Oates 1993b), les habitants du sud de la Mésopotamie avaient pris l'habitude de tirer profit de la Mésopotamie septentrionale (Algaze 1989a, 1993a, 1993b). Cette situation se serait en quelque sorte continuée au IIIème millénaire (Crawford 1992; Weiss et Courty 1993: 134). Elle aurait alors pris une forme différente avec l'apparition d'entités administratives et politiques locales qui auraient contrôlé les échanges commerciaux avec le sud, c'est-à-dire les routes commerciales et la production agricole qui était stockée dans les entrepôts (Rova 1988: 186-200). D'autre part, nous savons, par des textes du IIème millénaire, que les cités-états de la Basse Mésopotamie avaient fréquemment recours, à cette époque, à des expéditions vers la Haute Mésopotamie afin de s'approvisionner en grains lors de disettes alimentaires ou de famine. Il n'est pas interdit de supposer que la situation qui existait au IIIème millénaire ne devait pas être très différente de celle du IIème millénaire.

Suivant ce scénario, on ne peut passer outre la présence de Mari, ville commerçante et transitaire par excellence, stratégiquement localisée sur l'Euphrate en aval de la confluence du Khabour avec ce fleuve, lequel était relié avec son affluent par un important canal de navigation, le Nahr Daourîn, long de 120 km (Finet 1985; Geyer et Monchambert 1987: 306-15, 1990: 75-77; Monchambert 1990; Margueron 1987b: 498, 1988b: 52-54, 1989, 1990, 1991a sous presse),

4.   A l'encontre de Schwartz (1994a: 165) qui croit que les chefferies établies dans les plaines septentrionales du Haut Khabour auraient pu avoir expédié leurs surplus de production dans les dépôts du Moyen Khabour, ce qui aurait accru leur pouvoir et ainsi conduit à la formation de structures étatiques.

5.   L'outillage en silex de tell 'Atij, comprenant ces multiples éléments de faucille, est actuellement étudié par Jacques Chabot dans le cadre d'une thèse de doctorat qui sera bientôt défendue à l'Université Laval puis publiée dans la série des rapports définitifs de la mission canadienne en Syrie sur les sites de tell 'Atij et tell Gudeda.

dont l'entretien était une source de constantes préoccupations pour les rois de Mari (Birot 1974: 49; Dalley 1984: 169; Durand 1990: 136-37). Mais plus importantes encore sont les tablettes provenant des archives de son palais qui font état d'expéditions par bateau[6] vers les plaines du Haut Khabour (Dossin *et al.* 1964: 61; Finet 1969, 1984; Dalley 1984: 169-70; Birot 1993: 9), jusqu'à tell Brak-Nagar (Charpin 1994), pour aller y chercher du grain, notamment de l'orge. Qui plus est, certaines font carrément allusion à des expéditions militaires dirigées par le roi au début du IIème millénaire afin de s'approprier des pâturages d'été dans la région de tell Barri-Kahat pour les troupeaux d'ovins de la région de Mari qui devaient donc franchir cette distance lors de leur transhumance (Charpin 1990; Durand 1990: 104; Birot 1993: 9, 110). Une bulle-enveloppe inscrite trouvée à Chagar Bazar vient même nous confirmer que ces expéditions de grains par bateau sur le Khabour jusqu'à Mari se sont déroulées à l'époque akkadienne (Mallowan 1937: 96 et pl. XIIIB; Gadd 1937: 178; Mallowan 1966: 94; Weiss et Courty 1993: 148). Enfin, d'après la céramique du chantier B (Lebeau 1987), la ville de Mari aurait été fondée entre 3000 et 2800 av. J.-C. (Margueron 1987a: 22, 1987b: 493, 1988a: 43),[7] pour des raisons de contrôle du trafic fluviale commercial (Margueron 1990; Crawford 1992: 80), soit à peu près au même moment où le comptoir commercial de tell 'Atij était établi avec d'autres dans la moyenne vallée du Khabour.

Urbanisation et 'commerce'

Il me semble donc tout à fait possible que des relations commerciales quelconque, parfaitement bien attestées au début du IIème millénaire par des textes trouvés dans les archives du palais de Mari sur l'Euphrate, se soient développées entre cette cité-état et les dépôts à grains de la moyenne vallée du Khabour dès le début du IIIème millénaire (Margueron 1991a sous presse).

---

6. Au sujet de ce trafic fluviale et des sortes d'embarcations utilisées pour ce commerce, voir Margueron (1991b: 144-51).

7. Ce qui semble mis en doute par Schwartz (1994a: 158-66); un doute tout à fait injustifié selon le fouilleur de Mari, Jean Margueron (lettre à l'auteur datée du 4 février 1996).

Nous serions en présence, dans ce cas-ci, d'un commerce[8] dit de 'longue distance', selon la liste des diverses formes de commerce préparée par Beale (1973): *Long-Distance Organized Trade*, et dont les multiples aspects furent davantage expliqués par Kohl (1978). Plus précisément, ce modèle s'apparenterait à celui que Renfrew (1975) a désigné comme: *colonial enclave* ou encore *emissary trading*, selon le genre de relations sociales qu'il y avait entre le centre urbain et cette zone régionale. A ce sujet, Potts (1993: 395-96), dans une récente étude sur les relations commerciales entre la Mésopotamie et l'Iran au IIIème millénaire, a attiré l'attention sur l'existence assurée d'échanges non-réciproques notamment dans les cas où une entité politique puissante exerçait une forme de domination politique sur la région dont les produits étaient exploités. Une situation qui aurait existé à tepe Chenchi, un site contemporain près de Khorsabad, dans le nord de l'Irak, qu'Algaze (1989b: 15) vient d'interpréter comme un avant-poste spécialisé établi en périphérie par un état régional ou encore dans le Hamrin, au centre de l'Irak, avec le site de Gubba, parmi d'autres sites (tell Razuk, tell Maddhur) datés du début du IIIème millénaire, qui a produit un bâtiment circulaire qui fut interprété comme un grenier (Trümpelmann 1989: 72). En somme, les dépôts à grains du moyen Khabour auraient fait partie d'une structure organisationnelle simple, non compliquée comme North (1984: 261) les conçoit pour les économies pré-modernes, sans marché, selon Polanyi[9] (1957): soit une économie de redistribution (Oppenheim 1957; Hunt 1987: 181) à laquelle l'entreposage est intimement lié (Renger 1994: 178), d'autant que les terres qui auraient servi à garnir ces entrepôts auraient très bien pu appartenir en propre à l'Etat qui en tirait profit (Diakonoff 1974: 7-9, 1975; Renger 1994: 187-88).

J'ai de la difficulté à concevoir que des entrepreneurs privés (Foster 1977: 31-32),[10] indépendants,[11] autochtones aient pu prendre l'initiative

8.   Sur la définition encore vague chez les anthropologues du mot '*Trade*': Kipp et Schortman (1989: 372-73, 378). Pour Hunt (1987: 181 n. 35), il s'agirait plutôt d'un système de redistribution déterminé et administré par une autorité centrale.

9.   L'existence d'une économie sans marché en Mésopotamie, comme imaginée par Polanyi, semble être remise en question (Gledhill et Larsen 1982: 200-13).

10.   Quoique Adams (1974: 248) argumente en faveur d'entrepreneurs privés dans le cas de la Mésopotamie méridionale dès le milieu du IIIème millénaire pour le commerce de ville-à-ville avec Dilmun. Il a cependant reconnu par la suite (Adams 1984: 93) que leur liberté d'action devait être considérablement limitée.

11.   Même si la plupart des marchands qui se livraient au commerce à longue

de se lancer dans la construire de tant de grands greniers dans la moyenne vallée du Khabour; un tel programme d'investissement de longue durée comportait trop de risques et représentait des coûts trop importants. D'autre part, les produits comme le grain faisaient d'habitude partie des réseaux d'échanges publics (Zagarell 1986: 417). Je suis plutôt enclin à penser que des gens venant de l'entité politico-sociale à l'origine de tous ces établissements résidaient dans la vallée même pour assurer en quelque sorte le maintien du 'service' à longueur d'année: la saison des récoltes devait être aussi importante que celle du chargement des barques vu la quantité des produits stockés et le rôle vital joué par ces dépôts dans l'administration de la cité-état fondatrice. De plus, les grains analysés jusqu'à maintenant proviennent d'espèces qui poussaient lors des différentes saisons de l'année (McCorriston 1995). Les études traitant (Beale 1973: 143) du commerce à longue distance confirment que ce type de commerce nécessite un contrôle politique de la route et des zones où se trouvaient les ressources pour garantir un approvisionnement constant et suffisant.

Les quantités d'ossements d'animaux recueillis dans les couches du tell principal d'Atij m'ont amené à envisager la possibilité que les grains ensilés sur ce site aient pu avoir été utilisés comme fourrage pour des animaux, en l'occurrence des chèvres et des moutons, d'autant que les grains d'orge représentent un fort pourcentage. Or, l'orge est une plante céréalière facilement entreposable (Weiss 1986; McCorriston 1995: 42) et reconnue pour avoir servi de fourrage (Watson 1979: 68; Kramer 1982: 37). Les analyses de Zeder (1995) nous en apprendront sûrement plus en regard de cet 'entreposage indirect' (Flannery 1968: 87; Halstead et O'Shea 1982: 93; Halstead 1987: 83), c'est-à-dire cette transformation de denrées alimentaires périssables en produits plus stables comme des animaux qui eux peuvent être consommés au besoin et qui, en attendant, peuvent, de surcroît, fournir des produits secondaires tels le lait, le fromage et la laine (Andel et Runnels 1988: 242-44), comme cela a été vérifié dans le monde égéen (Halstead 1992, 1993, 1994: 208). A propos, McCorriston (1995) a déjà fait remarquer que les grains carbonisés recueillis à 'Atij, d'une part, proviennent surtout de coprolithes

distance en Mésopotamie méridionale au IIIème millénaire devaient dépendre d'une manière quelconque de cités-états (Snell 1977: 45-46), sans en être de simples agents (Powell 1977: 24-27), certains semblent n'avoir eu que des liens ponctuels avec des états (Yoffee 1981: 7-9).

d'animaux transformés en combustibles et, d'autre part, appartiennent à des espèces végétales qui poussent tellement au ras du sol qu'elles ont été forcément consommées par des animaux et non récoltées par des humains.

Les personnes requises pour faire fonctionner ces greniers de la moyenne vallée du Khabour n'avaient pas à être très nombreuses d'après des observations faites à Assiros, un établissement du Bronze Récent situé au nord de la Grèce (Jones *et al.* 1986: 84-85). Elles auraient constitué une classe sociale distincte, une élite formée, je pense, de bureaucrates (Hunt 1987), de marchands (Kupper 1989), ou de fonctionnaires, selon l'appellation que l'on veut leur donner, envoyés en mission par l'entité politique à l'origine des installations d'entreposage du moyen Khabour, à l'instar de la situation qui nous est rapportée dans les tablettes de Mari au IIème millénaire (Burke 1964): des marchands, originaires de la Mésopotamie méridionale auraient vécu à Mari même afin de veiller au bon déroulement des échanges commerciaux entre le nord et le sud (Crawford 1992: 81). Ces fonctionnaires étaient ainsi en mesure d'intégrer parfaitement bien les systèmes économiques régionaux à un centre politique puissant conformément au modèle 'centre-périphérie' (Rowlands 1987; Stanley et Alexander 1992). Ce sont probablement des membres de cette classe privilégiée de la société mariote dont on a retrouvé les tombes—une douzaine—sur le tell secondaire d'Atij et sur le tell principal même car plusieurs contenaient des marqueurs sociaux évidents tels des objets d'apparat, dont une parure ciselée dans un coquillage représentant un taureau (fig. 13) qui n'est sans rappeler celui découvert récemment à tell Brak (Oates et Oates 1992), ou des objets en bronze.

Conclusion

La moyenne vallée du Khabour se présentait, au IIIème millénaire, comme une zone écologique restreinte uniforme dans laquelle se trouvait une concentration importante de sites plutôt petits, espacés de quelques kilomètres seulement les uns des autres et répartis également sur les deux rives de la rivière, dont plusieurs étaient entièrement voués à l'entreposage et au traitement de grains, notamment d'orge, toute cette activité économique faisait manifestement l'objet d'un contrôle administratif (calculi, tablettes numérales, sceaux) de l'extérieur.

ATJ 87. D13A15. B 47

Figure 13.   Tell 'Atij: taureau en nacre de perle retrouvé parmi le mobilier funéraire d'une tombe.

Un tel type d'économie de subsistance spécialisée est un indicateur sûr de l'existence d'un État, du moins au Proche-Orient, comme Zeder (1988, 1991) l'a démontré lors de l'analyse des ossements d'animaux provenant de Malyan, en Iran. Cette spécialisation, dans le modèle que Zeder propose, ne comprend pas uniquement le produit lui-même des activités économiques d'une société mais aussi et surtout la spécialisation ou ségrégation des tâches liées à la production, au transport et au système de redistribution du produit en question; toutes ces opérations doivent en effet être accomplies par différents groupes de personnes, à des moments distincts et dans des endroits divers. Il va également de soi que si cette fragmentation des tâches est pour aboutir à un résultat productif et efficient, la prise de décision et l'administration de ces activités économiques doivent elles aussi être spécialisées et centralisées (Wright et Johnson 1975: 267; Wright 1978, 1984). A la lumière de ce modèle explicatif théorique, la situation qui avait cours dans la moyenne vallée du Khabour au IIIème millénaire semble donc indiquer l'existence d'un contrôle exercé par un état déjà bien établi dont le siège se trouvait dans un centre urbain à une distance appréciable de la vallée, ex. la ville de Mari, et avec laquelle elle entretenait des relations commerciales. La fondation de ce centre urbain aurait poussé ses occupants à chercher dans l'arrière-pays des

sources d'approvisonnment fiables ou complémentaires rendues néces-
saires par l'accroissement de sa population urbaine ou celle d'autres
cités avec lesquelles Mari entretenait des relations commerciales.

A tout événement, l'existence même de ces petits sites ruraux du
IIIème millénaire de la moyenne vallée du Khabour spécialisés dans le
stockage des grains et leur transformation ne s'explique que par le
développement de l'urbanisation en Mésopotamie septentrionale et les
problèmes qu'elle engendre en matière d'approvisionnement; une
catégorie de sites que Falconer et Savage (1995: 55) décrivent 'as a
supporting foundation for urbanism'.

BIBLIOGRAPHIE

Adams, R. McC.
1966 *The Evolution of Urban Society: Early Mesopotamia and Pre-hispanic Mexico* (Chicago: Aldine).
1972 'Patterns of Urbanization in Early Southern Mesopotamia', dans *Man, Settlement and Urbanism* (éd. P. Ucko; London: Duckworth): 735-50.
1974 'Anthropological Perspectives on Ancient Trade', *CA* 15: 239-58.
1981 *Heartland of Cities* (Chicago: University of Chicago Press).
1984 'Mesopotamian Social Evolution: Old Outlooks, New Goals', dans *On the Evolution of Complex Societies* (éd. T. Earle; Malibu: Undena): 79-129.
Adams, R. McC., et H.J. Nissen
1972 *The Uruk Countryside* (Chicago: University of Chicago Press).
Algaze, G.
1989a 'The Uruk Expansion: Cross-Cultural Exchange as a Factor in Early Mesopotamian Civilization', *CA* 30: 571-608.
1989b 'Tepe Chenchi: An Important Settlement near Khorsabad', dans *Essays in Ancient Civilization Presented to Helene J. Kantor* (éd. E. Leonard et B.B. Williams; Chicago: Oriental Institute): 1-25
1993a 'Expansionary Dynamics of Some Early Pristine States', *AA* 95: 304-33.
1993b *The Uruk World System: The Dynamics of Expansion of Early Mesopotamian Civilization* (Chicago: University of Chicago Press).
Andel, T.H., et C.N. Runnels
1988 'An Essay on the Emergence of Civilization in the Aegean World', *Ant* 62: 234-47.
Bayman, J.M.
1995 'Rethinking Redistribution in the Archaeological Record: Obsidian Exchange at the Marana Platform Mound', *JAR* 51: 37-63.
Beale, T.W.
1973 'Early Trade in Highland Iran: A View from a Source Area', *WA* 5: 133-48.

Beyer, D.
1993   'Mashnaqa 1993: rapport sommaire sur les travaux de la mission archéologique française', *Orient Express*: 7-8.
1995   'Mashnaqa (Syrie) 1994: rapport sommaire sur les travaux de la mission archéologique française', *Orient Express*: 43-46.

Bielinski, P.
1992   'The First Campaign of Excavations on Tell Rad Shaqrah (Haseke Southern Dam Basin)', *PAM* 3: 77-85.
1993   'Tell Rad Shaqrah 1992—The Fifth Season of Explorations in Northeast Syria', *PAM* 4: 119-27.
1994   'Tell Rad Shaqrah 1993', *PAM* 5: 154-63.
1995   'Tell Rad Shaqrah 1994', *PAM* 6: 109-17.

Birot, M.
1974   *Lettres de Yaqqim-Addu, Gouverneur de Sagarâtum* (Paris: Geuthner).
1993   *Correspondance des gouverneurs de Qattunân* (Paris: Editions Recherche sur les Civilisations).

Blackburn, M.
1995   'Environnement géomorphologique du centre de la moyenne vallée du Khabour, Syrie', *BCSMS* 29: 5-20.

Blackburn, M., et M. Fortin
1994   'Geomorphology of Tell Atij, Northern Syria', *Geo* 9: 57-74.

Bounni, A.
1990   'The Khabur and the Haseke Dam Projects and the Protection of Threatened Antiquities in the Region (A Preliminary Report), dans *Tall al-Hamidiya*. II. *Recent Excavations in the Upper Khaabur Region* (éd. S. Eichler *et al.*; Göttingen: Vandenhoeck & Ruprecht): 19-29.

Buccellati, G., et M. Kelly-Buccellatti
1988   *Mozan*. I. *The Soundings of the First Two Seasons* (Malibu: Undena).

Buccellati, G., D. Buia et S. Reimer (éds.)
1991   'Tell Ziyada: The First Three Seasons of Excavation (1988–1990)', *BCSMS* 21: 31-61.

Burke, M.L.
1964   'Lettres de Numusda-Nahrâri et de trois autres correspondants à Idiniatum', *Syria* 41: 67-103.

Charpin, D.
1990   'A Contribution to the Geography and History of the Kingdom of Kahat', dans *Tall Al-Hamadiya*, II (éd. S. Eichler *et al.*; Göttingen: Vandenhoeck & Ruprecht): 67-85.
1994   'Une campagne de Yahdun-Lîm en Haute-Mésopotamie', dans *Florilegium marianum. II. Recueil d'études à la mémoire de Maurice Birot* (éd. D. Charpin et J.-M. Durand; Paris: SEPOA): 177-200.

Charpin, D., F. Voannès, S. Lackenbacker et B. Lafort
1988   *Archives épistolaires de Mari I/2* (Paris: Editions Recherches sur les Civilisations).

Childe, V.G.
1936   *Man Makes Himself* (London: Watts).
1946   *What Happened in History* (Harmondsworth: Penguin Books).

1950 'The Urban Revolution', *The Town Planning Review* 21: 3-17.

1952 *New Light on the Most Ancient East* (New York: Praeger).

Crawford, H.

1992 'An Early Dynastic Trading Network in North Mesopotamia?', dans *La circulation des biens, des personnes et des idées dans le Proche-Orient ancien* (éd. D. Charpin et F. Joannès; Paris: Editions Recherche sur les Civilisations): 77-82.

Curvers, H.

1987 'The Middle Habur Salvage Operation: Excavations at Tell al-Raqa'i, 1986', *Akk* 55: 1-29.

Curvers, H., et G.M. Schwartz

1990 'Excavations at Tell al-Raqa'i: A small Rural Site of Early Urban Northern Mesopotamia', *AJA* 94: 3-23.

Dalley, S.

1984 *Mari and Karana: Two Old Babylonian Cities* (London et New York: Longman).

Diakonoff, I.M.

1974 *Structure of Society and State in Early Dynastic Sumer* (Los Angeles: Undena).

1975 'The Rural Community in the Ancient Near East', *JESHO* 18: 121-33.

Dossin, G., J. Bottéro, M. Birot, M. Lurton Burke, J. Kupper et A. Finet

1964 *Textes divers* (Paris: Geuthner).

Durand, J.-M.

1988 *Archives épistolaires de Mari*, I.1 (Paris: Editions Recherches sur les Civilisations).

1990 'Le sel à Mari (II): les salines sur les bords du Habur', *MARI* 6: 629-34.

Earle, T.

1987 'Chiefdoms in Archaeological and Ethnohistorical Perspective', *ARA* 16: 279-308.

1991 *Chiefdoms: Power, Economy, and Ideology* (Cambridge: Cambridge University Press).

Falconer, S.E., et S.H. Savage

1995 'Heartlands and Hinterlands: Alternative Trajectories of Early Urbanization in Mesopotamia and the Southern Levant', *AmAnt* 60: 37-58.

Finet, A.

1969 'L'Euphrate, route commerciale de la Mésopotamie', *AAAS* 19: 37-48.

1984 'Le Habur dans les archives de Mari', *AAAS* 34: 89-97.

1985 'Mari dans son contexte géographique', *MARI* 4: 41-44.

Flannery, K.V.

1968 'Origins and Ecological Effects of Early Near Eastern Domestication', dans *The Domestication and Exploitation of Plants and Animals* (éd. P. Ucko *et al.*; London: Duckworth): 73-100.

1972 'The Cultural Evolution of Civilization', *Annual Review of Ecology and Systematics* 3: 399-426.

Fortin, M.

1987 'Résultats de la première saison de fouilles de la mission canadienne à tell 'Atij, sur le Moyen Khabour, printemps 1986', *AAAS* 36-37: 144-63.

1988a   'Rapport préliminaire sur la première campagne de fouilles (printemps 1986) à tell 'Atij, sur le moyen Khabour (Syrie)', *Syria* 65: 139-71.

1988b   'Mission archéologique de l'université Laval en Syrie sur les sites de tell 'Atij et de tell Gudeda (IIIème millénaire av. J.-C.)', *Echos du Monde Classique/Classical Views* NS 32.7: 103-15.

1989   'Trois campagnes de fouilles à tell 'Atij: un comptoir commercial du IIIème millénaire av. J.-C. en Syrie du Nord', *BCSMS* 18: 35-56.

1990a   'Rapport préliminaire sur la seconde campagne de fouilles à tell 'Atij et la première à tell Gudeda (automne 1987), sur le moyen Khabour', *Syria* 67: 219-56.

1990b   'Résultats de la 3ème campagne de fouilles à tell 'Atij et de la 2ème à tell Gudeda, en Syrie du Nord', *Echos du Monde Classique/Classical Views* NS 34.9: 115-27.

1990c   'Rapport préliminaire sur la 3e campagne de fouilles à tell 'Atij et la 2e à tell Gudeda, sur le Khabour (automne 1988)', *Syria* 67: 535-57.

1991a   'Récentes recherches archéologiques dans la moyenne vallée du Khabour (Syrie)', *BCSMS* 21: 5-15.

1991b   'Tell Gudeda: un site 'industriel' du IIIème millénaire av. J.-C. dans la moyenne vallée du Khabour?', *BCSMS* 21: 63-77.

1994   'Rapport préliminaire sur la quatrième campagne à tell 'Atij et la troisième à tell Gudeda (printemps 1992)', *Syria* 71: 361-96.

1995   'Rapport préliminaire sur la cinquième campagne à tell 'Atij et la quatrième à tell Gudeda (printemps 1993)', *Syria* 72: 23-53.

Fortin, M., et L. Cooper
1994   'Canadian Excavations at Tell 'Atij (Syria) 1992–1993', *BCSMS* 27: 33-50.

Fortin, M., B. Routledge et C. Routledge
1994   'Canadian Excavations at Tell Gudeda (Syria) 1992–1993', *BCSMS* 27: 51-63.

Foster, B.R.
1977   'Commercial Activity in Sargonic Mesopotamia', *Iraq* 39: 31-43.

Fried, M.H.
1967   *The Evolution of Political Society: An Essay in Political Anthropology* (New York: Random House).

Gadd, C.J.
1937   'Tablets from Chagar Bazar, 1936', *Iraq* 4: 178-85.

Geyer, B., et J.-Y. Monchambert
1987   'Prospection de la moyenne vallée de l'Euphrate: rapport prélimi-naire: 1982–1985', *MARI* 5: 293-344.

1990   'Aménagements hydrauliques et terroir agricole dans la moyenne vallée de l'Euphrate', dans *Techniques et pratiques hydro-agricoles traditionnelles en domaine irrigué: Approche pluridisciplinaire des modes de culture avant la motorisation en Syrie. Actes du colloque de Damas 27 juin–1er juillet 1987* (éd. B. Geyer; Paris: Geuthner): 63-84.

Gledhill, J., et M. Larsen
1982   'The Polanyi Paradigm and a Dynamic Analysis of Archaic States', dans *Theory and Explanation in Archaeology* (éd. C. Renfrew *et al.*; New York: Academic Press): 197-299.

Graeve, M.-C. de
1981   *The Ships of the Ancient Near East (c.2000–500 BC)*, OLP 7.
Haas, J.
1982   *The Evolution of the Prehistoric State* (New York: Columbia University Press).
Halstead, P.
1987   Man and Other Animals in Later Greek Prehistory, BSA 82: 71-83.
1992   'Agriculture in the Bronze Age Aegean: Towards a Model of Palatial Economy', dans *Agriculture in Ancient Greece* (éd. B. Wells; Stockholm: Skrifter utgivna av Svenska institutet): 105-17.
1993   'Banking on Livestock: Indirect Storage in Greek Agriculture', *Bulletin on Sumerian Agriculture* 7: 63-75.
1994   'The North–South Divide: Regional Paths to Complexity in Prehistoric Greece', dans *Development and Decline in the Mediterranean Bronze Age* (éd. C. Mathers et S. Stoddard; Sheffield: Collins): 195-219.
Halstead, P., et J. O'Shea
1982   'A Friend in Need Is a Friend Indeed: Social Storage and the Origins of Social Ranking', dans *Ranking, Resource and Exchange: Aspects of the Archaeology of Early European Society* (éd. C. Renfrew et S.J. Shennan; Cambridge: Cambridge University Press): 92-99.
Hole, F.
1991   'Middle Habur Settlement and Agriculture in the Ninevite 5 Period', *BCSMS* 21: 17-29.
Hunt, R.C.
1987   'The Role of Bureaucracy in the Provisioning of Cities: A Framework for Analysis of the Ancient Near East', dans *The Organization of Power: Aspects of Bureaucracy in the Ancient Near East* (éd. McG. Gibson et R.D. Biggs; Chicago: Oriental Institute): 161-92.
Huot, J.-L.
1989   *Les Sumériens: Entre le Tigre et l'Euphrate* (Paris: Armand Colin).
1994   *Les premiers villageois de Mésopotamie: Du village à la ville* (Paris: Armand Colin).
Huot, J.-L. (éd.)
1988   *La ville neuve, une idée de l'Antiquité?* (Paris: Errance).
Huot, J.-L., J.-P. Thalmann et D. Valbelle
1990   *Naissance des cités* (Paris: Nathan).
Jawad, A.J.
1965   *The Advent of the Era of Townships in Northern Mesopotamia* (Leiden: Brill).
Jones, G. *et al.*
1986   'Le stockage des grains à Assiros', *Pour la Science* 103: 78-85.
Kelly-Buccellati, M.
1990a   'Trade in Metals in the Third Millennium: Northeastern Syria and Eastern Anatolia', dans *Resurrecting the Past: A Joint Tribute to Adnan Bounni* (éd. P. Matthiae *et al.*; Istanbul: Nederlands historisch–archaeologisch institut): 117-31
1990b   'Three Seasons of Excavation at Tell Mozan', dans *Tall Al-Hamadiya, II* (éd. S. Eicher *et al.*; Göttingen: Vandenhoeck & Ruprecht): 119-32.

Kipp, R.S., et E.M. Schortman
1989   'The Political Impact of Trade in Chiefdoms', *AA* 91: 370-85.
Klengel, H.
1984   'The Middle Euphrates and International Trade in the Old Babylonian Period', *AAAS* 34: 25-31.
Kohl, P.L.
1978   'The Balance of Trade in Southwestern Asia in the Third Millennium BC', *CA* 19: 463-92.
Kramer, C.
1982   *Village Ethnoarchaeology: Rural Iran in Archaeological Perspective* (New York: Academic Press).
Kühne, H.
1988   'The Reconstruction of Environment, Irrigation and Development of Settlement on the Habur in NE-Syria', dans *Conceptual Issues in Environmental Archaeology* (éd. J. Bintliff *et al.*; Edinburgh: University Press): 108-28.
Kühne, H., et W. Röllig
1974-75   'Zur historischen Geographie am Unteren Habur: Vorläufiger Bericht über die archäologische Geländebegehung', *AfO* 25: 249-55.
1977-78   'The Lower Habur: First Preliminary Report of a Survey in 1975', *AAAS* 27-28: 115-40.
1978-79   'Zur historischen Geographie am Unteren Habur: Zweiter, vorläufiger Bericht über eine archäologische Geländebegehung', *AfO* 26: 181-95.
1983   'The Lower Habur: Second Preliminary Report of a Survey in 1977', *AAAS* 33: 187-205.
Kupper, J.
1964   'Correspondance de Kibri-Dagan', *Syria* 41: 105-16.
1989   'Les marchands à Mari', dans M. Lebeau, *Reflets des deux fleuves: Volume de mélanges offerts à André Finet* (éd. P. Talon; Louvain: Peeters): 89-93
Lampl, P.
1968   *Cities and Planning in the Ancient Near East* (New York: Brazillier).
Lebeau, M.
1987   'Rapport préliminaire sur la céramique des premiers niveaux de Mari (Chantier B–1984)', *MARI* 5: 415-42.
Lewy, J.
1952   'Studies in the Historic Geography of the Ancient Near East', *Or* 21: 1-12.
Mallowan, M.E.L.
1936   'The Excavations at Tall Chagar Bazar, and an Archaeological Survey of the Habur Region, 1934–35', *Iraq* 3: 1-59.
1937   'The Excavations at Tall Chagar Bazar and an Archaeological Survey of the Habur Region: Second Campaign, 1936', *Iraq* 3: 1-59.
1966   'Tell Chuera in Nordost-Syrien', *Iraq* 28: 89-95.
Manzanilla, L. (éd.)
1987   *Studies in the Neolithic and Urban Revolutions: The V. Gordon Childe Colloquium Mexico, 1986* (Oxford: BAR International Series).

Margueron, J.
1987a   'Mari: rapport préliminaire sur la campagne de 1984', *MARI* 5: 5-36.
1987b   'Etat présent des recherches sur l'urbanisation de Mari. I', *MARI* 5: 483-98.
1988a   'Mari et Emar: deux villes neuves de la vallée de l'Euphrate à l'âge du bronze', dans *La ville neuve: Une idée de l'Antiquité?* (éd. J.-L. Huot; Paris: Errance): 37-60.
1988b   'Espace agricole et aménagement régional à Mari au début du IIIe millénaire', *Bulletin on Sumerian Agriculture* 4: 49-60.
1989   'Problèmes de transports au début de l'âge du bronze', dans *Reflets des deux fleuves: Volume de mélanges offerts à André Finet* (éd. M. Lebeau et P. Talmon; Louvain: Peeters): 119-26.
1990   'L'aménagement de la région de Mari: quelques considérations historiques', dans *Techniques et pratiques hydro-agricoles traditionnelles en domaine irrigué: Approche pluridisciplinaire des modes de culture avant la motorisation en Syrie. Actes du colloque de Damas 27 juin–1er juillet 1987* (éd. B. Geyer; Paris: Geuthner): 171-89.
1991a   'Mari, l'Euphrate, et le Khabur au milieu du IIIe millénaire', *BCSMS* 21: 79-100.
1991b   *Les Mésopotamiens* (2 vols.; Paris: Armand Colin).
sous presse 'Mari et le Khabur', dans *La Djazira et l'Euphrate syriens: Tendances dans l'interprétation historique des données nouvelles de la protohistoire à la fin du second millénaire av. J.-C.* (éd. O. Rouault et M. Wäfler; Paris: Editions Recherches sur les Civilisations).
McCorriston, J.
1995   'Preliminary Archaeobotanical Analysis in the Middle Habur Valley, Syria and Studies of Socioeconomic Change in the Early Third Millennium BC', *BCSMS* 29: 33-46.
McGuire, R.H.
1983   'Breaking Down Cultural Complexity: Inequality and Heterogeneity', *Advances in Archaeological Method and Theory* 6: 91-142.
Monchambert, J.-Y.
1983   'Le Moyen Khabour: prospection préliminaire à la construction d'un barrage', *AAAS* 33: 233-37.
1984a   'Prospection archéologique sur l'emplacement du futur lac du Moyen Khabour: Rapport préliminaire', *Akk* 39: 1-7.
1984b   'Le futur lac du Moyen Khabour: rapport sur la prospection archéologique menée en 1983', *Syria* 61: 181-218.
1990   'Réflexions à propos de la datation des canaux: le cas de la basse vallée de l'Euphrate syrien', dans *Techniques et pratiques hydro-agricoles traditionnelles en domaine irrigué: Approche pluridisciplinaire des modes de culture avant la motorisation en Syrie. Actes du colloque de Damas 27 juin–1er juillet 1987* (éd. B. Beyer; Paris: Geuthner): 87-99.

Moorey, P.R.S.
1993   'Iran: A Sumerian El-Dorado?', dans *Early Mesopotamia and Iran: Contact and Conflict 3500–1600 BC* (éd. J. Curtis; London: British Museum): 31-43.

Muhly, J.D.
1993   'Early Bronze Age Tin and the Taurus', *AJA* 97: 239-53.

Nissen, H.J.
1987   'The Urban Revolution of Mesopotamia—Reconsidered', dans *Studies in the Neolithic and Urban Revolutions: The V. Gordon Childe Colloquium, Mexico, 1986* (éd. L. Manzanilla; Oxford: BAR International Series): 287-94.

North, D.C.
1984   'Government and the Cost of Exchange in History', *Journal of Economic History* 44: 255-64.

Oates, J.
1985   'Tell Brak and Chronology: The Third Millennium', *MARI* 4: 137-44.
1986   'Tell Brak: The Uruk/Early Dynastic Sequence', dans W. Finkbeiner, *Gamdat Nasr: Period or Regional Style?* (éd. W. Röllig; Wiesbaden: Reichert): 245-73.
1990   'Tell Brak in the 4th and 3rd Millennia', dans *Tall al-Hamidiya*. II. *Recent Excavations in the Upper Khabur Region* (éd. S. Eichler *et al.*; Göttingen: Vandenhoeck & Ruprecht): 133-47.
1993a   'Il periodo protosiriano o protodinastico', dans *L'Eufrate e il tempo* (éd. O. Rouault et M. Masetti-Rouault; Milan: Electra): 51-53.
1993b   'Trade and Power in the Fifth and Fourth Millennia BC: New Evidence from Northern Mesopotamia', *WA* 24: 403-22.

Oates, D., et J. Oates
1992   'A Human-headed Bull Statue from Tell Brak', *Cambridge Archaeological Journal* 1: 131-39.
1994   'Tell Brak: A Stratigraphic Summary, 1976–1993', *Iraq* 56: 167-76.

Oppenheim, A.L.
1957   'A Bird's-Eye View of Mesopotamian Economic History', dans *Trade and Market in the Early Empires: Economies in History and Theory* (éd. K. Polanyi *et al.*; Glencoe: The Free Press et The Falcon's Wing Press): 27-37.

Orthmann, W.
1986   'The Origin of Tell Chuera', dans *The Origins of Cities in Dry-farming Syria and Mesopotamia in the Third Millennium BC* (éd. H. Weiss; Guildford: Four Quarters): 61-70
1990   *Tell Chuera. Ausgrabungen der Max Freiherr von Oppenheim-Stiftung in Nordost-Syrien* (Bonn: Rudolf Habelt Verlag).

Palmieri, A.M.
1985   'Eastern Anatolia and Early Mesopotamian Urbanization: Remarks on Changing Relations', dans *Studi di Paletnologia in onore di S.M. Puglisi* (éd. M. Liverani *et al.*; Rome: n.p.): 191-213.

Palmieri, A.M, K. Sertok et E. Chernykh
1993   'From Arslantepe Metalwork to Arsenical Copper Technology in Eastern Anatolia', dans *Between the Rivers and over the Mountains*.

Archaeologica Anatolica et Mesopotamica Alba Palmieri Dedicata (éd. M. Frangipane, *et al.*; Rome: Dipartimento di Scienze Storiche Archeologiche et Antropologiche dell'Antichità: Università di Roma La Sapienza): 573-99.

Paynter, R.
1989   'The Archaeology of Equality and Inequality', *ARA* 18: 369-99.

Polanyi, K.
1957   'Marketless Trading in Hammurabi's Time', dans *Trade and Market in the Early Empires. Economies in History and Theory* (éd. K. Polanyi; Glencoe: Free Press et Falcon's Wing Press): 12-26.

Posnansky, M.
1973   'Aspects of Early West African Trade', *WA* 5: 149-62.

Postgate, J.N.
1992   *Early Mesopotamia: Society and Economy at the Dawn of History* (London: Routledge).

Potts, T.F.
1993   'Patterns of Trade in Third-Millennium BC Mesopotamia and Iran', *WA* 24: 379-402.

Powell, M.A.
1977   'Sumerian Merchants and the Problem of Profit', *Iraq* 39: 23-29.

Price, B.
1978   'Secondary State Formation: An Explanatory Model', dans *Origins of the State: The Anthropology of Political Evolution* (éd. R. Cohen et E. Service; Philadelphia: Institute for the Study of Human Issues): 161-86.

Redman, C.L.
1978   *The Rise of Civilization* (San Francisco: W.H. Freeman).

Renfrew, C.
1975   'Trade as Action at a Distance: Questions of Integration and Communication', dans *Ancient Civilization and Trade* (éd. J. Sabaloff et C. Lamberg-Karlovsky; Albuquerque: University of New Mexico Press): 3-59.

Renger, J.
1994   'On Economic Structures in Ancient Mesopotamia', *Or* 63: 157-208.

Rova, E.
1988   *Distribution and Chronology of the Nineveh 5 Pottery and of its Culture* (Rome: Università degli studi di Roma La Sapienza).

Rowlands, M.
1987   'Center and Periphery: A Review of a Concept', dans *Centre and Periphery in the Ancient World* (éd. M. Rowlands *et al.*; Cambridge: Cambridge University Press): 1-11.

Saghié, M.
1991   'The Lebanese University Recent Excavations at Tell Kerma: A Salvage Operation on the Middle Khabur, N.E. Syria', *Mesopotamian History and Environment* 1: 171-84.

Schwartz, G.M.
1985   'The Ninevite V Period and Current Research', *Paléorient* 11: 53-70.

1987   'The Ninevite V Period and the Development of Complex Society in Northern Mesopotamia', *Paléorient* 13: 93-100.

1994a   'Before Ebla: Models of Pre-State Political Organization in Syria and Northern Mesopotamia', dans *Chiefdoms and Early States in the Near East: The Organizational Dynamics of Complexity* (éd. G. Stein et M.S. Rothman; Madison: Prehistory Press): 153-74.

1994b   'Rural Economic Specialization and Early Urbanization in the Khabur Valley, Syria', dans *Archaeological Views from the Countrysite: Village Communities in Early Complex Societies* (éd. G. Schwartz et S. Falconer; Washington: Smithsonian): 19-36.

Schwartz, G.M., et H. Curvers
1992   'Tell al-Raqa'i 1989 and 1990: Further Investigations at a Small Rural Site of Early Urban Northern Mesopotamia', *AJA* 96: 397-419.

1993-94   'Tell al-Raqa'i Excavations and Analyses: A Progress Report', *AfO* 40-41: 246-57.

Service, E.R.
1962   *Primitive Social Organization* (New York: Random House).
1975   *The Origins of the State and Civilization: The Process of Cultural Evolution* (New York: W.W. Norton).

Snell, D.C.
1977   'The Activities of Some Merchants of Umma', *Iraq* 39: 45-50.

Stange, G. le
1905   *Lands of the Eastern Caliphate* (Cambridge: Cambridge University Press).

Stanley, R.S., et R.T. Alexander
1992   'The Political Economy of Core-Periphery Systems', dans *Resources, Power, and Interregional Interaction* (éd. E. Schortman et P. Urban; New York: Plenum): 23-49.

Stein, G.
1994   'Segmentary States and Organizational Variation in Early Complex Societies: A Rural Perspective', dans *Archaeological Views from the Countrysite: Village Communities in Early Complex Societies* (éd. G. Schwartz et S. Falconer; Washington: Smithsonian): 10-18.

Stein, G., et P. Wattenmaker
1990   'The 1987 Tell Leilan Regional Survey: Preliminary Report', dans *Economy and Settlement in the Near East: Analyses of Ancient Sites and Materials* (éd. N. Miller; Philadelphia: University of Philadelphia); 8-18.

Trümpelmann, L.
1989   'Zum frühgeschichtlichen Silobau im alten Mesopotamien', dans *Archaeologica Iranica et Orientalis: Miscellanea in Honorem Louis Vanden Berghe*, I (éd. L. de Meyer et E. Haerinck; Gand: Peeters): 67-84.

Ucko, P.J., R. Tringham et G.W. Dimbleby (éds.)
1972   *Man, Settlement and Urbanism* (London: Duckworth).

Vandiver, P.B. *et al.*
1993   'Thermoluminescence Dating of a Crucible Fragment from an Early Processing Site in Turkey', *Archaeometry* 35: 295-98.

Watson, P.J.
  1979   *Archaeological Ethnography in Western Iran* (Tucson: University of Arizona Press).
Webb, M.C.
  1974   'Exchange Networks: Prehistory', *ARA* 3: 357-83.
  1975   'The Flag Follows Trade: An Essay on the Necessary Interaction of Military and Commercial Factors in State Formation', dans *Ancient Civilization and Trade* (éd. J. Sabloff et C. Lambergt-Karlovsky; Albuquerque: University of New Mexico Press): 155-209.
Weiss, H.
  1983   'Excavations at Tell Leilan and the Origins of North Mesopotamian Cities in the Third Millennium BC', *Paléorient* 9: 39-52.
  1985   'Tell Leilan on the Habur Plains of Syria', *BA* 48: 5-35.
  1986   'The Origins of Tell Leilan and the Conquest of Space in Third Millennium Mesopotamia', dans *The Origins of Cities in Dry-Farming Syria and Mesopotamia in the Third Millennium BC* (éd. H. Weiss; Guildford: Four Quarters): 71-108.
  1990a   ' "Civilizing" the Habur Plains: Mid-Third Millennium State Formation at Tell Leilan', dans *Resurrecting the Past: A Joint Tribute to Adnan Bounni* (éd. P. Mathiae *et al.*; Istanbul: Nederlands historisch-archaeologisch institut): 387-407.
  1990b   'Tell Leilan 1989: New Data for Mid-Third Millennium Urbanization and State Formation', MDOG 122: 193-218.
  1990c   'Third Millennium Urbanization: A Perspective from Tell Leilan', dans *Tall Al-Hamadiya*, II (éd. S. Eichler *et al.*; Göttingen: Vandenhoeck & Ruprecht): 159-66.
  1992   'Habur Triangles: Third Millennium Urban Settlement in Subir', *NABU* 4: 91-94.
  1993   'Subir *versus* Sumer: formazione secondaria e collasso dello stato nelle pianure del Khabur', dans *L'Eufrate e il tempo* (éd. O. Rouault et M. Masetti-Rouault; Milan: Electra): 40-50.
Weiss, H., et M.A. Courty
  1993   The Genesis and Collapse of the Akkadian Empire: The Accidental Refraction of Historical Law', dans *Akkad: The First World Empire* (éd. M. Lierani; Padoue: Sargon): 131-55.
Weiss, H., P. Akkermans, G. Stein, D. Parayre et R. Whiting
  1990   '1985 Excavations at Tell Leilan, Syria', *AJA* 94: 529-81.
Weiss, H. *et al.*
  1993   'The Genesis and Collapse of Third Millennium North Mesopotamian Civilization', *Science* 261: 995-1004.
Wilkinson, T.J.
  1994   'The Structure and Dynamics of Dry-Framing States in Upper Mesopotamia', *CA* 35: 483-520.
Wright, H.T.
  1978   'Toward an Explanation of the Origin of the State', dans *Origins of the State: The Anthropology of Political Evolution* (éd. R. Cohen et E. Service; Philadelphia: Institute for the Study of Human Issues): 49-68.

1984   'Prestate Political Formations', dans *On the Evolution of Complex Societies* (éd. T. Earle; Malibu: Undena; réimprimé, pp. 67-84) dans *Chiefdoms and Early States in the Near East: The Organizational Dynamics of Complexity* (éd. G. Stein et M. Rothman; Madison: Prehistory Press): 41-77.

Wright, H.T., et G.A. Johnson
1975   'Population, Exchange, and Early State Formation in Southwestern Iran', *AA* 77: 267-89.

Yener, K.A.
1995   'Swords, Armor, and Figurines: A Metalliferous View from the Central Taurus', *BA* 58: 101-107.

Yener, K.A., et M. Goodway
1992   'Response to M.E. Hall: S.R. Steadman "Tin and Anatolia: Another Look"', *JMA* 5: 77-90.

Yener, K.A., et H. Özbal
1987   'Tin in the Turkish Taurus Mountains: The Bolkardag Mining District', *Ant* 61: 220-26.

Yener, K.A., et P.B. Vandiver
1993a   'Tin Processing at Göltepe: An Early Bronze Age Site in Anatolia', *AJA* 97: 207-38.

1993b   'Reply to J.D. Muhly, "Early Bronze Age Tin and the Taurus"', *AJA* 97: 255-64.

Yener, K.A., E.V. Sayre, E.C. Joel, H. Özbal, I.L. Barnes et R.H. Brill
1991   'Stable Lead Isotope Studies of Central Taurus Ore Sources and Related Artifacts from Eastern Mediterranean Chalcolithic and Bronze Age Sites', *Journal of Archaeological Science* 18: 541-77.

Yoffee, N.
1979   'The Decline and Rise of Mesopotamian Civilization: An Ethnoarchaeological Perspective on the Evolution of Social Complexity', *AmAnt* 44: 5-35.

1981   *Explaining Trade in Ancient Western Asia* (Malibu: Undena).

1993   'Too Many Chiefs? (or, Safe Texts for the '90s)', dans *Archaeological Theory: Who Sets the Agenda?* (éd. N. Yoffee et A. Sherratt; Cambridge: Cambridge University Press): 60-78.

Zagarell, A.
1986   'Trade, Women, Class, and Society in Ancient Western Asia', *CA* 27: 415-30.

Zeder, M.A.
1988   'Understanding Urban Process through the Study of Specialized Subsistence Economy in the Near East', *JAA* 7: 1-55.

1991   *Feeding Cities: Specialized Animal Economy in the Ancient Near East* (Washington: Smithsonian).

1995   'The Archaeobiology of the Khabur Basin', *BCSMS* 29: 21-32.

CRAFT SPECIALIZATION AND THE RISE OF SECONDARY URBANISM: A VIEW FROM THE SOUTHERN LEVANT

Steven A. Rosen

In traditional formulations of the rise of the state, craft specialization has played a central role (e.g. Childe 1951: 134, 137, 182-83; Kempinski 1978; Tosi 1984; Shennan 1982; Johnson 1973). Historians, anthropologists, and archaeologists, have seen the rise of political hierarchy and centralization in a mutually reinforcing linkage with ever increasing specialization in production, especially of elite goods, or goods to which access was restricted for one reason or another. Control of specialized production has been construed as a prerequisite to greater socio-economic control, as well as a means of establishing the symbolic legitimacy of these control systems (e.g. Rowlands 1973; Shennan 1982; and compare to Brumfiel and Earle 1987). That is, the elite products of specialized production confer status. Copper and other metal goods have been especially the focus of such models (e.g. Renfrew 1984; Redman 1978: 70; Zaccagnini 1983; Kempinski 1989).

Although appealing in its apparent simple elegance, more critical reference to archaeological, historical, and anthropological data suggests that simple elegance is an inadequate criterion for acceptance of the model. The data suggest complexities on several levels that have not usually been considered in the more general discussions of the rise of the state (cf. Crumley 1995). These can be summarized as follows:

(1) Craft specialization as a phenomenon has been poorly defined anthropologically, and is even more difficult to define archaeologically (cf. Brumfiel and Earle 1987; Costin 1991; Tosi 1984; Cobb 1993: 87; Cross 1993: 63). In those cases where specialized production can be defined, elite control is not necessarily indicated.

(2) The classic model suggests a kind of linear evolution of craft specialization, concomitant with increasingly complex and centralized

political development. Yet craft specialization, either anthropologically or archaeologically recognized, clearly takes a variety of forms that do not describe a linear evolution, but rather a branching one.

(3) In direct relation to the above, different commodities, even when clearly the products of specialized manufacture, have very different potentials for either control of production, or for transmission as symbols of status.

(4) Finally, the developmental relation between political complexity and economic organization is not necessarily a direct one. In the case of the rise of secondary states, as opposed to that of the pristine states, state level political organization may be imposed from the outside, or in reaction to external forces. Commensurate economic complexity need not accompany the political changes immediately, although one may assume that for ultimate political stability, appropriate economic solutions to the problems of larger state organization must ultimately be devised (cf. Johnson 1982).

Definitions of craft specialization have always been tied to specific theoretical perspectives. Thus, Childe (1950) insisted that craft specialization needed to be a full-time occupation, tying it to the intensification of production under elite controls. The role of elites has been stressed by numerous other authors as well (e.g. Renfrew 1984; Tosi 1984; Shennan 1982), the general assumption being that only elites could actually pay for specialized goods. The Marxist or neo-Marxist frameworks are implicit. However, there are at least two unwarranted assumptions in this argument: first, that goods produced by specialists are also put to 'special' uses, primarily by elites; and secondly, that specialization demands some kind of centralized authority or organization for it even to function (compare to Brumfiel and Earle 1987; Costin 1991; Rosen 1993). A circular argument arises from the fact that production that does not meet these conditions is usually simply dismissed as not being fully specialized. However, there are numerous anthropological and archaeological examples of production which would seem, under common usage, to fall under the rubric of 'specialized', although they do not fit a strict definition; and they are clearly more complex than the term 'domestic production' (cf. Sahlins 1972) would imply.

Ethnographically, smithing in general and, particularly in the southern Levant, smithing by the Solubba Bedouin (Betts 1989), constitutes a good example of production beyond the level of household consumption, yet clearly does not fall into a preconceived framework of intensive specialized production. Smithing requires specialized knowledge, special equipment and special raw materials, yet is clearly not controlled by elites, either in terms of access to materials, nor in terms of distribution.

Archaeologically, the issue is even more problematic. Defining full-time occupation from the archaeological record is a virtual impossibility (cf. Tosi 1984). Furthermore, there are numerous examples of goods that were not produced by individual households, but by some more central producer. These goods were neither 'intensively' manufactured (e.g. Torrence 1986), nor produced by elites (or by elite support) (cf. Nassaney 1996). Thus, most pottery in the Early Bronze Age does not seem to reflect elite control, even though there is good evidence for mass manufacture (e.g. Esse 1989). Similarly, although sickle blades were produced in the thousands by a few craftsmen, and were distributed to farmers and in villages, towns and cities (Rosen 1989), it is difficult to see evidence for elite control. Grinding stones constitute another example of specialized and mass manufacture with little evidence for hierarchical controls. Indeed, recent evidence of grinding stone manufacture at the Camel site, a pastoral encampment in the central Negev, suggests that at least in some cases, manufacture was not intensive but opportunistic. Similar cases can be made for aspects of Chalcolithic and Early Bronze Age metallurgy (Rosen 1993).

Common usage dictates a looser definition that is easier to accommodate archaeologically. Briefly, craft specialization can be viewed as the restricted production of specific goods or a range of related goods for use beyond the immediate needs of the producer or his close household or relations. Archaeologically this is reflected in the differential distribution of manufacturing by-products and debris (i.e. the presence of workshops), in the widespread distribution of goods and in the general absence or scarcity of evidence for manufacture in association with those goods (cf. Tosi 1984; Evans 1978). Clearly, there are different degrees of intensity of manufacture, but it is not clear that these ought to be aligned on a linear scale, as one being more 'specialized' than the other.

The problem of definition, and the variability in type, suggests that craft specialization as an archaeological or anthropological phenomenon is complex (cf. Brumfiel 1995). This is because there is more than a single factor responsible for the rise of specialization, and the complexity arises from the different permutations and weights attached to different factors. Such factors include variability of access to raw materials; need for specialized knowledge; degree of capital investment; the quantity of goods produced and the distribution system tied to these goods; investment of time/labor in production; and the function, both utilitarian and symbolic, of the goods.

An obvious corollary of this complexity must be that it is impossible to view the rise of craft specialization as linear. Rather, it must be viewed as a form of economic adaptation to any number of different social and economic circumstances. While it is clear that there must be a general correlation between economic and socio-political complexity, the more interesting aspects of this relationship lie in the disconformities between the two. Thus, the rise of specialization in the Levant, as reflected in the archaeological record, in some cases seems clearly to predate the first cities, and seems to take several different forms. Although urbanization must unquestionably have affected economic organization, at least in some cases, the effects were indirect at best, if they existed at all.

To return to two of the examples noted above, Canaanean sickle blades constitute a prime case of a specialized product that preceded the rise of cities in the southern Levant (Rosen 1983, 1989). These sickle blades have been recovered in large quantities from the earliest layers of the Early Bronze I in exclusively village contexts (the only settlement type in the Early Bronze I); yet in the vast majority of these cases, no evidence for their manufacture, in the form of lithic waste (usually ubiquitous in lithic production areas), has been recovered from virtually any of these sites. Evidence for manufacture has been restricted to a few sites, such as Saida Dakerman (Hours 1979), Har Haruvim (Meyerhof 1960) and Gat Guvrin (Perrot, personal communication). Trade packets of unworked blades, that is, blades not yet hafted to sickles and lacking sickle gloss, have also been recovered at several sites, such as Motza (Eisenberg 1993), Lower Horvat Ilin (Marder, Braun and Milevski 1995), Nizzanim (Yekutieli and Gophna 1994) and Beth-Yerah (Rosen 1997). The type, and its production system, continue uninterrupted into the urban periods of the Early Bronze II and III (and then into the village system of the Early Bronze IV as well).

The grinding stone trade system evident at Arad (Amiran 1978: 57-58) also seems to reflect a specialized production that is unaffected by the rise of the city. The grinding stones there were manufactured from ferruginous sandstone, found in the craters of the central Negev. There is no evidence for their manufacture or modification at Arad, but there are two documented cases that show evidence of sandstone reduction at Early Bronze Age pastoral sites, the Camel site in Mitzpe Ramon and the site of Rekhes Nafha (B. Saidel, personal communication). Although these two sites do not constitute the entire trade system, and in fact present only the most incomplete of pictures, the points to be emphasized here are first, that there is a continuity of production from Early Bronze I to II at Arad; and secondly, that neither of the production sites reflects intensive production. Grinding stones are present in large quantities at Arad and all Early Bronze Age sites, yet seem to be the product of specialized but non-intensive production.

This analysis has deliberately stressed the utilitarian, especially the inelastic products made from stone. It is too easy to look with hindsight on the development of metallurgy and to attach to it overly great importance. There are also those who would claim that, as a lithic analyst, I see metallurgy as a competitor to flint, and therefore automatically reject the importance of metals! Whether or not this is true, the fact remains that both grinding stones and sickle blades constitute the products of specialized manufacture of one kind or another; and it is difficult, if not impossible, to see them as symbolically loaded, or prestige items. In fact, sickle blades are barely even visible once hafted in the shaft of the composite blade. They can hardly be considered as active carriers or transmitters of cultural information. Grinding stones are more visible, but it is hard to see any typological or decorative variability in these artifacts that might constitute symbolism. In other words, at least in the case of these objects, and presumably in the case of most other utilitarian objects, there can be little linkage between specialized production and status and its transmission. Obviously there will be objects that serve dual purposes, such as weapons, but to stress weapons and related objects in the rise of specialized production is to build a general model on an exceptional case.

The final point of this essay has to do with the relations between the political and economic systems in the rise of cities and the state. In the evolution of a 'pristine' state, one might expect the more or less simultaneous development of complexity in economic and political organization. The two systems are clearly related, and tend to develop in mutually reinforcing fashion. However, in the case of the secondary state, defined as the result of external stimuli, that linkage between economy and politics may not be as tight. Rapid political unification, especially under a military regime, need not have any economic correlates, and in fact may be detrimental to economic systems already in place (cf. Price 1978; Service 1975: 104-17).

Although the organization of sickle and grinding stone production seem not to have changed qualitatively from Chalcolithic to Early Bronze I–II–III, metallurgical production seems to have undergone major changes, changes that do not seem to conform to linear evolutionary expectations. Specifically, the major changes in metal production and distribution seem to have occurred at (1) the transition from Chalcolithic to Early Bronze I, and (2) the transition from Early Bronze II to III.

From the Chalcolithic to the Early Bronze I, lost wax production seems to have dropped out of the technological repertoire, along with the corresponding range of ceremonial objects (maceheads, scepters, etc.). The Early Bronze I shows a functionally restricted range of tool types, comprised almost exclusively of axes and awls (Ilan and Sebbane 1989). Although copper tools seem to be relatively abundant, evidence for production seems extensive, as opposed to intensive. Virtually all Early Bronze I–II copper working sites are small pastoral camps or perhaps trading stations, as in south Sinai (e.g. Amiran, Beit Arieh and Glass 1973), Timna (Rothenberg and Glass 1992), and, more recently, the Camel site in Mitzpe Ramon. Metal reworking is also present at Arad (Ilan and Sebbane 1989). Through the Early Bronze II, metallurgy seems primarily an extensive activity, not an intensive one, with at least a major part of the production carried out by peripheral pastoral elements.

The evidence from Wadi Feiran, still incompletely published, suggests intensive production beginning in the Early Bronze III, in significant contradistinction to the Early Bronze I–II (Hauptmann and Weisberger 1987), that is, intensification of production began several hundred years after urbanization. It is also notable that intensification seems to postdate the abandonment of Arad. The specific historical issues are beyond the scope of this paper, but the key point is that intensification of production was not an immediate concomitant of political complexity, as reflected in the rise of cities. Indeed, the apparent lag time in production intensification may well reflect specific processes of urbanization, that is, secondary urbanization and the rise of secondary state systems.

Finally, it should be noted that this critique of linear evolutionary models and one-to-one relationships between cultural subsystems should not be taken as a critique of models in general, in favor of historical particularism. It is clear that the processes are indeed general, but it is still necessary to understand how they integrate with the historical particulars.

ACKNOWLEDGMENTS

Isaac Gilead and Arlene M. Rosen read earlier drafts of this paper, and their discussions and comments were, as usual, invaluable. Benjamin Saidel served as my assistant during the Camel excavations, and I am grateful for his input and discussion.

BIBLIOGRAPHY

Amiran, R.
    1978   *Early Arad* (Jerusalem: Israel Exploration Society).
Amiran, R., I. Beit Arieh and J. Glass
    1973   'The Interrelationship between Arad and Sites in the Southern Sinai in the Early Bronze II', *IEJ* 23: 33-38.
Betts, A.V.G.
    1989   'The Solubba: Non-Pastoral Nomads in Arabia', *BASOR* 274: 61-70.
Brumfiel, E.M.
    1995   'Heterarchy and the Analysis of Complex Societies: Comments', in *Heterarchy and the Analysis of Complex Societies* (ed. R.M. Ehrenreich, C.L. Crumley and J.E. Levy; Arlington, VA: American Anthropological Society): 125-31.
Brumfiel, E.M., and T. Earle
    1987   'Specialization, Exchange, and Complex Societies: An Introduction', in *Specialization, Exchange and Complex Societies* (ed. E.M. Brumfiel and T. Earle; Cambridge: Cambridge University Press): 1-9.
Childe, V.G.
    1950   'The Urban Revolution', *Town Planning Review* 21: 3-17.
    1951   *Man Makes Himself* (New York: New American Library).
Cobb, C.
    1993   'Archaeological Approaches to the Political Economy of Non-Stratified Societies', *Archaeological Method and Theory* 5: 43-100.
Costin, C.L.
    1991   'Craft Specialization: Issues in Defining, Documenting, and Explaining the Organization of Production', *Archaeological Method and Theory* ?: 1-56.

Cross, J.
1993   'Craft Specialization in Non-stratified Societies', *Research in Eco-nomic Anthropology* 14: 61-84.

Crumley, C.L.
1995   'Heterarchy and the Analysis of Complex Societies', in *Heterarchy and the Analysis of Complex Societies* (ed. C.L. Crumley, R.M. Ehrenreich and J.E. Levy; Arlington, VA: American Anthropological Society): 1-7.

Eisenberg, E.
1993   'A Settlement from the Beginning of the Early Bronze Age I at Moza', *Atiqot* 22: 41-48.

Esse, D.L.
1989   'Secondary State Formation and Collapse in Early Bronze Age Palestine', in *L'urbanisation de la Palestine à l'âge du bronze ancien* (ed. P. de Miroschedji; Oxford: British Archaeological Reports): 81-96.

Evans, R.K.
1978   'Early Craft Specialization: An Example from the Balkan Chalcolithic', in *Social Archaeology, Beyond Dating and Subsistence* (ed. C.L. Redman *et al.*; New York: Academic Press); 113-30.

Hauptmann, A., and G. Weisberger
1987   'Archaeometallurgy and Mining—Archaeological Investigations in the Area of Feinan, Wadi 'Arabah (Jordan)', *ADAJ* 31: 419-37.

Hours, F.
1979   'L'industrie lithique de Saida-Dakerman', *Berytus* 27: 57-76.

Ilan, O., and M. Sebbane
1989   'Copper Metallurgy, Trade, and the Urbanization of Southern Canaan in the Chalcolithic and Early Bronze Age', in *L'urbanisation de la Palestine à l'âge du bronz ancien* (ed. P. de Miroschedji; Oxford: British Archaeological Reports): 139-62.

Johnson, G.A.
1973   *Local Exchange and Early State Development in Southwestern Iran* (Ann Arbor: University of Michigan, Museum of Anthropology).
1982   'Organizational Structure and Scalar Stress', in *Theory and Explanation in Archaeology: The Southampton Conference* (ed. C. Renfrew, M.J. Rowlands and B.A. Segraves-Whallon; New York: Academic Press): 389-421.

Kempinski, A.
1978   *The Rise of an Urban Culture: The Urbanization of Palestine in the Early Bronze Age* (Jerusalem: Israel Ethnographic Studies).
1989   'Urbanization and Metallurgy in Southern Canaan', in *L'urbanisation de la Palestine à l'âge du bronze ancien* (ed. P. de Miroschedji; Oxford: British Archaeological Reports): 163-68.

Marder, O., E. Braun and I. Milevski
1995   'The Flint Assemblage of Lower Horvat 'Illin: Some Technical and Economic Considerations', *Atiqot* 27: 63-93.

Meyerhof, E.
    1960   'Flint Cores at Har Haharuvim', *Mitekufat Haeven* 1: 23-26 (Hebrew).
Nassaney, M.S.
    1996   'The Role of Chipped Stone in the Political Economy of Social Rank-
                ing', in *Stone Tools: Theoretical Insights into Human Prehistory* (ed.
                G. Odell; New York: Plenum): 181-228.
Price, B.
    1978   'Secondary State Formation: An Explanatory Model', in *Origins of
                the State: The Anthropology of Political Evolution* (ed. R. Cohen and
                E.R. Service; Philadelphia: Institute for the Study of Human Issues):
                161-86.
Redman, C.L.
    1978   *The Rise of Civilization* (San Francisco: Freeman).
Renfrew, C.
    1984   'The Anatomy of Innovation' in *Approaches to Social Archaeology*
                (ed. C. Renfrew; Edinburgh: University Press): 390-418.
Rosen, S.A.
    1983   'The Canaanean Blade and the Early Bronze Age', *IEJ* 33: 15-29.
    1989   'The Analysis of Early Bronze Age Chipped Stone Industries: A
                Summary Statement' in *L'urbanisation de la Palestine à l'âge du
                bronze ancien* (ed. P. de Miroschedji; Oxford: British Archaeological
                Reports): 199-222.
    1993   'Metals, Rocks, Specialization and the Beginning of Urbanism in the
                Northern Negev' in *Biblical Archaeology Today 1990: Pre-Congress
                Symposium Supplement—Population, Production and Power* (ed. A.
                Biran and J. Aviram; Jerusalem: Israel Exploration Society): 41-56.
    1997   *Lithics after the Stone Age* (Walnut Creek: Altamira).
Rothenberg, B., and J. Glass
    1992   'The Beginnings and Development of Early Metallurgy and the Settle-
                ment and Chronology of the Western Arabah from the Chalcolithic
                Period to the Early Bronze IV', *Lev* 24: 141-57.
Rowlands, M.J.
    1973   'Modes of Exchange and Incentives for Trade, with Reference to Late
                European Prehistory', in *The Explanation of Culture Change: Models
                in Prehistory* (ed. C. Renfrew; London: Duckworth): 589-600.
Sahlins, M.D.
    1972   *Stone Age Economics* (Chicago: Aldine).
Service, E.R.
    1975   *The Origins of the State and Civilization* (New York: Norton).
Shennan, S.
    1982   'Exchange and Ranking: The Role of Amber in the Earlier Bronze
                Age of Europe', in *Ranking, Resource, and Exchange* (ed. C. Renfrew
                and S. Shennan; Cambridge: University Press): 33-45.
Torrence, R.
    1986   *Production and Exchange of Stone Tools* (Cambridge: Cambridge
                University Press).

Tosi, M.
  1984   'The Notion of Craft Specialization and its Representation in the
               Archaeological Record of Early States in the Turanian Basin', in
               Marxist Perspectives in Archaeology (ed. M. Spriggs; Cambridge:
               Cambridge University Press): 22-52.
Yekutieli, Y., and R. Gophna
  1994   'Excavations at an Early Bronze Age Site near Nizzanim', *TA* 21:
               162-85.

Zaccagnini, C.
  1983   'Patterns of Mobility among Ancient Near Eastern Craftsmen', *JNES*
               42: 245-64.

THE AGRICULTURAL BASE OF URBANISM
IN THE EARLY BRONZE II–III LEVANT

Arlene Miller Rosen

Much of the literature on early urbanism is concerned with the development of models of the processes and factors that brought about this phenomenon. However explanatory these models, it is equally important to understand some of the 'urbanizing' mechanisms that functioned in different cultural spheres. The following is an attempt to explore several aspects of the agricultural economy that supported the early urbanism of the Early Bronze Age in the southern Levant from the point of view of environment and social complexity.

The Southern Levant

This area is unlike neighboring regions in which urbanization also took place. On the one hand, it is a marginal farming zone subject to periodic droughts that would cause significant instability in a large settled population. On the other hand, it can be a rich mosaic landscape with environmental niches to support a wide variety of crops for subsistence as well as for markets and trade. This potential for agricultural diversity was undoubtedly recognized and exploited by the upper echelons of the social hierarchy for revenues to support their base of power (Stager 1985; Esse 1991). This power base is manifested materially in the massive public architecture at such sites as Yarmouth in the Shephelah region of Israel, and Megiddo in the Jezreel Valley (de Miroschedji 1988; Kempinski 1992). However, in order to maximize effectively the potential of this region for market production and maintenance of a sizable population, it would have been necessary to intensify agricultural productivity, thereby increasing the risk of periodic crop failure and famine. The mechanisms by which this unique agricultural economy functioned and maintained relative stability for close to 1000 years are of importance for understanding the character of Early Bronze Age society.

In the light of this perspective there are three issues that need to be explored: (1) the intensification of agricultural production in what is traditionally assumed to have been an exclusively dry-farming region; (2) the social and agrarian dichotomy between the production of cash crops, such as olives and grapes, and the production of subsistence crops, primarily cereals; and (3) social hierarchies and the control of agricultural production, storage, taxation and redistribution of agricultural produce.

Environmental Setting of Third Millennium BCE Canaan

The importance of the geographical setting in understanding Early Bronze Age urbanization goes beyond that of a stage scene for the political events of the time period. The landscape and environment played an active role in the character and maintenance of Early Bronze Age urbanism. The southern Levantine environment contrasts in significant ways with that of early urban societies in the neighboring Mesopotamian and Egyptian irrigation spheres. The latter are situated on broad flat flood plains dominated by major rivers, but receive little or no rainfall. The southern Levant is a semi-arid zone with modern yearly rainfall averages ranging from 200 mm per year in the northern Negev up to 800 mm per year in the Galilee, and there is much proxy evidence from environmental data that indicates higher rainfall averages throughout much of the third millennium BCE (A. Rosen 1995). These figures, however, are misleading since in any given year there can be variations of up to hundreds of millimeters in rainfall. Likewise, rainfall patterns (i.e. amount and timing of storm episodes) vary a great deal in this region, and it is possible that the distribution of the rain within a particular year would be unfavorable for high crop yields. This leads to situations in which it is difficult to predict if the harvest will result in an abundant yield or a possible famine. In the past this uncertainty would have required adjustments in agricultural strategies on the part of any society existing in the region in order to support the relatively large settled populations, and the Early Bronze Age towns were no exception.

The other unique aspect of the geography is the marked topographical, soil and vegetation differences grading from the flat coastal plain in the west to the Shephela foothills and then the hilly region in the east. This mosaic of landscapes and soils allowed for a dual agricultural system that could produce tree and vine crops (primarily olives and grapes, but also such fruits as figs and dates) as cash crops in the hilly zones and cereals as subsistence crops in the lowland valleys (Stager 1985; Zohary and Spiegel-Roy 1975). Furthermore, in the Early Bronze Age, the lowland valleys were physiographically different from those we know today. In today's landscape, drainages are narrow and deeply incised, with a hydrological regime of winter flash-flooding and summer-dry channels. Geomorphological studies have shown, however, that in the third millennium BCE the situation was quite different. Today's perennially dry abandoned flood plains were then actively being flooded throughout the winter, creating moist alluvial soils for cultivation (A. Rosen 1989, 1991). This had great significance for the agricultural potential of the Early Bronze Age hinterland. It indicates that the soils of the valley bottoms were rich zones for the production of high-yield cereal crops, and provided a buffer against drought years when rain-fed crops produced only low yields (A. Rosen 1995).

Agricultural Intensification

This is clearly a necessary part of the development of complex civilizations on the rainless alluvial flood plains of Mesopotamia and Egypt. Without irrigation there could be no large settled villages, towns and cities. Perhaps less obvious would be the need for some kind of intensification in areas that today seem capable of supporting small towns and villages through simple dry-farming techniques. In the Levantine situation, pre-modern observations of village farmers in Palestine (cited by Esse 1991) showed that dry-farming of cereals was widespread and this has been generally assumed to be the case for the early agricultural towns of the Early Bronze as well. Given the uncertainties of the rainfall regime in this region, small-scale subsistence farmers are able to make do in times of drought through storage of seeds, selling off of material goods or livestock, or in dire situations, by abandoning their homes (Dirks 1980). In a non-industrial urban situation, however, there are relatively large populations, many of whom are non-producers and in order to maintain social stability the yearly grain yields must be predictable and secure. It is therefore reasonable to expect that water manipulation was taking place, even at the low technological level of floodwater farming. At the very least, the alluvial valley bottoms were probably exploited for the production of cereals, and perhaps even altered for better water capture. Indeed, it has been shown (A. Rosen 1995) that wheat phytoliths from Early Bronze Age sites are indicative of those found in irrigated cereals. Perhaps the introduction of the plow in this period can be partly explained by the need to cultivate the very heavy clay soils of the alluvial valley bottoms.

Agricultural Dichotomy

Another aspect of the agricultural economy that requires elucidation is the dichotomy between cash crops used for inter- and intra-regional trade and that of subsistence crops. Unfortunately, there are only a few archaeobotanical reports from Early Bronze II and III sites, and, given the lack of data, it is necessary to speculate that the hilly areas were exploited primarily for olive tree production and the inter-montaine valleys and coastal plain for cereals—a model also taken from observations of pre-modern agriculture in Ottoman Palestine (Esse 1991). If this were indeed the case in the Early Bronze Age, then sites located in the Shephela foothills with easy access to both lowland valleys and hilly regions, such as Yarmouth and Lachish, would be in an ideal position to exploit both ecological zones. Numerous olive pits were recovered from the charred macro-botanical remains at Yarmouth (de Miroschedji, personal communication), as well as a large number of wheat phytoliths. Likewise, the two most important macro-botanical remains from the site of Lachish were emmer wheat and olives, which illustrates the importance of these two crops. Sites that are firmly set in the heart of the mountainous zone, such as 'Ai, might have depended partially on inter-regional trade for an adequate supply of staples. One can assume that the administrative control over cash crop production of olives and grapes was greater than that over cereal production, which was probably conducted at the family or small village level.

Social Hierarchies and Control over Agricultural Production

There are three basic areas in which the elite segments of the society could have maintained control over the subsistence farmers. The first was by the extraction of cereals in the form of a tax due to the state; the second was the temple/fertility cults holding a monopoly; and the third was the exploitation of labor for maintaining cash cropping operations.

Cereal production was almost certainly left under the control of subsistence farmers at the family group level of organization. Studies of proto-state societies or principalities in southern Mesopotamia have shown that the additional administrative hierarchy required for control over subsistence production would have overtaxed the bureaucratic capabilities of the system (Wright 1984). Therefore, the Levantine lowland alluvium and upland alluvial valleys were probably heavily exploited by family farmers who seem, for the most part, to have lived within the Early Bronze II and III towns themselves, judging from (1) the large number of sickles found at these sites (S. Rosen 1989), and (2) the fact that the occurrences of Early Bronze II/III small farming village sites were reduced from those of the Early Bronze I and there were relatively more large town sites in Early Bronze II/III (Gophna and Portugali 1988). Farmers at Shephela towns such as Yarmouth and Lachish, would not have had to walk more than 3–7 km in order to reach the fertile soils of the lowland valleys. These farmers apparently utilized the very lowest level of irrigation agriculture, that is, floodwater farming. Yet the increased stability in cereal yields from this procedure served as a sufficient buffer against drought years. If the huge granaries from Beth-yerah can be taken as a general example, then a portion of the cereal produce was extracted from the subsistence farmers as a tax by the elite administrators. This would have decreased the surplus under the direct control of individual farmers and added to their vulnerability in times of drought.

But what was the incentive for farmers to live in these towns relatively far from their fields and provide the administrators with a yearly tariff? One motivation might well have been defence from marauders. However, another major inducement could have derived from the fertility cult, which, according to ancient Mesopotamian texts and some artifactual remains from the southern Levant, played an important role in the agricultural life of the peasant farmers (Amiran 1972). It was perceived as contributing to high yields in the same way that modern farmers rely on fertilizers and chemical nutrients. Control over the population and their produce in this manner is more efficient and effective than physical coercion. Another mode of integrating the farmers into the social hierarchy might have been the redistribution of cereals to the lowest social levels in times of drought and famine. This in itself would have been an incentive for farmers to remain enmeshed within the society and contribute to the public store-houses as well as the private coffers of the elite.

In contrast to the strategies for production and redistribution of subsistence crops, the cash crops of olives and grapes, were apparently controlled by elite managers and produced for trade at first on an inter-regional basis for the Egyptian market and later in Early Bronze III for intra-regional trade, the purpose of which, according to Joffe (1993), was to consolidate the wealth and power of the elite and to continue to support the institutions developed in the period of international trade. The production of these cash crops would have entailed the control of labor for growth and processing of these products, perhaps with the same social mechanisms that were used to exact labor for the building of fortifications, temples and other public construction projects.

Conclusions

In conclusion, the uniquely marginal environment of the southern Levant required equally unique adaptations on the part of urban societies inhabiting the region in order to maintain and support the large base populations required by such complex levels of social organization. With the help of floodwater farming in the rich alluvial valleys, the society was able to maintain a large and stable population that overcame periods of drought by a system of food redistribution on the part of the elite managerial classes. These classes consolidated their position of power by revenues from the production of olive oil and wine, and through control of the population by co-opting temple fertility cults and the redistribution of staples in the semi-regular drought regime.

BIBLIOGRAPHY

Amiran, R.B.K.
    1972   'A Cult Stela from Arad', *IEJ* 22: 86-88.

Dirks, R.
1980   'Social Responses During Severe Food Shortages and Famine', *CA* 21: 21-44.
Esse, D.L.
1991   *Subsistence, Trade, and Social Change in Early Bronze Age Palestine* (Chicago: Chicago University Press).
Gophna, R., and Y. Portugali
1988   'Settlement and Demographic Processes in Israel's Coastal Plain from the Chalcolithic to the Middle Bronze Age', *BASOR* 269: 11-28.
Joffe, A.H.
1993   *Settlement and Society in the Early Bronze Age I and II, Southern Levant* (MMA, 4; Sheffield: Sheffield Academic Press).
Kempinski, A.
1992   'Fortifications, Public Buildings, and Town Planning in the Early Bronze Age', in *The Architecture of Ancient Israel: From Prehistoric to the Persian Periods* (ed. A. Kempinski and R. Reich; Jerusalem: Israel Exploration Society): 68-80.
Miroschedji, P. de
1998   *Yarmouth 1: Rapport sur les trois premières campagnes de fouilles à Tel Yarmouth (Israël) (1980–1982)* (Paris: Editions recherche sur les civilisations).
Rosen, A.M.
1989   'Environmental change at the end of the Early Bronze Age in Palestine', in *L'urbanisation de la Palestine à l'âge du bronze ancien* (ed. P. de Miroschedji; Oxford: British Archaeological Reports): 247-55.
1991   'Early Bronze Age Tel Erani: An Environmental Perspective', *TA* 18: 192-204.
1995   'The Social Response to Environmental Change in Early Bronze Age Canaan', *JAA* 14: 26-44.
Rosen, S.A.
1989   'The Analysis of Early Bronze Age Chipped Stone Industries: A Summary Statement', in *L'urbanisation de la Palestine à l'âge du bronze ancien* (ed. P. de Miroschedji; Oxford: British Archaeological Reports): 199-222.
Stager, L.E.
1985   'The Firstfruits of Civilization', in *Palestine in the Bronze and Iron Ages: Papers in Honor of Olga Tufnell* (ed. J. Tubb; London: Institute of Archaeology): 172-88.
Wright, H.T.
1984   'Prestate Political Formations', in *On the Evolution of Complex Societies: Essays in Honor of Harry Hoijer, 1982* (ed. T. Earle; Los Angeles: Udena): 41-77.
Zohary, D., and P. Spiegel-Roy
1975   'Beginnings of Fruit Growing in the Old World', *Science* 187: 319-27.

THE SOCIAL CONTEXT OF EARLY IRON WORKING IN THE LEVANT

Neil A. Mirau

The importance of metal and metalworking technologies to the development of complex urban societies is difficult to estimate in any objective manner. That said, there is no question that metal, particularly iron, was an integral part of the material culture of almost all complex and many other societies in antiquity. This fact is illustrated by the ancient Greek poet Hesiod, who acknowledged and exploited the cultural importance of metals by using them as metaphors in his view of the human condition. In *Works and Days*, written in the early first millennium BCE, Hesiod described the ages of gods and men from the original paramount Age of Gold down through the Age of Silver and the Age of Bronze to the dark and dangerous Age of Iron of Hesiod's own time. Since before Hesiod's time the working of iron and the use of goods produced from iron has been a central element of the technology of many cultures and by extension of those cultures themselves.

In the ancient world perhaps no region experienced more profound changes during the period of the introduction of iron than the Near East. It is in this region that culture change and the genesis of large-scale iron working appear to be the most closely linked. That is not to say that the emergence of iron working caused major socioeconomic or other shifts in the cultures of Early Iron Age in the Near East. At some level, however, culture change precipitated the emergence of the widespread use of iron for the production of utilitarian goods in the centuries following c. 1200 BCE (McNutt 1990; Muhly 1992; Waldbaum 1980). These changes were ultimately responsible for the emergence of large-scale iron working. By the same token, large-scale iron working caused changes in the economics, politics and perhaps the ideology of Near Eastern cultures after c. 1200 BCE.[1]

1.   The linkage between iron and ideology has been examined ethnographically in many societies, particularly in Africa where metalworking and concepts of the

These issues of the origins, development and effects of iron working in the Near East are complex, and many researchers have noted that the textual and archaeological data are unclear, often contradictory and, despite outstanding research by archaeologists and other scholars, still poorly understood.[2] The following examines some of the implications of those issues and related problems, and in so doing attempts to contribute to an understanding of the relationship between the origin of large-scale (that is, the production of utilitarian goods, such as tools and weapons) iron working and culture change in the Levant following c. 1200 BCE.

The beginning of large-scale iron working in the Levant is linked to economic shifts which occurred as a consequence of cultural changes in the period following ca. 1200 BCE, but it cannot be solely attributed to economic upheaval. While it is important to consider such factors as supply and demand, cost of production, diffusion of metalworking knowledge and advances in metallurgical processes via experimentation and innovation, these factors alone cannot adequately explain the emergence of iron as the material of choice for utilitarian goods. There were apparently more factors at work than those which could reasonably be attributed to the economic sphere of culture. Furthermore, no single ethnic group or culture was responsible for the emergence of large-scale iron working in the Levant, even though some groups may have been able to produce more and better iron products than others at certain times in the Late Bronze and Early Iron Ages.

To understand the issue of the emergence of iron working in the Levant and, by extension, the rest of the Near East, it is necessary to go beyond simple models of technological progress facilitated by diffusion, experimentation and economics. Rather, it is necessary to examine the issue from a perspective that includes a broader consideration of the social systems of the Levant during the Late Bronze and

supernatural are especially connected (see e.g. Kense 1983). McNutt (1990) in fact examines the symbolism in African iron working to inform her research on symbolism of iron in Ancient Israel.

2.   The problems associated with determining causalities for the beginning of *large-scale* iron working have been dealt with directly and indirectly by many including, but not limited to Dayton (1973), Forbes (1972), McNutt (1990), Maddin, Muhly and Wheeler (1977), Muhly (1982, 1985, 1992), Muhly *et al.* (1985), Stech-Wheeler *et al.* (1981), Wertime (1973), Wertime and Muhly (1980), and Wright (1938, 1939).

Early Iron Ages. This approach follows Budd and Taylor (1995) and more generally employs a contextual approach to archaeological interpretation as advocated by Hodder (1992). It should be noted that some leading archaeometallurgical scholars of the Near East have also stated that the questions and issues of metalworking need to be more inclusive and not examined only from a perspective of technological evolution (Smith *et al.* 1984: 236). Notwithstanding this holistic approach, any attempt to understand the emergence of large-scale iron working requires a brief discussion of pyrotechnology and related iron working procedures.

Pyrotechnology and the Prerequisites to Iron Working

Iron is the fourth most common element on earth, but it is rarely found in a pure enough form that it is malleable or otherwise usable as a utilitarian material. Like other metallic elements, potentially usable iron is most commonly found as a constituent of metalliferous mineral ores. In order to produce iron metal from ore, the ore must be subjected to temperatures high enough to extract the elemental iron from other material in the ore body. Iron bearing ores are not ubiquitous in the Levant, although they are present. The greater eastern Mediterranean area, however, most notably Anatolia, is rich in iron ore deposits. Eastern Mediterranean iron ores vary greatly in quality and iron content, and most iron ores in the Levant are low quality (Liebowitz and Folk 1984: 275-76; Wertime 1973a: 885). The fact that iron bearing ores are highly variable in terms of their elemental constitution and the percentage of iron that they contain means that large-scale iron production became viable only when metal workers acquired the expertise necessary to deal with the inevitable vagaries presented by the variable nature of individual ore bodies. The difficulties of ancient iron working were further exacerbated by the high melting point of iron in comparison with other metals known to ancient cultures (Wertime 1973b).

Iron becomes molten at a temperature of 1537°C, considerably higher than the melting point of copper at 1083°C. Copper, of course, was the predominant metal in the ancient Near East, primarily as the most important component of bronze, an alloy of copper and arsenic or tin prior to the advent of iron. The difference in the respective melting temperatures meant that copper and bronze goods could be produced by casting, whereas the high melting point of iron was beyond the normal capability of metal working furnaces of the ancient Near East. Iron could therefore not be cast to form utilitarian (or other) products (Tylecote 1980). Usable iron metal had to be produced in a series of steps that were much different and more complex than the production of copper, lead, tin, silver, gold or even alloys, such as bronze, all of which could be cast.

The production of iron requires heating ferrous ores to a temperature where impurities reach a liquid or near-liquid state and then separate from the metal, forming a slag at the bottom of the smelting furnace. The variety of ore and a number of other chemical factors dictate the temperature at which separation of the iron from other matter in the ore occurs. These temperatures range from about 900°C for an iron-rich magnetite ore to 1200°C or more for hematite, limonite and other ores that typically contain lower percentages of iron (Wertime 1973a, 1973b). Ore reduction can be aided by fluxing. Fluxing is a process whereby a material, or 'flux', is placed in the smelting furnace with the ore and fuel and, via a chemical reaction, reduces the temperature at which impurities become separated from the ore.

The heat-driven separation process resulted in the formation of lump of spongy iron. This lump would have been of variable quality, depending upon the heat capability of the furnace, the type of fluxing agent used, the fuel-to-ore ratio, the quality of ore and the expertise of the metal workers. This iron lump or 'bloom' would then be reheated and hammered in a forge to eliminate air pockets present in the bloom and to further remove impurities. Reheating and hammering were carried out until the product that remained was of sufficiently pure iron that it was ductile enough to be formed into a usable tool (Tylecote 1980).

The process of separating the iron from other elements in the ore without liquefying the metal and then repeatedly reheating and hammering the iron bloom until it is ductile produces wrought iron. Wrought iron, while capable of being used for tools and weapons, is both softer and less able to hold a sharp edge than most bronzes.

Iron can be made harder by 'carburizing', a process that impregnates wrought iron with elemental carbon. This process, which occurs during smelting, results in the production of the iron-carbon alloy known commonly as steel. Carburization of iron occurs when the iron bloom is in prolonged contact with burning charcoal and the bloom absorbs the carbon given off as a result of the chemical reactions within the charcoal (Stech-Wheeler *et al.* 1981: 246). Carburization can also occur in the forge (Smith *et al.* 1984). Carburized iron can be made harder still by quenching, that is, plunging the forged item into water immediately after removal from the forge. Quenching however causes the iron to become brittle, and brittleness obviously decreases durability. The brittleness of carburized iron can be reduced by tempering, that is, reheating the carburized and quenched iron to a relatively low temperature. This process reduces iron's hardness as well as its brittleness. Metal smiths had to have a thorough under-standing of the behavior and results of the many production steps before high-quality iron that was hard but not brittle could be produced consistently.[3]

The exact production sequence and procedure would vary sig-nificantly depending upon the ore used, the fluxing agent, the capa-bility of the furnace and a number of other factors. From this it is likely that many of the earliest known examples of carburized iron goods found in the Near East were produced unintentionally (Clough 1987).

The vagaries of production and the level of iron working knowl-edge required to consistently produce a usable metal suggests that there must have been a social infrastructure capable of and willing to support such experimentation. It is likely that iron working innova-tions and experimentation occurred over generations, and therefore the demand for usable iron products and economic circumstances which resulted in such demand were consequences of fundamental changes in the social infrastructure.[4] Having said this it should also be noted that modern concepts of supply and demand and related issues, such as specialized, intense production, are conditioned by our parti-cipation in modern industrial/post-industrial society. It should not be

---

3.   For a more complete discussion on the process of producing carburized or steeled iron see Maddin, Muhly and Wheeler (1977), Tylecote (1980) and Wheeler and Madden (1980).

4.   That fundamental social changes occurred in the Levant during the transition from the Late Bronze Age to the early Iron Age is axiomatic. It is the exact nature of the changes, their causes and consequences that are the subject of ongoing debate and research in modern Syro-Palestinian archaeology. See, for example, Ward and Joukowsky (1992).

presumed that ancient cultures had or adhered to similar concepts. Members of ancient societies, notably those of the Levant of the Early Iron Age simply did not experience the nuances of large-scale 'industrial-like' economies and the consequences thereof.[5]

Explanations for the Beginnings of Large-Scale Iron Production

What social and economic conditions either directly or indirectly encouraged the development of iron working technology in the Near East in the period after c. 1200 BCE? Many theories have been proposed to account for the beginnings of large-scale iron production in this region, but the processes and history of the beginnings of the technology are still poorly understood. The written record from the region is essentially mute on the matter of the introduction of iron technology (McNutt 1990: 144). An explanation or explanations for the origins of iron technology must therefore rely on archaeological inference even though the material culture record of the early iron working industry in the eastern Mediterranean is still incomplete (Hallo 1992; McNutt 1990; Muhly 1982: 54; Smith *et al.* 1984). This does not mean that there is little to say on the issue of the origins of large-scale iron working. It is possible to examine this issue contextually and develop models, albeit incomplete and perhaps somewhat oversimplified, which can help explain the origins of the Levantine iron working.

A view that might now be characterized as the traditional one in archaeometallurgical studies of the eastern Mediterranean suggests that the widespread use of iron for utilitarian purposes began relatively suddenly, when the copper and tin supply, most notably the latter, could no longer meet the demand for bronze. This supposed material shortage was seen as wholly or partially due to disruptions in international trade that occurred with the social upheavals suffered by the Late Bronze Age urban cultures of the eastern Mediterranean.[6]

---

5. As noted earlier this view employs a perspective advocated by Budd and Taylor (1995) which in effect suggests that many, if not most, archaeometallurgical studies employ a view of industrial development and scientific progress which fails to consider the historical context of the cultures being examined. Hodder (1992) has of course long advocated the importance of situating archaeological inferences contextually.

6. A number of researchers have utilized the theory of a tin shortage as the

That is, the perceived sequence of urban destruction and abandonment and the collapse of the control of Late Bronze Age eastern Mediterranean states led to an interruption in trade and transportation of metals used in the production of bronze. As a result, metal smiths turned to the production of iron as a substitute for bronze primarily because iron bearing ores were more widely available. This in turn allowed the development of iron working technology and the evolution of metal production processes which eventually allowed metalworkers to consistently produce 'steeled' iron.

This view of widespread shortages of copper and tin is no longer tenable. It appears that there were no large-scale or long-term interruptions in the copper and tin trade, and therefore bronze production c. 1200 BCE was not significantly affected. While sporadic supply problems must have occurred before, during, and after the Late Bronze–Early Iron transition, there are no archaeological or textual data that support the view of a sustained collapse in either copper or tin production in the eastern Mediterranean during this period (Muhly 1992; Waldbaum 1987). For iron to emerge as the dominant form of utilitarian metal as a direct consequence of a copper and tin shortage, the interruption in copper–tin supplies would have to have been catastrophic and long. Some researchers have used the limited textual evidence to substantiate such a supply problem, but as Muhly (1992) has shown, the small amount of textual evidence that has been claimed as supporting the theory of a raw material shortage is itself open to other interpretations. Even if there was a supply shortage in the crucial period in question, the archaeological record suggests it was not severe enough to cause a determined and widespread program of iron working experimentation. If copper and/or tin shortages forced the advent of iron working in the Levant and elsewhere, there should have been a relatively sudden increase in the number of iron smelting facilities in these regions. Furthermore, the remains of furnaces and the slags which they produced should exist in areas with a tradition of bronze working, because bronze metal workers would (at least theoretically)

primary causative factor in the emergence of iron as the dominant metal for utilitarian purposes in the Near East including Maddin, Muhly and Wheeler (1977), Muhly (1980) and Snodgrass (1980, 1989). It should be noted, however, that many of these researchers now reject the theory of a shortage of tin as the primary cause for the origins of iron working in the Near East (Muhly 1992; Smith *et al.* 1987; Waldbaum 1987).

have been forced to turn to the use of iron ore. So far, very few furnaces or other facilities that were demonstrably used for iron working have been found that date to this period (Muhly *et al.* 1990). There is little or nothing in the archaeological record that indicates a pattern of bronze smelting being replaced or superseded by iron smelting in the same location. The absence of iron working facilities, of course, does not disprove the copper–tin shortage theory, but if iron working began in the Levant as a replacement for bronze, the technological shift should be archaeologically manifested in the sudden appearance of Late Bronze–Early Iron Age iron smelting furnaces. Rather, the lack of Late Bronze–Early Iron Age iron working furnaces suggests that the shift to iron was gradual and therefore is not likely linked to abrupt interruptions in the supply of copper and tin associated with the breakdown of international trade at the end of the Late Bronze. Furthermore as Muhly (1992: 17) has indicated, there is no evidence of a shortage of copper in the eastern Mediterranean in the thirteenth and twelfth centuries BCE. Cypriot copper production and export actually expanded during this period. In addition, Waldbaum's (1987) research indicates that the tin content of twelfth- and eleventh-century BCE bronzes is higher than bronzes from earlier periods and so a tin shortage in the Late Bronze and Early Iron Ages appears as unlikely as a copper shortage.

The relatively simple cause–effect explanation for the beginning of the use of iron for utilitarian purposes because of a shortage of copper and/or tin has been perhaps attractive because it is a unidimensional explanation. It is therefore easy to understand and logical in our own supply and demand-driven society, but, like most unidimensional answers, it is probably too simple.

Other unidimensional explanations for the emergence of iron working in the Levant and elsewhere in the Near East have been offered. Stager (1985) and Wertime (1983) have suggested that iron superseded bronze for large-scale metal production because iron production is more fuel efficient than copper/bronze production. According to this theory, charcoal, the fuel with which virtually all ancient metals were smelted, was in short supply, as demand for wood resulted in widespread deforestation in the region. As a consequence, ancient smelters sought to reduce their fuel requirements by switching to iron production from bronze. This explanation can be questioned on a number of grounds. First, there is evidence that widespread deforestation of the Mediterranean lands occurred only about the nineteenth century CE (Thirgood 1981), and therefore the theory of deforestation in the late second millennium BCE is difficult to support. Secondly, although iron production is more fuel efficient, the increasing incidence of iron artifacts in the region, especially after the tenth century BCE, indicates that the production of metal was on the rise. Any saving in fuel associated with a switch from bronze production to iron would have been more than offset by the increase in the amount of iron produced (Miller 1986). A fuel shortage scenario is simply not supportable as an overarching cause for the emergence of iron working.

Another explanation for the supposedly sudden onset of iron working in the Levant is the theory that the Hittites developed the ability to smelt iron and were successful in retaining the 'secrets' of iron working until their collapse and following that collapse iron working diffused to other cultures in the region. As a number of authors have pointed out (e.g. Muhly *et al.* 1985, 1990), the idea of a Hittite iron monopoly is no longer regarded as plausible. It has been demonstrated that, while the Hittites were capable metal workers, there is no evidence that they produced more or better iron than other groups.

The theory of monopolistic knowledge of iron working is not restricted to the Hittites. Several researchers have suggested the Philistines possessed some form of a monopoly on iron working and were able to control the early Iron Age iron industry of the Levant, excluding other ethnic groups, such as the proto-Israelites, from access to the technology (see e.g. Wright 1939, 1943; Dothan 1982; Muhly 1982).

The data used to support the claim of Philistine control of iron working, or at least control over the distribution of iron weapons, are ambiguous. On the one hand, there is little archaeological evidence to support the theory that the Philistines brought an effective large-scale iron working industry to the Levant and for some period had exclusive access to that technology. On the other hand, there is some textual evidence that seems to suggest that the Philistines exercised control over the early iron working industry in the Levant. This of course is the oft-mentioned passage in 1 Samuel (Wright 1943; McNutt 1990; Muhly 1982). This passage suggests that sometime during Saul's lifetime the Philistines were able to restrict the Israelites' access to iron weapons and the Israelites relied on Philistine smiths for their other utilitarian metal needs. The archaeological evidence does not seem to support this interpretation of the passage in the book of Samuel. McNutt (1990) has examined the distribution of iron goods in Early Iron Age Palestine and her data suggest Philistines and non-Philistines alike were using iron and that both had access to iron weapons. The evidence is slim given the relatively small number of iron goods (approximately 350 iron artifacts from both Philistine and non-Philistine sites for all of the twelfth, eleventh and tenth centuries BCE), but again, the distribution of iron artifacts data indicate that the Philistines did not have greater access to iron tools or weapons than other non-Philistines living in the region.

The Philistines may have been able to dominate other ethnic groups in the region in the Early Iron Age, but their success in doing so apparently did not lie with greater access to or use of iron weapons or tools, despite the passage in 1 Samuel. It therefore appears that no one group, at least in the Levant, was able to exercise monopolistic control over the emergent iron working technology of the Early Iron Age.

As a number of authors have noted, the causes of the changes that accompanied the beginnings of the Iron Age and iron usage in the Levant were very complex and therefore our explanatory models and answers must be more sophisticated and flexible than simple single mechanism explanations (e.g. Dever 1992: 99). With this in mind, a more holistic explanation is required and there is a need to consider the social context within which metal production occurred in order to go beyond these unidimensional explanations.

Toward a More Holistic Theory for the Introduction of Large-Scale Iron Working in the Levant

If the beginnings of an effective utilitarian iron industry in the Levant cannot be attributed to the interruption of international trade in the twelfth century BCE, the problem of fuel shortages, the Hittite collapse and subsequent diffusion of iron working knowledge or the invasion of the Philistines, to what *can* it be attributed? In order to attempt an explanation for the emergence of iron working, it is necessary to examine briefly conditions in the Levant c. 1200 BCE, and look a little more closely at iron working as part of society and how it was impacted by the social change of the Late Bronze–Early Iron Age transition.

The Levant in the twelfth century BCE was undergoing significant social upheaval. Dever (1992: 107) and Finkelstein (1995: 354) refer to this upheaval as a 'collapse' and Dothan (1992: 93) refers to it as a 'breakdown of cultural coherence'. Whatever the terminology applied, clearly there was social disjunction at the temporal boundary between the Late Bronze and the Early Iron Ages. The Late Bronze Age city-states had collapsed or were collapsing; Egyptian control in the region was deteriorating (Weinstein 1981); and deurbanization was occurring as cities were destroyed or abandoned (Aharoni 1970; Fritz 1987; Mazar 1990). At the same time as the population of the area was shifting away from urban areas, it was apparently expanding due to the arrival of immigrants from adjacent regions. This changing demographic situation was a result of and contributed to a decentralization of authority. Those segments of society that, in the Late Bronze Age, were accountable to Egyptian overlords and Canaanite rulers were no longer under the hegemonic controls of those rulers and princes. As Dever (1992: 107) has noted, new settlement patterns, new socio-economic structures, less formal and more flexible political systems and generally new ideas emerged from the chaos of the Late Bronze–Early Iron transition.

These new, more flexible political systems were the product of the end of Egyptian dominance in the region and the breakdown of political control wielded by Late Bronze Levantine city-states (Bunimovitz 1995: 324-27; Dever 1992: 105-107; LaBianca and Younker 1995: 399). The new political entities, whatever their form, for example, the so-called 'tribal kingdoms' of Transjordan (LaBianca and Younker 1995), the integrated, regional political system of Philistia or the 'segmentary lineage system' of the emerging Israelites (Stager 1985: 260), represented more decentralized systems, which presumably were, as Dever (1992: 107) puts it, more 'flexible' systems of political and socio-economic control than those which dominated the Late Bronze Age Levant. These political entities and those that controlled them were apparently less interested in, and/or less capable of, extracting and exploiting the human and natural resources of the Levant than their Late Bronze predecessors had been. The consequences of the emergent Early Iron Age political systems of the Levant were many and varied. However, it may be that decentralization of the political and socio-economic systems meant that many segments of society were encouraged to engage in activities which would facilitate their autonomy and enhance their own social position. Such emphasis on locally autonomous systems may have encouraged interest in the production of iron as a utilitarian metal.

That being said, new socio-political systems, even if they do encourage technological, and for that matter ideological, economic and other systemic change, do not actually produce those changes. Such changes must and do come from other social developments and pressures. Two interrelated pressures that may have pushed iron to the forefront are population increases and the concomitant demands on supply and production.

Before going into this issue further, it is necessary to very briefly examine iron production and its circumstances in the preceding Bronze Age. The ability to produce iron from the smelting of terrestrial ores was not suddenly discovered at the beginning of the Iron Age. While Bronze Age iron is relatively rare, Wertime (1973a) and Davis *et al.* (1985) note that iron artifacts produced from terrestrial iron ores occur in archaeological deposits that date to the Early and Middle Bronze Ages of the Levant and elsewhere. These pre-Iron Age iron artifacts appear to be primarily ceremonial (Muhly 1982; Wertime 1973a; Smith *et al.* 1984), but some are made from steeled iron and may well have been used for utilitarian purposes. The existence, but relative rarity of iron artifacts from this period suggests that while iron working was known in the Bronze Age, production was extremely limited. The reasons for the limited use of iron in the Bronze Age may be related to the inherent difficulty in producing a relatively pure iron product from terrestrial ores, the lack of incentive to innovate and experiment with iron ores and the generally conservative nature of the dominant socio-political system. In other words, the lack of iron production in the Bronze Age may have been as much as result of socio-economic, demographic and political factors as it was technological.

Even in the Bronze Age, bronze was a metal of the elite, expensive to produce and of limited utilitarian use other than weapons (Muhly, Maddin and Stech 1985; Wertime 1979). The primary material for the majority of utilitarian tasks such as agriculture during the Bronze Age in the Near East was stone (Muhly *et al.* 1990; Stech-Wheeler *et al.* 1981; Wertime 1979). Bronze Age metal workers therefore probably had a limited number of 'customers' and were probably tied to those customers in a patron–client relationship (Budd and Taylor 1995). In the Late Bronze Age of the Levant, therefore, bronze metal production was centralized at locations where copper and especially tin were readily available, and where the wealthy elite had ready access to metal workers. Perhaps the supply of copper and tin were limited, but given this model, so was the demand due to the cost of producing bronze.

With the disruption of the Late Bronze Age collapse and deurbanization, metal workers became less tied to their patrons and, like the rest of society, metal working became less centralized. This decentralization no doubt meant less ready access to copper and tin sources, but, more importantly, it meant that metal workers became part of a different social system, one less dependent on client–patron relations and perhaps one where new ideas could be explored more readily. Iron working, although a relatively complex technology, was possible because iron ores, albeit of variable quality, were widely and easily available (Forbes 1950: 385; Liebowitz and Folk 1984: 275). This meant that local metal workers with small-scale smelting facilities could experiment with, work and produce iron at a cost low enough that utilitarian iron use became a possibility. Gradually, metal smiths, via innovation and the diffusion of technological advances, learned to produce a hard, durable iron product using these locally available ores.

The proposition of widespread local experimentation with iron ores implies that there must have been a demand for utilitarian iron products. As a number of researchers have noted, the early Iron Age population of the Levant was significantly higher than that of the Late Bronze Age (Bunimovitz 1995; Finkelstein 1995; Stager 1985, 1995). This demographic shift was a result of migration into the region and the expansion of *in situ* populations. The increasing population would have increased the demand for utilitarian products, particularly those that could enhance agricultural productivity, and perhaps those that aided defensibility, such as iron weapons. Iron eventually replaced bronze for utilitarian purposes, but it is more likely that a primary initial impetus for iron production was that it could be produced locally by local metal workers and that it was producible at a cost low enough that it could replace stone tools and weapons (Muhly, Maddin and Stech 1990).

Again, as Budd and Taylor (1995) point out, the theory that large-scale iron working emerged simply due to the ubiquity of iron ore alone is not a convincing nor sufficient explanation in itself. Iron ore was after all just as common in the Bronze Age as it was in the Iron Age. Nor is the theory that progressive linear technological evolution finally permitted ancient smelters to produce iron consistently sufficient to explain the origins of iron working. This evolutionary view is grounded in our modern industrial/post-industrial world and ignores the context of ancient metal workers. These smiths were not the ancient equivalent of research and development scientists. Clearly ancient metal workers experimented and developed metallurgical innovations, but progress was undoubtedly slow, sporadic and spanned generations. Useful knowledge of iron working procedures was probably learned in very small incremental stages, and this knowledge was probably slow to disseminate.

This suggests that it would have difficult or impossible for one culture to develop and control knowledge of iron working for any length of time. Iron working probably only became an important technology when many smiths over a wide area discovered that they could produce iron consistently and that their product was cheap enough that it was viable to use it to replace stone a the primary utilitarian material.

Conclusion

The emergence of iron working for utilitarian purposes was a consequence of the transition from the cultural systems of the Late Bronze to those of the Iron Age, not a primary or even secondary cause of that transition. There is no evidence to suggest that the upheaval that occurred c. 1200 BCE in the Levant was in any way related to one group's access to iron. While there is still much to know about the cultural causes and consequences of the beginning of iron working, the archaeological record suggests that none of the unidimensional models are viable explanations for the beginnings of this singularly important technology.

A final point should be made concerning the connection of iron working and urbanization in the Levant. It appears likely that the initial impetus for iron working was more a consequence of shifting demographic patterns, and perhaps even deurbanization, than a consequence of urban growth and development. However, with a return to political centralization and urban development in the Iron Age, the emerging iron working industry may have taken off as demand for steel tools and weapons increased and as small incremental increases in iron working technology eventually permitted large-scale iron and steel production.

BIBLIOGRAPHY

Aharoni, Y.
1970   'New Aspects of the Israelite Occupation in the North', in *Near Eastern Archaeology in the Twentieth Century: Essays in Honor of Nelson Glueck* (ed. J.A. Sanders; New York: Doubleday): 254-65.

Budd, P., and T. Taylor
1995   'The Faerie Smith Meets the Bronze Industry: Magic versus Science in the Interpretation of Prehistoric Metal-making', *WA* 27: 133-43.

Bunimovitz, S.
1995   'On the Edge of Empires—Late Bronze Age (1500–1200 BCE)', in *ASHL*: 320-31.

Clough, R.E.
1987   'The Bloomery Process—Observations on the Use of Rich Ores and the Production of Natural Steel', in *The Crafts of the Blacksmith* (ed. B.G. Scott and H. Cleere; Belfast: 1984 Symposium of the UISPP, Comité pour la Sidérurgie Ancienne): 19-27.

Davis, D., R. Maddin, J.D. Muhly and T. Stech
1985   'A Steel Pick from Mt. Adir in Palestine', *JNES* 44: 41-51.

Dayton, J.
1973   'The Problem of Tin in the Ancient World', *WA* 5: 123-25.

Dever, W.G.
1992   'The Late Bronze–Early Iron I Horizon in Syria–Palestine: Egyptians, Canaanites, "Sea Peoples", and Proto Israelites', in *TCY*: 99-110.

Dothan, T.
1982   *The Philistines and their Material Culture* (Jerusalem: Israel Exploration Society).
1992   'Social Dislocation and Cultural Change in the 12th Century BCE', in *TCY*: 93-98.

Finkelstein, I.
1995   'The Great Transformation: The "Conquest" of the Highland Frontiers and the Rise of Territorial States', in *ASHL*; 349-67.

Forbes, R.J.
1950   *Metallurgy in Antiquity* (Leiden: Brill).
1972   *Studies in Ancient Technology* (Leiden: Brill).

Fritz, V.
1987   'Conquest or Settlement? The Early Iron Age in Palestine', *BA* 50: 84-100.

Hallo, W.W.
1992   'From Bronze Age to Iron Age in Western Asia: Defining the Problem', in *TCY*: 1-9.

Hodder, I.
1992   *Theory and Practice in Archaeology* (London: Routledge).

Kense, F.
1983   *Traditional African Iron Working* (African Occasional Papers, 1; Calgary: Department of Archaeology, University of Calgary).
LaBianca, Ø.S., and R.W. Younker
1995   'The Kingdoms of Ammon, Moab and Edom: The Archaeology of Society in Late Bronze/Iron Age Transjordan (ca. 1400–500 BCE)', in *ASHL*: 399-415.
Liebowitz, H., and R. Folk
1984   'The Dawn of Iron Smelting in Palestine: The Late Bronze Age Smelter at Tel Yin'am', Preliminary Report, *JFA* 11: 265-80.
Maddin, R., J.D. Muhly and T. Wheeler
1977   'How the Iron Age Began', *SciAm* 237: 122-30.
Mazar, A.
1990   *Archaeology of the Land of the Bible 10,000–586 BCE* (New York: Doubleday).
McNutt, P.M.
1990   *The Foraging of Israel* (Sheffield: JSOT).
Miller, R.
1986   'Elephants, Ivory and Charcoal: An Ecological Perspective', *BASOR* 264: 29-43.
Muhly, J.D.
1982   'How Iron Technology Changed the Ancient World and Gave the Philistines a Military Edge', *BAR* 8.6: 42-54.
1985   'Sources of Tin and the Beginnings of Bronze Metallurgy', *AJA* 89: 275-91.
1992   'The Crisis Years in the Mediterranean World: Transition or Cultural Disintegration', in *TCY*: 10-26.
Muhly, J.D., R. Maddin and T. Stech
1990   'The Metal Artifacts', in *Kinneret: Ergebnisse der Ausgrabungen auf dem Tell el 'Oreme am See Genneserat 1982–1985* (ed. V. Fritz; Wiesbaden: Harrassowitz): 159-75.
Muhly, J.D., R. Maddin, T. Stech and E. Özgen
1985   'Iron in Anatolia and the Nature of the Hittite Iron Industry', *AS* 35: 67-84.
Smith, R.H., R. Maddin, J.D. Muhly and T. Stech
1984   'Bronze Age Steel from Pella, Jordan', *CA* 25: 234-36.
Snodgrass, A.M.
1980   'Iron and Early Metallurgy in the Mediterranean', in *TCY*: 335-74.
1989   'The Coming of the Iron Age in Greece: Europe's Earliest Bronze/Iron Transition', in *The Bronze Age/Iron Age Transition in Europe: Aspects of Continuity and Exchange in European Societies, c. 1200 to 500 BC* (ed. M.L.S. Sorenson and R. Thomas; Oxford: British Archaeological Reports): 22-35.
Stager, L.E.
1985   'The Archaeology of the Family in Ancient Israel', *BASOR* 260: 1-3.
1995   'The Impact of the Sea Peoples (1185–1050 BCE)', in *ASHL*: 332-48.

Stech, T., J.D. Muhly and R. Maddin
    1985   'The Analysis of Iron Artifacts from Palaepahos—*Skales*', RDAC: 192-202.
Stech-Wheeler, T., J.D. Muhly, K. Maxwell-Hyslop and R. Maddin
    1981   'Iron at Taanach and Early Iron Metallurgy in the Eastern Mediterranean', *AJA* 85: 245-68.
Thirgood, J.V.
    1981   *Man and the Mediterranean Forest* (London: Academic Press).
Tylecote, R.F.
    1980   'Furnaces, Crucibles and Slags', in *The Coming of the Age of Iron* (ed. T.A. Wertime and J.D. Muhly; New Haven: Yale); 183-228.
Waldbaum, J.C.
    1980   'The First Archaeological Appearance of Iron', in *The Coming of the Age of Iron* (ed. T.A. Wertime and J.D. Muhly; New Haven: Yale); 69-98.
    1987   'Copper, Iron, Tin, Wood: The Start of the Iron Age in the Eastern Mediterranean', *AJA* 91: 285.
Ward, W.A., and M.S. Joukowsky (eds.)
    1992   *The Crisis Years: The Twelfth Century BC* (Dububque: Kendall Hunt).
Weinstein, J.M.
    1985   'The Egyptian Empire in Palestine: A Reassessment', *BASOR* 241: 1-28.
Wertime, T.A.
    1973a   'The Beginnings of Metallurgy: A New Look', *Science* 182: 875-87.
    1973b   'Pyrotechnology: Man's First Industrial Uses of Fire', *American Scientist* 61: 670-82.
    1979   'Pyrotechnology: Man's Fire-Using Crafts', in *Early Technologies: Invited Lectures on the Middle East at the University of Texas at Austin*, III (ed. D. Schmandt-Besserat; Malibu, CA: Undena): 17-21.
    1983   'The Furnace Versus the Goat: The Pyrotechnologic Industries and Mediterranean Deforestation in Antiquity', *JFA* 10: 445-52.
Wertime, T.A., and J.D. Muhly (eds.)
    1980   *The Coming of the Age of Iron* (New Haven: Yale).
Wheeler, T., and R. Maddin
    1980   'Metallurgy and Ancient Man', in *The Coming of the Age of Iron* (ed. T.A. Wertime and J.D. Muhly; New Haven: Yale): 99-126.
Wright, G.E.
    1938   'Iron in Israel', *BA* 1: 5-12.
    1939   'Iron: The Date of its Introduction into Common Use in Palestine', *AJA* 43: 458-13.
    1943   'I Sam. 13:19-20', *BA* 6: 34.

URBANIZATION AND NORTHWEST SEMITIC INSCRIPTIONS OF THE LATE BRONZE AND IRON AGES

Walter E. Aufrecht

Epigraphy in the broadest sense is the study of ancient texts, and an epigrapher is one who studies the form and content of these texts, the materials on which they were written, the kind of writing that appears and the language to which the words belong (Naveh 1982: 1-12). For the Northwest Semitic inscriptions of the Late Bronze and Iron Ages, that means texts written on stone, pottery, papyrus and metal in the languages of Ugaritic, Aramaic, Phoenician, Hebrew, Moabite, Ammonite and Edomite.

Epigraphy is related to both archaeology and history. Epigraphers usually are dependent on archaeologists to discover the texts to be translated and interpreted. Historians are dependent on epigraphers for translations and interpretations of the primary documents of the past upon which histories are based.[1]

In its most narrow sense, epigraphy is the study of letters, their evolution and development. For the Northwest Semitic epigrapher, this means for the most part, study of the alphabet. Often, the alphabet is not fully considered in discussions of the creation of human culture, though of course, it is no less an artifact than a stone scraper, potsherd or grain silo. Despite this, handbooks of archaeology give the invention and development of the alphabet little or no attention.[2] When they

---

1. The most recent, clearest presentations of the relationship between Syro-Palestinian archaeology and history may be found in Dever (1995b, 1996): '...Syro-Palestinian archaeologists must contribute [to scholarship]...as historians... Syro-Palestinian archaeology is "history" [or it is] "nothing"' (Dever 1995b: 70).

2. For example, see the otherwise splendid handbook by Levy (1995), which presents extensive discussions of stone tools and their development, accompanied by at least 18 plates (one in color!); but only one paragraph of discussion on alphabetic origins and one plate, which does not even show the complete development of the

list the truly great moments or turning points of human invention that created and shaped civilization (or as we now say, *complex society*), they do not include the alphabet along with the domestication of plants and animals, and the invention of pottery and metallurgy. The following will compensate for that omission by showing that the alphabet was not only a factor which led to the development of human society as we know it, but was an *essential* factor.

The creation of the alphabet was 'a singular event in human history, occurring probably in the eighteenth century BC... [It was] invented only once' (Cross 1989).[3] The alphabet is simplicity itself. Unlike the elaborate and complicated graphic systems of Egypt, Mesopotamia, India, Anatolia and China, which were the domain of professional writers and readers, the alphabet contained relatively few characters or signs, which were easy to recognize, memorize and write (Cross 1967, 1989). Once learned, they could be adapted to any language or linguistic system. They were first adapted, apparently, to the Canaanite languages of the Late Bronze and early Iron Ages.

The consequences of the invention of this graphic system are enormous. For example, anyone can learn to read and write. By learning the alphabet and how to use it, one does not have to resort to a professional class of scribes.[4] Of course, professional scribes and readers continued to exist and perform their traditional tasks even after the invention of the alphabet, and likely were its first users. It should not be imagined that everyone instantly took up reading and writing in the Late Bronze Levant. On the other hand, alphabetic writing was adopted quickly in a wide range of locales. Many have confused the

letters (Ilan 1995: 311, pl. 9). In the same book, the discussion of Northwest Semitic texts is relegated to the Iron Age II in the careful but brief treatment by Dever (1995a: 425-29); but no author deals with *how* or *why* alphabetic writing developed up to that point. Standard handbooks appear equally as reticent to discuss these subjects, despite elaborate typologies, analyses and interpretations of the cultural significance of all manner of human creations, such as pottery, tools, architecture, tombs and other artifacts.

3.   There is an enormous literature on the subject of the origins of the alphabet. For the technical discussion, see Cross (1967, 1979, 1980) and Sass (1988, 1991a, 1991b). For less technical exposition, see Naveh (1982: 23-42), Cross (1989) and Healey (1990).

4.   For recent discussion of scribes and scribal education in the Iron Age Levant, see Lemaire (1981), Millard (1982, 1985), Demsky (1988: 10-14), Greenfield (1991), Greenstein (1996) and Niditch (1996).

temporal and geographical spread of the alphabet with its spread within a society. Temporally, the spread of the alphabet was very rapid if measured in centuries rather than millennia (Cross 1985, 1989). Geographically, the spread also was wide, for example, from Canaan to Greece. But neither of these are the same thing as spreading rapidly among social classes within a society. Well into the Iron Age and beyond, large numbers of people could neither read nor write, and were dependent on those who could. Irrespective of how long it took for (some or all) Levantine peoples to develop the skills of alphabetic reading and writing, two facts remain: (1) the alphabet was a simple system, and (2) because of this simplicity, increasing numbers of people who were not scribes eventually *could* and *did* read and write. It is ironic that the simplicity of the alphabet should be an important factor in the complexity of human society.

The term *complexity* is used in modern social scientific study to denote what used to be called 'civilization'. It signifies at least two things: (1) urbanization, the movement toward city or 'city-state' social structures (Dever 1993: 89-101); and (2) social stratification, 'the process by which groups within a society become differentiated, elite classes... In a complex society, elite classes may not be born as such, but may become so through craft specialization, entrepreneurship, the accumulation of capital, the wielding of power in a variety of ways, or through other means' (Dever 1993: 101). Writing was then (as it is now) a means of wielding power. '...In any society where non-literate people are the majority, literacy was virtually synonymous with power and authority, and consequently considered a special mark of social prestige' (Uehlinger 1993: 284). Of course, from the end of the Late Bronze Age, through the Iron Age in the Levant and beyond, the elite were the royal and priestly strata of society, and their agents, the scribes. But by the end of the Iron Age, writing was no longer exclusively the domain of these classes. Even though writing and reading remained an indicator of elite status in society, there now began to develop a more a varied corps of elite persons.

Before dealing further with the issue of literacy, however, several factors must be recognized. First, while it is clear that a society cannot pass beyond a certain threshold of complexity with *only* a professionally trained corps of writers and readers, that threshold seldom (if ever) can be recognized or even characterized. Secondly, the steps leading up to that threshold seldom (if ever) can be detailed and analysed. Third, that threshold will be different for each society, making systemic analysis more difficult if not impossible. These factors not withstanding, it is clear that a society with only a trained scribal corps is different from one in which non-scribes are able to read and write. Thus, despite our inability to trace in every detail the evolution and development of alphabetic writing in the Levant from the Late Bronze Age through its adoption and transformation into the ninth century BCE 'national' scripts of Phoenicia, Aram and Israel, to the development of the eighth- through sixth-century BCE scripts of Ammon, Edom and Moab and beyond, many stages in that development are clear; and even if they were not, the fact that there *was* a development would still be clear.[5]

Furthermore, that development does not proceed simply from literacy by a professional class in the twelfth century BCE to literacy by everyone in the sixth century BCE. The development was much more nuanced than that linear model suggests. Professional scribes and interpreters continued to be employed in the Iron Age and beyond, but there developed alongside of them (and, no doubt, interacting with them), an increasing number of people who needed first to read and then to write. The indisputable evidence of this is found in two sorts of epigraphic evidence: (1) the most mundane of epigraphic sources, personal seals, and (2) the sophisticated and rapid development and spread of script types.

In the Levant, beginning in the second half of the ninth century BCE, precisely the time when the Phoenician, Aramaic and Hebrew 'national' scripts become distinguishable (Naveh 1982; Bordreuil 1992: 138-39), there was a progression from personal seals containing

---

5.   Among the clear stages are the place of origin of the pictographs, the meaning of the pictographs, the adoption of the acrophonic principle, the fixing of the direction of alphabetic writing, the evolution and development of (most) alphabetic characters, the appropriation of the alphabet for the writing of different languages and the development of distinct alphabetic scripts. However, it is not necessary to see and detail all (or any) of the steps leading up to the moment when society is transformed by the adoption of alphabetic writing or even the moment of transformation itself, to recognize *that* the transformation took place. The issue is analogous to one confronted by biologists who cannot determine the exact moment of (let alone the steps leading up to) the creation of eukaryotes, that is, cells with nuclei and other specialized internal bodies. Nevertheless, such a moment (and preparation) did take place, and it created a new threshold in the development of life on earth, the consequences of which appeared only 700 million or so years later (Dennett 1995: 86).

only designs to seals containing personal names in alphabetic script (Naveh 1982: 4). By the end of the Iron Age, three interesting features are discernible. First, the quantity of inscribed seals and seal impressions increases steadily from the ninth to the sixth centuries BCE as attested by the present corpus of over 1200 seals and impressions (Avigad and Sass 1997), a corpus which is only a fraction of the seals that existed and/or still await discovery. Secondly, seals and the level of literacy they represent were socially diffuse (Bordreuil 1992: 182-99). Thirdly, in Judah at least, there was a development toward aniconic name-seals, a circumstance now taken to be evidence of more widespread literacy (Demsky 1985; Uehlinger 1993).[6] Evidently, it became increasingly important for people not only to have name-identifers, but to be able to read them. The level of literacy which this represents has been called 'functional literacy' (Dever 1995a: 426) or 'popular literacy' (Demsky 1985: 351, 1988: 15), as opposed to the kind of literacy represented by a professional scribal corps.

Further evidence for this distinction is found in the sophisticated and rapid development and spread of script types. Based on the work of Cross (1961, 1962a, 1962b, 1996), Naveh (1968; 1982: 6-8) and others, it is now possible to distinguish at least four script types: (1) lapidary (the equivalent of printing), the use of which was confined to engraving on stone by a professional writer; (2) formal cursive (variously called 'conservative', 'chancellery' or 'professional'), the handwriting of the professional scribe; (3) free cursive (variously called 'extreme' or simply 'cursive'), the handwriting used by the educated upper classes; and (4) vulgar cursive, the handwriting adopted by the less well-educated.[7] It is the latter that is of special interest for understanding the development of literacy. The relative ubiquity of documents written in the vulgar cursive script, which existed *at the same time* as documents written in the formal scripts and in a variety of genres, tells that not all writing was done by professional scribes

6.   The older view that the tendency toward aniconism on late Judean name-seals is an indication of the biblical ban on making images (Reifenberg 1950) can no longer be maintained in the light of archaeological evidence that illuminates so-called popular Israelite religion, the most recent treatment of which is Dever (1995c: 40-54), to which should be added Albertz (1994).

7.   For examples of Hebrew texts written in each of these scripts and a discussion of how they illustrate the development of literacy in Iron Age Israel, see the important paper by Naveh (1968).

and the well-educated classes, but by farmers and craftsmen, such as potters, ivory joiners and builders (Demsky 1985; Millard 1985). And although this evidence makes clear that popular literacy was widespread, the important issue is not how widespread literacy was, but what writing and reading accomplished for people. This is because 'differences in the mode of communication...involve developments in the storing, analysis, and creation of human knowledge, as well as the relationships between individuals involved' (Goody 1977: 37).[8]

In the ancient Levant, what 'functional' or 'popular' literacy accomplished for people was to make the world more 'accessible' to the individual. People were able to appropriate information with less mediation from a writer and/or interpreter. For example, business and commerce no longer need be controlled exclusively by royalty and priesthood, originally the only groups or classes who could afford to employ professional record keepers (scribes). Individuals could enter into contracts and other relationships by virtue of their ability to write or sign (i.e. use a personal name seal) and read (another's stamp seal). To be sure, there was still the need for a professional class of writers and interpreters (lawyers and judges), whose numbers no doubt increased exponentially with these (now) more literate individuals. But these professionals began to serve not just crown and priesthood, but the 'new elite', individuals who could read and write. In the Levant, the Bronze Age lasted approximately two thousand years with an economy monopolized by an elite who were dependent on a professional scribal class. But in the few centuries of the Iron Age, there appeared what clearly can be recognized as 'private' persons who engage in enterprise. They are recognized because they can read and write and have left a record for us. As Millard (1985: 304) put it,

> Can it really be supposed that Israelite scribes did no more than write such trifles as the list of names from Tel Masos, or the incoherent complaint about a sequestrated cloak from Mesad Hashavyahu, or scribbled notes about the class of wine in various jugs? Were potsherds really their normal writing material...?

These examples could be multiplied with references to other 'functional' or 'popular' or 'vulgar' Northwest Semitic inscriptions from

---

8.   Estimates regarding the extent of popular literacy are highly subjective, and should be abandoned because 'there are no direct, absolute or objective criteria for measuring literacy' (Demsky 1988: 15).

the Iron Age.[9] But the point is clear. The epigraphic evidence tells that many more people than scribes could read and write at the end of the Iron Age in the Levant. To focus only on literature produced by professional scribes (e.g. the biblical texts) will ignore the evidence of popular, non-professional literacy, and distort the picture of the development of reading and writing.

As literacy increased and society was made up more and more of individuals who could read and write, there was a need to have more and better access to reading and writing. Complexity speeded up, so to speak. A class of teachers was necessary and with them institutions, such as schools. This in turn resulted in specialized branches of learning and knowledge which required further specialists (e.g. administrators), who wielded power (though, as in any era, administrators were not necessarily literate), which led to more institutions and more specialists, and so on. Of course, this did not happen overnight, but the evidence is clear: just as there is a literary movement in the southern Levant from Late Bronze Age oral traditions to Iron Age written traditions (Cross 1995), there is a movement from a system of reading and writing by professional scribes to one of reading writing by an increasingly literate non-scribal corps. The two movements are obviously related.

A similar movement took place outside of the Levant, which also is the story of the alphabet. The alphabet moved to Greece,[10] where it eventually contributed to the expression and creation of such things as critical thought (philosophy, education), experimentation in the social realm (democracy), development in the physical realm (aesthetics, architecture) and expression of the aesthetic realm (art, literature, drama, poetry). All of these are societal phenomena which were expressed, transmitted and received in Greek society in alphabetic

9.   For a convenient list of Hebrew ostraca and graffiti from the Iron Age, see Millard (1985: 310-11). For recent collections of Northwest Semitic inscriptions see the following: Herr (1978), Aufrecht (1989), Timm (1989), Davies (1991: 1-263), Fitzmyer and Kaufman (1992), Hübner (1992) and Avigad and Sass (1997).

10.   It is neither necessary nor possible here to detail the arguments regarding the Greek adoption and adaption (or invention, cf. Powell 1991) of the alphabet. See Cross (1979) and Isserlin (1991) for discussion of and bibliography on this subject. Is it also not necessary to describe the mechanisms which caused and abetted the development of literacy within Greek society, on which see Baslez and Briquel Chatonnet (1991) and Collombier (1991).

writing by a new elite who were not professional scribes.[11] And when, some centuries later, Greek ideas and culture entered the Near East, they had an enormous influence, the results of which are with us to this day. As F.E. Peters (1970: 22-23) has written,

> Eastern Hellenism has left its mark on all the lands once conquered by Alexander: on Buddhist art, the Zoroastrian Scriptures, the preaching of Mani, the spirituality of Christianity, the theology of Judaism, the palace architecture of Arab *shaykhs*. It produced Zeno (and through him Seneca), Apollonius of Rhodes (and through him Vergil), Posidonius (and through him Cicero), Plotinus (and through him Augustine). Its monuments are gnosticism, the university, the catechetical school, pastoral poetry, monasticism, the romance, grammar, lexicography, city planning, theology, canon law, heresy and scholasticism.

And all this because some Middle Bronze Age Canaanite invented the alphabet. If the alphabet does not qualify as a cultural artifact, then nothing does.

But in what kind of culture did this artifact first develop and thrive? Certainly not an exclusively rural one. People within 'closed' rural environments like the village do not need written documents like contracts in order to interact with each other. They only need mutually agreed-upon reliable witnesses who they know and who know them (such as patriarch and deity). This is good enough for village culture, because most people in a village are bound by kinship regulations or are so proximate that everyone in the village will know everyone else's business anyway. Paradoxically, when people in a 'closed' community (in which interaction with others is 'public') want to deal with outsiders, they enter an 'open' community (in which interaction with others is 'private'). This requires a more or less arbitrary, but still mutually agreed-upon, means of establishing and maintaining relationships. Written documents accomplish this. The new elite emerge because they can write and read, and the society in which this takes place is one that allows for the externally *protected* establishment of rights and responsibilities between people who need not know each other and who interact with each other under well-defined but limited circumstances. Village culture begins to give way to urban culture.[12]

---

11. The debate on Greek literacy has centered on how widespread it was in any given period of Greek history. See Millard (1985: 306) for a discussion. But the issue should be what writing and reading accomplished for people.

12. Unfortunately, a full-scale treatment of the city in the Late Bronze and Iron

In the Levant, it is clear that 'vulgar' documents illustrating 'popular' literacy are the product of urban, or better, *urbanizing* culture. They are the artifacts of impersonal culture typical of urban not rural environments, developed initially for inter-village (and subsequently inter-society) commerce, business, governments and other human activities.

If one plows a field each day and sells (or trades) one's produce to one's immediate neighbors, there is no need for identification and no need to document a transaction, because everyone in the village will know it (if they haven't watched it). But if one wants to conduct a transaction with a stranger, a mechanism for protecting the parties is necessary, and this, it seems, involves writing. One consequence of this is that skilled persons (who come to form the new elite classes and guilds) arise, persons whose jobs, like so many other jobs in urban environments, exist only because of the urban environment. In rural settings, one does not need a trained scribal class with special skills like seal cutting (or making telephone calling cards, a modern equivalent, that contain identification of an individual, but are not created by that individual). In urban environments these special skills are a necessity.

The movement from village to urban life (or at least its beginnings) in the Levant is illustrated by the epigraphic evidence from the Late Bronze and Iron Ages. The simple fact of these epigraphic documents tells about the development toward literacy, complexity and urbanization. Their *contents* tell the same thing. The ancients themselves were aware of a distinction between a 'village' and 'city' (Dreyer 1961; Zimmerman 1967; Na'aman 1991; Lemaire 1995; Hoftijzer and Jongeling 1995).

The invention of the alphabet is one of the great accomplishments of human invention and creativity. Like the others, the domestication of plants and animals and the invention of pottery and metallurgy, it put humanity on a new course. That it occurred considerably later than

Age Levant emphasizing both archaeological and epigraphic evidence has yet to appear. Provisionally, see the excellent treatments by Beaudry (1994), which emphasizes the archaeological evidence; and Lemaire (1995), which emphasizes (the monumental) epigraphical evidence. Other treatments of the city in the Late Bronze and Iron Age Levant usually belong to the genre 'Biblical Archaeology' (e.g. Neufeld 1960; Evans 1962–63; Frick 1977; Herzog 1992; Fritz 1995; Rouillard-Bonraisin 1995), with all the attendant problems derived therefrom (Dever 1990: 8-11).

these others should not obscure recognition of its importance, nor the fact that since its invention, it has been *the* essential creator, carrier and maintainer of human culture, first in Bronze and Iron Age Canaan; second in Iron Age, Classical and Hellenistic Greece; third in lands impacted by Arabic language and literature; and now throughout the world.

ACKNOWLEDGMENTS

I wish to thank Professors Larry G. Herr and Neil A. Mirau, Ms Wendy D. Shury and Mr Steven W. Gauley for suggestions which have improved this paper in numerous ways.

BIBLIOGRAPHY

Albertz, R.
   1994   *A History of Israelite Religion in the Old Testament Period*. II. *From the Exile to the Maccabees* (Louisville: Westminster; Richmond, VA: John Knox).

Aufrecht, W.E.
   1989   *A Corpus of Ammonite Inscriptions* (Lewiston, NY: Edwin Mellen).

Avigad, N., and B. Sass
   1997   *Corpus of West Semitic Stamp Seals* (2 vols.; Jerusalem: Israel Academy of Sciences and Humanities).

Baslez, M.-F., and F. Briquel Chatonnet
   1991   'De l'oral à l'écrit: le bilinguisme de Phéniciens en Grèce', in *PGL*: 372-86.

Beaudry, M.
   1994   'L'urbanisaton à l'époque du Fer', in *«Où demeures-tu?»* (Jn *1, 38)*: *La maison depuis le monde biblique. en hommage au professeur Guy Couturier à l'occasion de ses soixante-cinq ans* (ed. J.-C. Petit *et al.*; Québec: Fides): 31-51.

Bordreuil, P.
   1992   'Sceaux inscrits des pay du Levant', *Dictionnaire de la Bible, Supplément* 12.66: 86-211.

Collombier, A.-M.
   1991   'Écritures et sociétés à Chypre à l'âge du Fer', in *PGL*: 425-47.

Cross, F.M.
   1961   'Epigraphic Notes on Hebrew Documents of the Eighth–Sixth Centuries BC: I. A New Reading of a Place Name in the Samaria Ostraca', *BASOR* 163: 12-14.

   1962a   'Epigraphic Notes on Hebrew Documents of the Eighth–Sixth Centuries BC: II. The Murabb'ât Papyrus and the Letter Found near Yabneh-yam', *BASOR* 165: 34-46.

1962b   'Epigraphic Notes on Hebrew Documents of the Eighth–Sixth Centuries BC: III. The Inscribed Jar Handles from Gibeon', *BASOR* 168: 18-23.

1967   'The Origin and Early Evolution of the Alphabet', *Er-Is* 8: 8*-24*.

1979   'Early Alphabetic Scripts', in *Symposia Celebrating the Seventy-fifth Anniversary of the Founding of the American Schools of Oriental Research (1900–1975)*. I. *Archaeology and Early Israelite History*; II. *Archaeology and the Sanctuaries of Israel* (ed. F.M. Cross; Cambridge, MA: American Schools of Oriental Research): 95-123.

1980   'Newly Found Inscriptions in Old Canaanite and Early Phoenician Scripts', *BASOR* 238: 1-20.

1985   Response, in *BAT*: 367.

1989   'The Invention and Development of the Alphabet', in *The Origins of Writing* (ed. W.M. Senner; Lincoln, NB: University of Nebraska): 77-90.

1995   'Toward a History of Hebrew Prosdy', in *Fortunate the Eyes that See: Essays in Honor of David Noel Freedman in Celebration of his Seventieth Birthday* (ed. A.B. Beck *et al.*; Grand Rapids, MI: Eerdmans): 298-309.

1996   'A Papyrus Recording a Divine Legal Decision and the Root *rhq* in Biblical and Near Eastern Legal Usage', in *Texts, Temples, and Traditions: A Tribute to Menahem Haran* (ed. M.V. Fox *et al.*; Winona Lake, IN: Eisenbrauns): 311-20.

Davies, G.I.

1991   *Ancient Hebrew Inscriptions, Corpus and Concordance* (Cambridge: Cambridge University Press).

Demsky, A.

1985   'On the Extent of Literacy in Ancient Israel', in *BAT*: 349-53.

1988   'Writing in Ancient Israel and Early Judaism. Part One: The Biblical Period', in *Mikra: Text, Translation, Reading and Interpretation of the Hebrew Bible in Ancient Judaism and Early Christianity* (ed. M.J. Mulder; Assen: Van Gorcum; Philadelphia: Fortress Press): 2-20.

Dennett, D.C.

1995   *Darwin's Dangerous Idea: Evolution and the Meanings of Life* (New York: Simon and Schuster).

Dever, W.

1990   *Recent Archaeological Discoveries and Biblical Research* (Seattle: University of Washington).

1993   'The Rise of Complexity in the Land of Israel in the Early Second Millennium BCE', in *BATS*: 98-109.

1995a   'Social Structure in Palestine in the Iron II Period on the Eve of Destruction', in *ASHL*: 416-30.

1995b   ' "Will the Real Israel Please Stand Up?" Archaeology and Israelite Historiography: Part I', *BASOR* 297: 61-80.

1995c   'Will the Real Israel Please Stand Up?' Part II: Archaeology and the Religions of Ancient Israel', *BASOR* 298: 58.

1996   'Archaeology and the current Crisis in Israelite Historiography', *Er-Is* 25: 18*-27*.

Dreyer, H.J.
1961   The Roots qr, ʿr, ġr and ṣ/ṭr = "Stone, Wall City" etc.', in *De fructu oris sui: Essays in Honor of Adrianus van Selms* (ed. I.H. Eybers *et al.*; Leiden: Brill): 17-25.

Evans, G.
1962–63   ' "Gates" and "Streets": Urban Institutions in Old Testament Times', *JRS* 2: 1-12.

Fitzmyer, J.A., and S.A. Kaufman
1992   *An Aramaic Bibliography. Part I. Old, Official, and Biblical Aramaic* (Baltimore: Johns Hopkins University Press).

Frick, F.S.
1997   *The City in Ancient Israel* (Missoula, MT: Scholars Press).

Fritz, V.
1995   *The City in Ancient Israel* (Sheffield: Sheffield Academic Press).

Goody, J.
1977   *The Domestication of the Savage Mind* (New York: Columbia University Press).

Greenfield, J.C.
1991   'Of Scribes, Scripts and Languages', in *PGL*: 173-85.

Greenstein, E.L.
1996   'The Canaanite Literary Heritage in Ancient Hebrew Writing', *Michmanim* 10: 19-38 (Hebrew).

Healey, J.F.
1990   *The Early Alphabet* (Berkeley: University of California; London: British Museum).

Herr, L.G.
1978   *The Scripts of Ancient Northwest Semitic Seals* (Missoula, MT: Scholars Press).

Herzog, Z.
1992   'Cities', in *ABD*, I: 1031-43.

Hoftijzer, J., and K. Jongeling
1995   *Dictionary of the North-West Semitic Insciptions* (2 vols.; Leiden: Brill).

Hübner, U.
1992   *Die Ammoniter: Untersuchungen zur Geschichte, Kultur und Religion eines transjordanischen Volkes im 1. Jahrtausend V. Chr.* (Wiesbaden: Otto Harrassowitz).

Ilan, D.
1995   'The Dawn of Internationalism—The Middle Bronze Age', in *ASHL*: 297-315.

Isserlin, B.S.J.
1991   'The Transfer of the Alphabet to the Greeks. The State of Documentation', in *PGL*: 283-91.

Lemaire, A.
1981   *Les Écoles et la formation de la Bible dans l'ancien Israël* (Fribourg: University Press; Göttingen: Vandenhoeck & Ruprecht).

1995   'Villes, rois et gouverneurs au Levant d'après les inscriptions monu-
            mentales ouest-sémitiques (IXe–VIIe siècles av. J.-C.)', *Sem* 43–44:
            21-36.

Levy, T.E. (ed.)
1995   *The Archaeology of Society in the Holy Land* (New York: Facts on
            File).

Millard, A.R.
1982   'In Praise of Ancient Scribes', *BA* 45: 143-53.
1985   'An Assessment of the Evidence for Writing in Ancient Israel', in
            BAT: 301-12.

Na'aman, N.
1991   'Amarna *ālāni pu-ru-zi* (EA 137) and Biblical '*ry hprzy/hprzwt*
            ("Rural Settlements")', *ZAH* 4: 72-75.

Naveh, J.
1968   'A Palaeographic Note on the Distribution of the Hebrew Script', *HTR*
            61: 68-74.
1982   *Early History of the Alphabet: An Introduction to West Semitic
            Epigraphy and Palaeography* (Jerusalem: Magnes; Leiden: Brill).

Neufeld, E.
1960   'The Emergence of a Royal-Urban Society in Ancient Israel', *HUCA*
            31: 31-53.

Niditch, S.
1996   *Oral World and Written Word* (Louisville: Westminster/John Knox
            Press).

Peters, F.E.
1970   *The Harvest of Hellenism: A History of the Near East from Alexander
            the Great to the Triumph of Christianity* (New York: Simon &
            Schuster).

Powell, B.B.
1991   'The Origins of Alphabetic Literacy among the Greeks', in *PGL*: 357-
            70.

Reifenberg, A.
1950   *Ancient Hebrew Seals* (London: East and West Library).

Rouillard-Bonraisin, H.
1995   'Les relations villes—rois en Juda et in Israël des débuts à la chute de
            la monarchie', *Sem* 43-44: 53-62.

Sass, B.
1988   *The Genesis of the Alphabet and its Development in the Second
            Millennium BC* (Wiesbaden: Otto Harrassowitz).
1991a   'The Beth Shemesh Tablet and the Early History of the Proto-
            Canaanite, Cuneiform and South Semitic Alphabets', *UF* 23: 315-26.
1991b   *Studia Alphabetica: On the Origin and Early History of Northwest
            Semitic, South Semitic and Greek Alphabets* (Fribourg: University
            Press; Göttingen: Vandenhoeck & Ruprecht).

Timm, S.
1989   *Moab Zwischen den Mächten: Studien zu historischen Denkmälern
            und Texten* (Wiesbaden: Otto Harrassowitz).

Uehlinger, C.

1993   'Northwest Semitic Inscribed Seals, Iconography and Syro-Palestinian Religions of Iron Age II: Some Afterthoughts and Conclusions', in *Studies in the Iconography of Northwest Semitic Inscribed Seals* (ed. B. Sass and C. Uehlinger; Fribourg: University Press; Göttingen: Vandenhoeck & Ruprecht): 257-88.

Zimmerman, F.

1967   'קיר, עיר and Related Forms', in *The Seventy-Fifth Anniversary Volume of the Jewish Quarterly Review* (ed. A.A. Neuman and S. Zeitlin; Philadelphia: Jewish Quarterly Review): 582-92.

LEARNING TO LOVE THE KING:
URBANISM AND THE STATE IN IRON AGE MOAB

Bruce Routledge

During the Iron Age II–III (c. 950–500 BCE), territorial states arose for the first time in Jordan's history.[1] Given the apparent novelty of these Iron Age political institutions, one might reasonably ask how these 'new states' encouraged and maintained political legitimacy through time. In other words, how did these Iron Age states blend their political structures into the regional landscape in such a way that the resultant social hierarchy was seen as 'not merely important but in some odd fashion connected with the way the world [was] built' (Geertz 1983: 124)?

The following will suggest that this legitimacy was achieved and maintained by the inscription of state hierarchy onto the process of urbanization. Indeed, in the case of the Moab, state hierarchy and urbanism developed as linked, mutually reinforcing phenomena during the latter part of the Iron Age.

What Is Urbanism?

Urbanization as a process, and urbanism as a phenomenon, are notoriously slippery terms to define. Certainly these terms imply a regional system distinguished by the presence of cities (Redman 1978: 216). However, this is not a particularly informative statement, as the burden of definition is simply shifted onto the equally indeterminate term 'city'. More promising is a core set of characteristics that researchers have tended to employ when defining a settlement system as urban: (1) the dense concentration of population in a limited number of settlements; (2) heterogeneity within and between settlements; and

---

1. A short, but useful summary of the textual and archaeological evidence relevant to the states of Ammon, Moab and Edom can be found in Lemaire (1987).

(3) the existence of a regional spatial hierarchy (Wheatley 1972).

Each of these three characteristics can be understood in both absolute and relative terms (Redman 1978: 215-16). For example, Maisels (1993: 12-13, 155, 254-61) draws a distinction between the nature of early Mesopotamian and Chinese state development (characterized as 'city-state' and 'village-state' patterns, respectively) primarily on the quantitatively greater degree to which these three characteristics were manifest in the urban system of Sumer. Furthermore, Falconer (1987, 1994; Falconer and Savage 1995) has repeatedly emphasized the absolute distinctions to be found between the distribution of Bronze Age site sizes in southern Mesopotamia and the southern Levant.

In recognizing the absolute differences in scale that separate 'truly urban' societies like Early Dynastic Sumer from so many other complex preindustrial societies, one must not lose sight of the relative sense in which these latter societies are themselves urban. Indeed, the three characteristics given above could, at least theoretically, exist relative to a given settlement system of almost any scale (that is, settlements can be densely populated and socially heterogenous relative to the rest of the region to which they are hierarchically linked). This relative form of urbanism is recognized, at least implicitly, in Fox's (1977) typology of urban social systems. Here the 'regal-ritual' cities of segmentary states (Fox 1977: 39-43) are characterized not by absolute distinctions in population, but rather by their central position in an ideologically defined spatial hierarchy.

When conceived in this relative sense, the three characteristics of urbanism can be seen to reflect different aspects of a settlement's 'nodality'. Nodality refers to the degree to which a settlement serves as the point of intersection (and hence concentration) for the overlapping networks of social relations found in any given society. When certain settlements in a region serve as nodal points, concentrating activity within regional networks of economic production, commodity exchange, political power, jural authority or religious practice, these centers can be said to be urban in at least a relative sense.

Urbanism and Political Hierarchy

Returning to the question of state legitimacy in Iron Age Moab, one can now see the role that urban centers can play in reifying and extending political hierarchies. As nodal points in regional networks of social relations, urban centers are places where people learn the nature and distribution of social power through everyday experience (Roscoe 1993: 112-16). For nascent states this fact presents both a challenge and an opportunity. The challenge is to inscribe state political authority onto the regional landscape so as to co-opt or undermine the alternative sources of authority latent in the regional urban system. The opportunity lies in the fact that once spatial and state political hierarchies are linked, urbanization can serve as a vehicle for the expansion of state authority.

Moab

This dynamic can be illustrated fairly clearly in the case of the Iron Age state of Moab, where the growth of spatial hierarchy and the growth of the state would appear to have progressed hand in hand. On the Kerak Plateau, the only extensively studied portion of Moab, Miller's (1991) survey of the central core indicated a general, but not marked, increase in settlement through the Iron Age. However, if one includes survey work on the dry margins that bracket all four sides of the Kerak Plateau (Clark *et al.* 1994; Clark, Koucky and Parker n.d.; Jacobs 1983; Worschech 1985), it becomes clear that the extent and density of human settlement in the region expanded dramatically during Iron Age II, peaking in the late seventh through mid-sixth centuries BCE (B. Routledge 1996). Given the broadly similar results of surveys in the vicinity of Hesban (Ibach 1987) and Tell el-'Umeiri (Geraty *et al.* 1989; Herr *et al.* 1991), it seems likely that the intervening territory of northern Moab will also show evidence of significant settlement expansion during late Iron Age II, when properly explored.

Unlike the neighbouring states of Edom (Bienkowski 1990) and Ammon (Herr 1993), settlement in southern Moab seems to decline precipitously after the middle of the sixth century BCE, with little clear fifth-century BCE material known at the present time (Mattingly 1990). This settlement chronology seems to match well with the chronology of our textual evidence for the historical development of the Moabite state (Lemaire 1994: 22-23; Timm 1989).

Post-Iron Age occupation prevents us from determining, without excavation, the nature of Iron Age settlement at most sites yielding Iron Age sherds in the fertile core of the Karak Plateau. However, Iron Age settlement is exceptionally prominent and accessible on the dry margins of this region. Here we have a hint that some rather significant changes occurred through the course of the Iron Age. During Iron Age I there are at least eight similar sites[2] located on the margins of the Kerak Plateau and the north bank of Wadi Mujib (fig. 1),

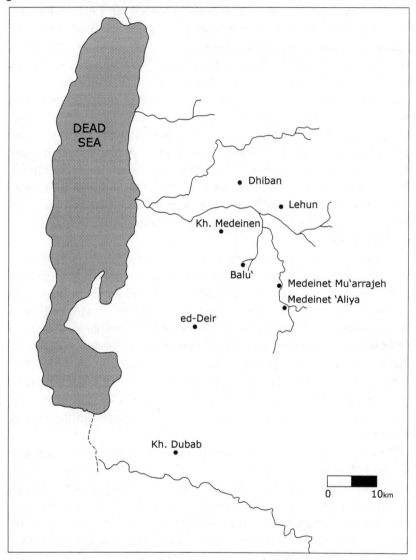

Figure 1.   Important Iron I/early Iron II sites in south-central Jordan.

    2.   This only includes sites whose surface remains and occupational histories allow some reasonable estimate of Iron I site size.

including Kh. Dubab (but cf. Bienkowksi 1996), Medeinet 'Aliya, Medeinet Mu'arrajeh, Qasr Abu Kharaqeh, Bālū', Lehun, Medeineh on the Wadi Mujib and ed-Deir. These sites share a common isolated location and relatively large size of between 1.5 and 2.5 ha.

Iron Age I architecture has been recorded at Lehun (Homès-Fredrique 1992: fig. 16.11), Medeinet Mu'arrajeh (Olávarri 1983: fig. 3) and at Medeinet 'Aliya (B. Routledge 1996: fig. 4.6). All three sites have a casemate fortification wall with attached, primarily domestic, buildings (see C. Routledge 1995: 236).

Although one must be aware of the significant sampling problems that accompany the currently available evidence, it does seem that spatial hierarchy during this period was relatively limited. Small sites and farmsteads are only represented equivocally in the archaeological record and sites larger than 2.5 ha have not been clearly identified. Of course, large modern towns such as el-Kerak and er-Rabbah may well cover large Iron Age I sites, but even if future research identifies such settlements, the degree of spatial hierarchy in the region would remain limited.

Perhaps even more important is the internal organization of these sites. Medeinet 'Aliya has produced evidence for public administration in the form of seal impressions, and possible public storage space in the form of large casemate rooms not attached to any buildings (B. Routledge in press). However, it is important to note that the largest buildings at the site are still recognizable as elaborate four-room houses, rather than as special public or royal buildings set off by their size and plan. Hence architectural hierarchy at the site is not particularly pronounced. Both excavated (Olávarri 1977–78, 1983) and surface remains at Medeinet Mu'arrajeh suggest a rather similar internal organization.

The date of this settlement system cannot be securely fixed due to a lack of published data. At Medeinet 'Aliya there is a period of occupation stretching from the end of the eleventh century BCE to perhaps the third quarter of the tenth century BCE. Published evidence from Medeinet Mu'arrajeh (Olávarri 1977–78: fig. 2; 1983: fig. 6) could support a late eleventh-century date, while claims for a Late Bronze II/early Iron Age I foundation at Lehun (Homès-Fredrique 1992: 195) have yet to be supported by published pottery.

Sometime in the tenth century there seems to have been a dramatic change in the settlement patterns of the region (fig. 2). Sites such as

Medeinet 'Aliya and Medeinet Mu'arrajeh are permanently abandoned, while at Lehun the Iron Age I settlement is replaced by a much smaller Iron Age II fort. Only Bālū' shows signs of growth in the early part of Iron II Age (Worschech 1990: 91-92).

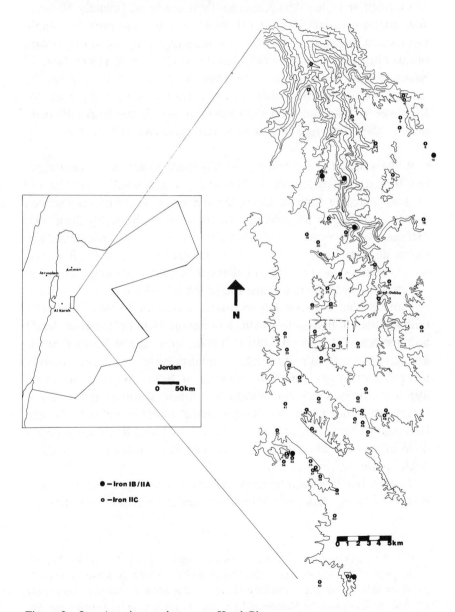

Figure 2. Iron Age sites on the eastern Kerak Plateau.

By the last phase of the Iron Age, during the seventh and sixth centuries BCE, the settlement landscape of Moab under the mature
Moabite state is radically changed. On the eastern Kerak Plateau,
in place of the nucleated villages of Medeinet 'Aliya, Medeinet
Mu'arrajeh and Qasr Abu Kharaqeh there are approximately 58 small
sites founded in late Iron Age II, most of which are probably single
farmsteads engaged in a relatively intensive form of agro-pastoral
production (B. Routledge 1996). Similarly, Clark *et al.* (1994: table 2)
have, at least preliminarily, identified 97 Iron Age II sites on the
north bank of the Wadi el-Hasa, in contrast to the 12 identified for
Iron Age I. Like those on the eastern fringe of the Karak Plateau,
most of these Iron Age II sites are small farmsteads (Clark *et al.* 1994:
46).

While small 'towers' and farmsteads predominate in the landscape,
late Iron Age II settlement is not limited to such small sites. The site
of Bālū' expands dramatically in the late seventh century (Worschech
1990), growing to as much as 10 ha in area. Between these two
extremes we have many mid-sized sites, such as 'Adir, Mudeibi', Kh.
Faris, el-Mreigha and Um Hamāt. Therefore, despite limited evidence, there is good reason to believe that spatial hierarchy increased
significantly in Moab during the life of the Moabite state.

Some evidence also exists to link this increased spatial hierarchy
with the developed state political hierarchy. Unlike the Iron Age I
architecture of Medeinet 'Aliya, in late Iron Age II Moab there is
architectural differentiation that is qualitatively rather than merely
quantitatively significant. For example, at Bālū', Worschech (1990:
89) has credited the foundation and basic form of the massive
Nabataean through Mamluke 'Qasr el-Bālū'' tower complex to the late
Iron Age II. Similarly, at Dhibân, the largely unpublished excavations
of William Morton (1989: fig. 13) revealed a massive 21 × 43 m
public building.[3]

Reinforcing this architectural evidence is the fact that the word
melek or 'king' has been found on Iron II inscriptions at Dhibân

---

3. The exact date of this building remains uncertain. Morton (1989: 241, cf.
Tushingham 1990) has suggested that this is the palace built by Mesha in Qirhoh.
However, this has not been established in terms of published evidence, and pottery
selected for illustration by Morton (n.d.) before his death includes a significant proportion of Iron I, eighth-century and seventh-century forms.

(Mesha Inscription), Bālū'[4] (Zayadine 1986) and el-Kerak (Reed and Winnett 1963), pointing to a close association between Moabite royalty and the apex of spatial hierarchy in Moab. Interestingly, the site of Mudeibi', the largest Iron II site in the dry eastern margins[5] of the Kerak Plateau, has at least three proto-aeolic column capitals visible on the site's surface (Negueruela 1982). In Cisjordan such capitals are always associated with Iron II royal architecture (Shiloh 1979).[6]

In summary, although the archaeological evidence is meager, it seems undeniable that during the seventh and sixth centuries BCE there was (1) a marked growth in spatial hierarchy congruent with the growth of the state of Moab, and (2) a connection forged between nodal points (urban centers) in this hierarchy and social groups at the apex of state authority.

Thus far, only an apparent correlation between the processes of urbanization and state development, rather than a causal link, has been demonstrated. In order to be able to say that urbanization was a means by which state authority was extended and reinforced, we must produce evidence for both political underdevelopment prior to Iron II 'urbanization' and the strategic manipulation of site 'nodality' in the process of state development. While conclusive evidence of this kind cannot yet be mustered, partial evidence may be found in a careful reading of the Mesha Inscription.

4. The Bālū' example is open to question as it reads *tmlk* and could be a word or a name fragment (Zayadine 1986: 304).

5. East of the 200 mm isohyet.

6. This pattern of association between urban centers and state hierarchy is, of course, not limited to Moab. The word *melek*, or the name of someone mentioned elsewhere as a king, has been found on inscriptions, ostracta, seals and bullae in Ammon (Aufrecht 1989: 368; Herr 1985) and Edom (Bennett 1966: 399-400; Puech 1977: 12-13). Most sites where these inscriptions were found can be considered important Iron II urban centers, be they full-fledged royal capitals, or local administrative centers. Similarly, the spatial dominance of public and royal architecture is also widespread. For example, at Busierah in Edom, between 40 and 50 per cent of the site's walled area is taken up by the citadel with its monumental 'palaces' (Bennett 1974: fig. 1).

Urbanism in Antiquity

The Mesha Inscription

The Mesha Inscription (henceforth MI) is a ninth-century BCE[7] memorial stelae (Miller 1974) from Dhibân commemorating the reign of Mesha, king of Moab. It focuses in particular on Mesha's 'revolt' against Israel and his subsequent unification of Moab under his own authority.

Recent scholarship (LaBianca and Younker 1995: 408-409; Knauf 1992: 49-50; Miller 1992: 86; B. Routledge 1996) has emphasized the unique role given to Mesha's 'hometown' of Dibon in the MI. He not only refers to himself as a 'Dibonite' (MI: 1), but also records conquering and annexing neighbouring towns to the territory of Dibon (MI: 20-21, 28-29), while specifically noting that all of Dibon was 'loyal' or 'subject' to him (MI: 28).[8] When considered beside the episodal nature[9] of Mesha's campaigns against individual settlements and the use of the phrase 'land of (city name)' to designate certain territories (MI: 7-8, 10), this evidence points to a segmented political landscape based upon the affiliation of individuals with one of a number of larger settlements on the northern plateau.[10] Within this territory, the MI seems to recognize a number of distinct group identities (i.e. Moab, Israel, men of Gad, men of Sharon and men of

7.   The exact date of the events related in the MI cannot be fixed with certainty. However, a date between the last years of Ahab's reign and the initial years of Jehu's reign, that is, between c. 855 and c. 835 BCE, would seem to make the best sense of both the MI and biblical evidence (Dearman 1989: 163; Smelik 1992: 80-83; but cf. Lemaire 1991: 146-50).

8.   While Lipiński's (1971: 339-40) syntactical argument for reinterpreting lines 28-29 (and especially the translation of *hmšn*) has some merit, his narrow interpretation of *mšm't* as 'body-guard' seems unnecessary given its use in Isa. 11.4. This would seem to be the position of Smelik (1992: 66), who otherwise follows Lipiński's interpretation of these lines (Smelik 1992: 71-72).

9.   For the most part, each of Mesha's campaigns against a major settlement in Moab are syntactically marked as separate sections of the text. See the very similar subdivisions of Smelik (1992: 61-66) and Niccacci (1994: 227-31), including most particularly the explicit analysis of syntax offered by the latter scholar.

10.   This political structure underlies Israel's dominance in the north of the plateau (perhaps through the allegiance or vassalhood of individual town rulers). The king of Israel's rule is expressed in terms of dominance over particular settlements and their territories in the MI. Furthermore, the 'men of Gad' are distinguished from the king of Israel and specifically designated as residents of the 'land of Ataroth' (MI: 10-11).

Maharith), and distinct settlement histories. This would seem to echo the segmented Iron I settlement pattern noted above. As such, Mesha's strategy for integrating this segmented landscape into what must have been a novel regional political structure is clearly something that should be considered.

Mesha's Achievements

One side of Mesha's integrative strategy is all too familiar, namely the slaughter of the conquered settlement's citizens followed by the forcible resettlement of others in their place (MI:11-14, 16-17). This is the brutal side of a 'carrot and stick' equation. More subtle are Mesha's efforts to integrate by instilling an ideology of legitimacy. It is these strategies that underlie the political aspects of Iron Age urbanism, and hence it is these strategies that must be addressed.[11]

In the first four lines Mesha establishes both his patrimonial legitimacy (his father 'ruled over Moab') and his sacral legitimacy (he built a high-place for Kemosh). Most interesting for us are the deeds claimed by Mesha in the second biographical statement in lines 22–30. Here Mesha claims to have built fortification walls, towers, a royal palace and water works at Qirhoh,[12] while organizing citizens in the excavation of cisterns for each house. He also claims to have constructed a road in Wadi Mujib and to have initiated construction projects in at least seven other settlements (MI: 9-10, 26-30), perhaps including the building of several temples (Ahlström 1982: 15).

Public construction is a kingly act of near-monotonous commonality in the ancient Near East. Certainly Ahlström (1982: 1-8) is correct to emphasize the ideological significance of these acts in a cosmology whereby the king is legitimized through his establishment and care of the person and property of the deity on earth. However, too singular

11. A fundamental division exists within the MI between those biographical sections characterized by the fronting of the first person singular pronoun *'nk*, and those sections narrating military action characterized by *wayyiqtol* sequences (Niccacci 1994: 226-27; Smelik 1992: 66-67). The biographical sections amount to something of a *curriculum vitae* for Mesha's claims to authority, and hence provide some insight into his legitimizing strategies.

12. The exact relationship of Qirhoh to Dibon in the MI remains unclear. The suggestion of many scholars (e.g. Ahlström 1982: 16; Dearman 1989: 173-74; Tushingham 1990) that Qirhoh is an acropolis or quarter within Dibon has been followed in this study.

an emphasis on the formal and explicitly articulated cosmological 'logic' of public construction loses sight of the practical, and even non-verbal, impact of such endeavours. By associating himself with the built environment of an urban center, the king is inserting himself into the everyday experience of all those oriented towards that center. In the case of Mesha, his public construction marks his claim to the loyalty of the conquered towns of Moab. Consequently, people's experience of these settlements as centers for economic exchange and jural or religious authority now occurred in a built environment physically marked with Mesha's presence. As is true every time power is effectively wielded, Mesha literally became part of the scenery.

The inscription of Mesha's authority onto local hierarchies also meant their subjugation to a new, more elaborate, spatial hierarchy centered on Dibon/Qirhoh. This fact is witnessed literally by the concept of annexation to Dibon expressed in the MI (20–21) and figuratively by the central position given to Qirhoh in the description of Mesha's public building program. Hence in the MI we see Mesha overcoming the political challenge of urbanism by making the competing regional centers of northern Moab both officially Moabite and subordinate to Dibon.

Conclusions

The archaeological and textual evidence brought together in this study do not mesh seamlessly. The MI is concerned primarily with the north of Moab, while the archaeological evidence is largely from the south. Furthermore, the archaeological evidence brackets the MI in time rather than being contemporary with it. Apparently the triumphant message of the MI did not become the reality 'on the ground' in the south of Moab until the seventh century BCE. At the same time, in Mesha's strategy, one can recognize the seeds of the social order in the seventh and sixth centuries BCE. Indeed, it seems that by the end of the seventh century BCE, political and spatial hierarchy were largely indistinguishable in that the former was completely inscribed upon the latter. Urban centers were dominated by the name and symbolics of royalty simply because, by late Iron II, political centeredness was the measure of spatial centrality. The degree to which the two might have been separated, for example, in the distribution of goods and services, cannot be measured given current knowledge. However, one is tempted to see in the brevity and fragility of Iron Age urban traditions in Transjordan evidence for very little in the way of separation. Indeed, in contrast to the continuous urban traditions of southern Mesopotamia, the urban system in Transjordan collapses in tandem with the political systems of the Iron Age states.

Urbanism in Iron Age Transjordan was a political phenomenon, not in the simple causal sense that the state stimulated spatial hierarchy, but rather in the more subtle sense that political and spatial hierarchies developed as inextricable phenomena. Each proved necessary for the growth, stability and continued existence of the other. Future research must treat political and spatial hierarchies together if our rather limited understanding of the historical development of Transjordan's Iron Age states is to be increased.

BIBLIOGRAPHY

Ahlström, G.
1982   *Royal Administration and National Religion in Ancient Palestine* (Leiden: Brill).
Aufrecht, W.E.
1989   *A Corpus of Ammonite Inscriptions* (Lewiston, NY: Edwin Mellon).
Bennett, C.-M.
1966   'Fouilles d'Umm el-Biyara: Rapport Préliminaire', *RB* 73: 372-403.
1974   'Excavations at Buseirah, Southern Jordan 1972: Preliminary Report', *Lev* 6: 1-24.
Bienkowski, P.
1990   'The Chronology of Tawilan and the "Dark Age" of Edom', *ARAM* 2: 35-44.
1996   'Ash-Shorabat and Khirbet Dubab, Wadi Hasa', *AJA* 100: 523.
Clark, G., D. Olszewski, J. Schuldenrein, N. Rida and J. Eighmey
1994   'Survey and Excavation in Wadi al-Hasa: A Preliminary Report of the 1993 Field Season', ADAJ 38: 41-55.
Clark, V., F. Koucky and S.T. Parker
n.d.   'The Survey', in *The Roman Frontier in Central Jordan: Final Report on the Limes Arabicus Project, 1980–1989* (2 vols.; ed. S.T. Parker; Washington: Dumbarton Oaks).
Dearman, J.A.
1989   'Historical Reconstruction and the Mesha' Inscription', in *Studies in the Mesha Inscription and Moab* (ed. J.A. Dearman; Atlanta, GA: Scholars Press): 155-210.
Falconer, S.
1987   'Heartland of Villages: Reconsidering Early Urbanism in the Southern Levant' (unpublished PhD dissertation, University of Arizona).

1994   'The Development and Decline of Bronze Age Civilization in the Southern Levant: A Reassessment of Urbanism and Ruralism', in *Development and Decline in the Mediterranean Bronze Age* (ed. C. Mathers and S. Stoddart; Sheffield: J.R. Collis): 305-33.

Falconer, S., and S.H. Savage
1995   'Heartlands and Hinterlands: Alternative Trajectories of Early Urbanization in Mesopotamia and the Southern Levant', *AmAnt* 60: 37-58.

Fox, R.
1977   *Urban Anthropology* (Englewood Cliffs, NJ: Prentice–Hall).

Geertz, C.
1983   *Local Knowledge: Further Essays in Interpretive Anthropology* (New York: Torch).

Geraty, L., L.G. Herr, Ø.S. LaBianca and R.W. Younker
1989   *Madaba Plains Project 1: The 1984 Season at Tell el-'Umeiri and Vicinity and Subsequent Studies* (Berrien Springs: Andrews University).

Herr, L.G.
1985   'The Servant of Baalis', *BA* 48: 169-72.
1993   'Whatever Happened to the Ammonites?', *BAR* 19.6: 26-35, 68.

Herr, L.G., L. Geraty, Ø.S. LaBianca and R.W. Younker
1991   *Madaba Plains Project 2: The 1987 Season at Tell el-'Umeiri and Vicinity and Subsequent Studies* (Berrien Springs: Andrews University).

Homès-Fredericq, D.
1992   'Late Bronze and Iron Age Evidence from Lehun in Moab', in *Early Edom and Moab: The Beginning of the Iron Age in Southern Jordan* (ed. P. Bienkowski; Sheffield: J.R. Collis): 187-202.

Ibach, R.
1987   *Archaeological Survey of the Hesban Region: Heshban 5* (Berrien Springs: Andrews University).

Jacobs, L.
1983   'Survey of the South Ridge of the Wadi 'Isal, 1981', ADAJ 27: 245-74.

Knauf, E.A.
1992   'The Cultural Impact of Secondary State Formation: The Cases of the Edomites and the Moabites', in *Early Edom and Moab: The Beginning of the Iron Age in Southern Jordan* (ed. P. Bienkowski; Sheffield: J.R. Collis): 47-54.

LaBianca, Ø.S., and R.W. Younker
1995   'The Kingdoms of Ammon, Moab and Edom: The Archaeology of Society in Late Bronze/Iron Age Transjordan (ca. 1400–500 BCE)', in *ASHL*: 399-415.

Lemaire, A.
1987   'Ammon, Moab, Edom: l'Epoque du Fer en Jordanie', in *La Jordanie de l'Âge de la Pierre à l'Époque Byzantine* (Paris: École du Louvre): 47-74.

1991   'La Stèle de Mésha de l'histoire de l'Ancien Israël', in *Storia e Tradizioni de Israele: scritti in onore di J. Alberto Soggin* (ed. D. Garrone and F. Israel; Brescia: Paideia): 143-69.
1994   'Les transformations politiques et culturelles de la Transjordanie au Vi^e Siècle av. J.–C.', *Trans* 8: 9-27.

Lipiński, E.
1971   'Etymological and Exegetical Notes on the Mesha' Inscription', *Or* 40: 325-40.

Maisels, C.
1993   *The Emergence of Civilization* (London: Routledge).

Mattingly, G.
1990   'Settlement on Jordan's Kerak Plateau from Iron Age IIC through the Early Roman Period', *ARAM* 2: 309-35.

Miller, J.M.
1974   'The Moabite Stone as a Memorial Stele', *PEQ* 106: 9-18.
1991   'Archaeological Survey of the Kerak Plateau' (Atlanta, GA: Scholars Press).
1992   'Early Monarchy in Moab?', in *Early Edom and Moab: The Beginning of the Iron Age in Southern Jordan* (ed. P. Bienkowski; Sheffield: J.R. Collis): 77-91.

Morton, W.
1989   'A Summary of the 1955, 1956 and 1965 Excavations at Dhiban', in *Studies in the Mesha Inscription and Moab* (ed. J.A. Dearman; Atlanta, GA: Scholars Press): 239-46.
n.d.   *Unpublished Pottery Drawings from the 1955, 1956, and 1965 Seasons of Excavation at Dhiban.*

Negueruela, I.
1982   'The Proto-Aeolic Capitals from Mudeibi'a, in Moab', ADAJ 26: 395-401.

Niccacci, A.
1994   'The Stele of Mesha and the Bible: Verbal System and Narrativity', *Or* 63: 226-48.

Olávarri, E.
1977–78   'Sondeo arqueologico en Khirbet Medeineh junto a Smakieh (Jordania)', ADAJ 22: 136-49.
1983   'La Campagne de Fouilles 1982 à Khirbet Medeinet al-Mu'arradjeh prés de Smakieh (Kerak)', ADAJ 27: 165-78.

Puech, E.
1977   'Documents épigraphiques de Buseirah', *Lev* 9:11-20.
Redman, C.L.
1978   *The Rise of Civilization* (San Francisco: Freeman).
Reed, W., and F.V. Winnett
1963   'A Fragment of an Early Moabite Inscription from Kerak', *BASOR* 172: 1-9.

Roscoe, P.
1993   'Practice and Political Centralization: A New Approach to Political Evolution', *CA* 34: 111-40.

Routledge, B.
1996   'Intermittent Agriculture and the Political Economy of Iron Age
            Moab' (unpublished PhD dissertation, University of Toronto).
in press   'Khirbet Medeinet 'Aliya', *The Archaeology of the Levant: Encyclo-*
            paedia (ed. S. Richard; New York: Garland).
Routledge, C.
1995   'Pillared Buildings in Iron Age Moab', *BA* 58: 236.
Shiloh, Y.
1979   *The Proto-Aeolic Capital and Israelite Ashlar Masonry* (Jerusalem:
            Hebrew University Institute of Archaeology).
Smelik, K.A.D.
1992   'King Mesha's Inscription', in *Converting the Past: Studies in Ancient*
            Israelite and Moabite Historiography (ed. K.A.D. Smelik; Leiden:
            Brill): 59-92.
Timm, S.
1989   *Moab Zwischen den Mächten* (Wiesbaden: Otto Harrassowitz).
Tushingham, A.D.
1990   'Dhibān Reconsidered: King Mesha and his Works', ADAJ 34: 183-
            92.
Wheatley, P.
1972   'The Concept of Urbanism', in *Man, Settlement and Urbanism* (ed. P.
            Ucko, R. Trigham and G. Dumbely; London: Duckworth): 601-37.
Worschech, U.
1985   *Northwest Ard el-Kerak 1983 and 1984: A Preliminary Report*
            (Munich: Manfred Görg).
1990   'Ergebnisse de Grabungen in el-Bālū' 1987: Ein Vorbericht', *ZDPV*:
            106: 86-113.
Zayadine, F.
1986   'The Moabite Inscription', ADAJ 30: 302-304.

URBANISM AT TELL EL-'UMEIRI
DURING THE LATE BRONZE IIB–IRON IA TRANSITION

Larry G. Herr

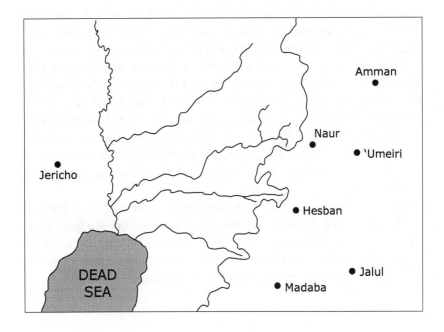

Figure 1. The Madaba Plains region.

Fortified sites on the Transjordanian plateau from Late Bronze II and Iron I are rare. So far, Tell el-'Umeiri is the only one to have been excavated with significant enough horizontal exposure to say anything about urbanism (fig. 1). Other sites in the Amman area are too small, for example, the Amman Airport (Herr 1983); were excavated with little horizontal exposure, for example, the Amman Citadel (Bennett 1978:8), Sahab (Ibrahim 1972, 1974, 1975) and Umm el-Dananir (McGovern 1989); were preserved in only small pockets at multiperiod sites, for example, Hesban (Fisher 1995); produced pottery but no *in situ* remains, for example, Jawa (Daviau, personal communication); or are unexcavated except for tombs, for example, Amman (Dajani 1966b), Sahab (Dajani 1970a) and Madaba (Harding and Isserlin 1953; Thompson 1986; Piccirillo 1975). Moreover, several of these publications present pottery that is somewhat later than the Late Bronze–Iron I transition, for example, Sahab (personal observation confirmed by Ibrahim) and the Madaba tombs published by Piccirillo and Thompson. The problems in other regions of Transjordan are similar or worse; only the Irbid region has produced some finds in the form of tomb furnishings (Dajani 1966a).

Indeed, in all of the southern Levant, there are very few fortified highland sites during the Late Bronze–Iron I transition, and, when excavated, they usually produce a material culture more akin to the coastal and valley urban sites. Usually, a burgeoning scatter of small villages is encountered, especially in the northern hill country of Cisjordan. The same phenomenon has yet to be identified in Transjordan. It is therefore surprising that at Tell el-'Umeiri we should find a strongly fortified highland site with a material culture strikingly similar to the villages in Cisjordan, but very different than the contemporary coastal and valley urban centers, including those of the Jordan Valley.

The following will describe the emerging features of the urban plan at Tell el-'Umeiri, as excavated by the on-going Madaba Plains Project over five seasons (1984, 1987, 1989, 1992 and 1994).[1] More of the plan will be excavated in future seasons, and some of the discussion here will undoubtedly have to be altered.

1.   The project is sponsored by Andrews University in consortium with Canadian Union College, LaSierra University, Walla Walla College, Levant Foundation Poland and the University of Eastern Africa, and is directed by L. Geraty (Senior Project Director), L. Herr ('Umeiri excavations), R. Younker (Jalul excavations), Ø. LaBianca (hinterland survey) and D. Clark (consortium). Full reports have been published for the first season (1984: Geraty *et al.* 1986) and the second season (1987: Herr *et al.* 1991a). Preliminary reports have also been published (1984: Geraty 1985; Geraty, Herr and LaBianca 1986; Geraty, Herr and LaBianca 1987; 1987: Geraty, Herr and LaBianca 1988; Geraty, Herr and LaBianca 1989; Geraty, Herr and Labianca 1990; 1989: Younker *et al.* 1990; Herr *et al.* 1991b; LaBianca *et al.* 1995; 1992; Younker *et al.* 1993; Herr *et al.* 1994).

Tell el-'Umeiri

The Late Bronze Age IIB settlers encountered a ridge above the only spring between Amman and Madaba. It had last been occupied toward the end of the Middle Bronze Age, when the ridge was fortified on its western and most vulnerable side with an artificial rampart and a moat that isolated the settled area from the rest of the ridge. Combining the depth of the moat with the height of the rampart, the Middle Bronze Age builders had created an artificial obstruction about 10 m high (fig. 2, nos. 10 and 15). Elsewhere, it seems the natural slopes of the ridge afforded a sufficiently fortified slope. The Late Bronze IIB settlers reused this defensive system after the site had been unoccupied during the Late Bronze I–IIA Periods.

So far, very little is known of this settlement, but it was apparently destroyed toward the end of the thirteenth century BCE by an earthquake that exhibited itself in a large slab of fallen bedrock and the subsequent erosion of the Middle Bronze Age rampart (fig. 2, no. 10).[2] Much of this settlement was found in secondary deposit in the debris layers making up the subsequent rampart (fig. 2, no. 9). The date of this first settlement is best determined by the pottery, which clearly represents material from the thirteenth century BCE, the very end of the Late Bronze Age. Many of the cooking pots still retain the triangular section of the Late Bronze Age, while a few anticipate the longer, flanged sections of early Iron I.

After the earthquake, a vigorous reconstruction took place which re-excavated most of the Middle Bronze Age moat (fig. 2, no. 14) and rebuilt the rampart (fig. 2, no. 9), filling the earthquake crack and raising the rampart about 1.5 m. At the bottom of the rampart a retaining wall (fig. 2, no. 12) kept the rampart from eroding into the moat. Although prior to this time the occupation level inside the Middle Bronze Age rampart was apparently below its crest (fig. 2, no. 6) much like the interior of a crater, post-quake floors were laid above the rampart's crest. This caused the need for a fortification wall on top of the rampart, which is the earliest example of a casemate wall so far found. It was made up of a continuous outer wall (fig. 2, no. 8;

---

2. Note the fallen slab of bedrock in Square 7J87 which had originally been level with that in Square 7J88.

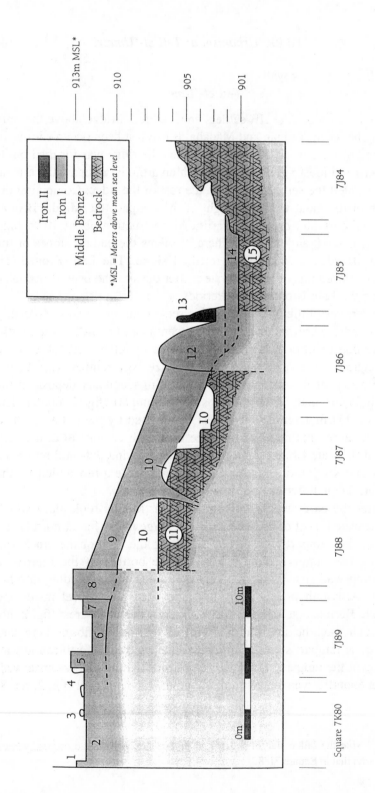

Figure 2.   Section of fortifications on the western edge of Tell el-ʻUmeiri, defence system—Field B.

fig. 3, the leftmost wall) and an inner wall (fig. 2, no. 5; figure 3, the two aligned walls to the right of Rooms A3 and B4). Although some visitors to the site have proposed that this is not a casemate wall system, images from ground penetrating radar on the southern side of the site show a distinctly similar pattern there. In any case, more of the system will be excavated in subsequent seasons.

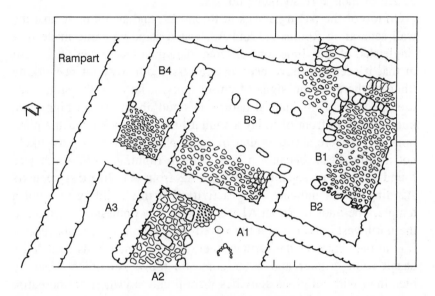

Figure 3. Plan of residences inside the fortifications (Tell el-'Umeiri, field B—
western perimeter Early Iron I buildings A and B).

It is with the houses inside the fortifications (of which the casemate Rooms A3 and B4 form a part) that one gets the first glimpse of the 'urban' plan of a very early highland fortified settlement in Transjordan. Portions of two (possibly three) houses have been excavated so far. No clear sign of a street has been discovered, but, in the 6m excavated to the east of the buildings, no contemporary remains have yet been found, suggesting that either the level of buildings inside the Middle Bronze Age rampart were still at a lower level than those on the crest or that a street existed there. Both explanations may be correct.

Both of the casemate rooms (fig. 3, Rooms A3 and B4) contained quantities of storage vessels in the form of collared pithoi. About 13 were clumped together in the northern half of Room A3, and 20 lined all walls of Room B4, ignoring the curious division of the room into two parts by a flagstone pavement and two pillar bases along the wall in front of the pavement. In the southern end of Room A3 was a stone platform with a large flat stone on top and a series of three shallow steps leading up to it. It may have been a platform for ladder access to the second floor. Others might suggest it to be a platform for votive gifts. Both casemate rooms should be seen as 'inner rooms' (1 Kgs 22.25) of their corresponding houses.

On top of the paving stones in Room A2, and standing against the wall separating Rooms A3 and A2, was a standing stone made of a single slab of gray limestone different than the other stones at 'Umeiri in that it seems to have been naturally smooth, without re-working (that is, there are no signs of chisel marks). Perhaps the stone was used because of its special nature. It stood about 90 cm high, and, immediately in front of it, lay a similar limestone rock in such a position as if it were a votive altar or small platform. It was most likely not a pillar base, because a line of them running north–south was found to the east separating Rooms A2 from A1. In most contexts standing stones indicate cultic activity, but this building was not a temple. The finds in Room A1 were completely domestic in nature: in the northwest corner was a bin paved with pebbles, a circular hearth was in the center of the earthen floor, and the small finds included a basalt food grinder and other domestic tools. No objects usually identified with religious activities were found anywhere in the entire house. However, this does not necessarily negate a religious function for the standing stone; it may have simply been an object of prayer with small offerings of a biodegradable nature, such as food offerings. A cultic corner in a residential building reminds one of the biblical story in Judges 17 where a man named Micah made an image of Yahweh, installed it in a shrine connected with his house and hired a Levite to serve at the shrine. Family religious expression appears to have been a part of our site as well.

Building B was a four-room house with an interesting twist. With casemate Room B4 as the broad or 'inner' room, post bases subdivide Room B3 into the three long rooms normally seen in these houses, so typical of Iron Age Cisjordan. But the eastern wall of the building does not fully enclose it. One suspects that this is an early example of a four-room house, and the evolution of the plan was still in its beginning stages. It is possible that the house continued into Rooms B1 and B2, but it is more likely that this area was an open courtyard with a small walled enclosure for animals paved with flagstones. Perhaps the remainder of the wall between Rooms B1 and B3 was separated by a curtain or was simply open. It is unclear at present whether the eastern wall depicted at the right edge of fig. 3 was the eastern wall of Building B. No sign of it has so far been found in the neighboring excavation unit; but if it is, the substantial raised threshold in the northern wall of the building would be the entrance to Building B, and the area to the north of the building would be a street or alleyway.

However, if the eastern extent of Courtyard B1–B2 has not yet been determined, the threshold most likely led into another house (Building C, not labelled on fig. 3) sharing Courtyard B1–B2 with Building B. If this is the case, Buildings B and C were probably inhabited by relatives of an extended family.

The destruction of the site took place soon after it was built; there was very little difference in the pottery found in the rampart from the vessels buried in the destruction. The presence of weapons in the casemate rooms suggest it was a military destruction, and our discovery of butchered animal shank bones, piles of barley grains and the burned bones of at least two individuals caught in the destruction show it to have been quickly accomplished. Within the destruction layer, which was over 2m thick in places, were the broken remains of over 30 collared pithoi (5 in Room A3, 20 in Room B4, and about another 5 in Room B3 along the southern edge), showing that the upper floors were used for food storage as well as the casemate rooms. In one of the bases of a fallen collared pithos were burned barley seeds.

Conclusion

The date of this group of buildings is clearly established by the pottery which bridges the transition period from Late Bronze II to Iron I and must date to the late thirteenth century BCE and/or early twelfth century BCE. The best parallels to the pottery and some of the objects come from the earliest highland settlements in Cisjordan, such as Mt Ebal, where a potter's mark identical to two from 'Umeiri was found. The pottery contains very early forms of collared pithoi and a mixture of Late Bronze and Iron I cooking pots. The two most prominent types of bowls are the typical early Iron Age carinated forms and a type otherwise found only in the northern hills of Cisjordan, the so-called 'Manasseh bowl' (Zertal 1987). A quantitative analysis of the ceramic forms confirms the connection with Cisjordanian highland sites. Following are the percentages (with sherd counts) of early Iron I vessel types within the total assemblage of 3883 pieces of pottery, published and unpublished: collared pithoi: 19.19 per cent (745), jars: 11.41 per cent (443), jugs: 21.43 per cent (832), juglets: 0.67 per cent (26), kraters: 5.79 per cent (225), bowls: 22.56 per cent (876), cooking pots: 15.92 per cent (618), pyxides: 0.15 per cent (6), lamps: 2.60 per cent (101), flasks: 0.10 per cent (4), chalice: 0.03 per cent (1), stand: 0.03 per cent (1). There are high percentages of utilitarian types, such as collared pithoi, jugs, cooking pots, and bowls, which make up approximately 75 per cent of the total, connecting the assemblage with simple highland sites rather than the more complex coastal and valley sites (Mazar 1981: 31; Zertal 1987: 138; Finkelstein 1988: 177-204). Moreover, 'Umeiri's location in the hilly terrain south of Amman and its small size (1.5 ha) make it hard to connect the site with coastal and valley sites (Finkelstein 1994).

Despite this, the site was earlier, larger, and more prosperous than other highland settlements in Cisjordan. The impressive fortifications suggest, furthermore, that the inhabitants could marshall enough social and economic potential to construct the casemate wall, rampart and retaining wall at least on the western edge of the site. Although some aspects of the settlement suggest a recently settled pastoral/nomadic population, such as the possible use of a curtain in Building B to separate space, the cultic corner in a residential building and the possible kinship-based architecture between Buildings B and C (if it is another house), the fortifications indicate a population concerned with security and willing to pay for it with organized labor. Elsewhere these socio-economic questions have been discussed within a tribal model to describe the settlement of tribes that later became the small national groups of the southern Levant in Iron II (Herr in press). In terms of the process of a society's urbanism, it is most relevant to note that the urban feature of a significant fortification system was incorporated rather soon in the process at 'Umeiri. It is not necessary to expect a linear development of urban elements within a society, as they go through the process of sedentarization. Rather, whatever particular features or strategies are necessary for survival may be addressed by a sedentarizing society at a site within their own set of priorities.

It is too early to be sure of the overall plan of the settlement, but in the excavation unit east of Room B1 ruins from this stratum were not found even though excavation had easily reached the level of the destruction in Room B1. This could be explained by the 'cratering' effect of the Middle Bronze Age rampart east of its crest, or possibly by a street adjacent to the building at a lower level, or even the absence of any buildings there. If the last option is true, the site may have been made up of a ring of houses around the perimeter with a more-or-less open area inside, such as has been proposed for some Cisjordanian sites (Finkelstein 1988: 243).

BIBLIOGRAPHY

Bennett, C.-M.
    1978   'Excavations at the Citadel (El Qal'ah), Amman', *Lev* 10: 1-9.
Dajani, R.W.
    1966a   'Four Iron Age Tombs from Irbid', ADAJ 11: 88-101.
    1966b   'Jebel Nuzha Tomb at Amman', ADAJ 11: 48-52.
    1970a   'Late Bronze–Iron Age Tomb Excavated at Sahab, 1968', ADAJ 15: 29-34.
Finkelstein, I.
    1988   *The Archaeology of the Israelite Settlement* (Jerusalem: Israel Exploration Society).
    1994   'The Great Transformation: The "Conquest" of the Highlands Frontiers and the Rise of the Territorial States', in *ASHL*: 350-65.
Fisher, J.R.
    1995   'Hesban and the Ammonites during the Iron Age', in *Hesban after 25 Years* (ed. D. Merling and L.T. Geraty; Berrien Springs, MI: Andrews University): 81-95.
Geraty, L.T.
    1985   'The Andrews University Madaba Plains Project: A Preliminary Report on the First Season at Tell el-'Umeiri', *AUSS* 23: 85-110.
Geraty, L.T., L.G. Herr and Ø.S. LaBianca
    1986   'Madaba Plains Project: A Preliminary Report of the 1984 Season at Tell el-'Umeiri and Vicinity', *BASOR Supp* 24: 117-19.
    1987   'The Madaba Plains Project: A Preliminary Report on the First Season at Tell el-'Umeiri and Vicinity', ADAJ 31: 187-99.
    1988   'The Joint Madaba Plains Project: A Preliminary Report on the Second Season at Tell el-'Umeiri and Vicinity (June 18 to August 6, 1987)', *AUSS* 26: 217-52.
    1989   'Madaba Plains Project: The 1987 Season at Tell el-'Umeiri and Vicinity', ADAJ 33: 145-76.

Geraty, L.T., L.G. Herr, Ø.S. LaBianca and R.W. Younker
    1989   *Madaba Plains Project 1: The 1984 Season at Tell el-'Umeiri and Vicinity and Subsequent Studies* (Berrien Springs, MI: Andrews University).
Geraty, L.T. *et al.*
    1990   Madaba Plains Project: A Preliminary Report of the 1987 Season at Tell el-'Umeiri and Vicinity', *BASOR Supp* 26: 59-88.
Harding, G.L., and B.S.J.Isserlin
    1953   'An Early Iron Age Tomb at Madaba', PEFA 6: 27-41.
Herr, L.G.
    in press   'Tell el-'Umeiri and the Madaba Plains Region during the Late Bronze–Iron I Transition', *The Eastern Mediterranean in Transition: Essays in Honor of Trude Dothan* (ed. S. Gitin and A. Mazar; Jerusalem: Hebrew University).
Herr, L.G., (ed.)
    1983   *The Amman Airport Excavations, 1976*, AASOR 48 (Winona Lake, IN: Eisenbrauns).
Herr, L.G., L.T. Geraty, Ø.S. LaBianca and R.W. Younker
    1991a   *Madaba Plains Project 2: The 1987 Season at Tell el-'Umeiri and Vicinity and Subsequent Studies* (Berrien Springs, MI: Andrews University).
    1991b   'Madaba Plains Project: The 1989 Excavations at Tell el-'Umeiri and Vicinity', ADAJ 35: 155-80.
    1994   'Madaba Plains Project: The 1992 Excavations at Tell el-'Umeiri, Tell Jalul, and Vicinity', ADAJ 38: 147-72.
Ibrahim, M.
    1972   'Archaeological Excavations at Sahab, 1972', ADAJ 17: 23-36.
    1974   'Second Season of Excavation at Sahab, 1973', ADAJ 19: 55-62.
    1975   'Third Season of Excavations at Sahab, 1975 (Preliminary Report)', ADAJ 20: 69-82.
LaBianca, Ø.S. *et al.*
    1995   'Madaba Plains Project: A Preliminary Report on the 1989 Season at Tell el-'Umeiri and Hinterland', in *Preliminary Excavation Reports* (ed. W.G. Dever; AASOR, 52; Atlanta: Scholars Press): 93-120.
Mazar, A.
    1981   'Giloh: An Early Israelite Settlement Site near Jerusalem', *IEJ* 31: 1-36.
McGovern, P.E.
    1989   'The Baq'ah Valley Project 1987, Khirbet Umm ad-Dananir and el-Qesir', ADAJ 33: 123-36.
Piccirillo, M.
    1975   'Una tomba del ferro I a Madaba', *LASBF* 25: 199-224.
Thompson, H.O.
    1986   'An Iron Age Tomb at Madaba', in *The Archaeology of Jordan and Other Studies* (ed. L.T. Geraty and L.G. Herr; Berrien Springs, MI: Andrews University): 331-64.

Younker, R.W., L.G. Herr, L.T. Geraty and Ø.S. LaBianca
    1990   'The Joint Madaba Plains Project: A Preliminary Report of the 1989 Season, Including the Regional Survey and Excavations at El-Dreijat, Tell Jawa, and Tell el-'Umeiri (June 19 to August 8, 1989)', *AUSS* 28: 5-52.
    1993   'The Joint Madaba Plains Project: A Preliminary Report of the 1992 Season, Including the Regional Survey and Excavations at Tell Jalul and Tell El-'Umeiri (June 16 to July 31, 1992)', *AUSS* 31: 205-38.
Zertal, A.
    1987   'An Early Iron Age Cultic Site on Mout Ebal: Excavation Seasons 1982-1987', *TA* 13-14: 105-65.

TELL JAWA:
A CASE STUDY OF AMMONITE URBANISM DURING IRON AGE II

P.M. Michèle Daviau

In his classic study of the emergence of urbanism in Mesopotamia, Redman (1978: 215) put forward the hypothesis that the minimal population for a city was 5000 persons. As this study will demonstrate, such a criterion would eliminate most Iron Age sites in Transjordan from the ranks of urban settlements. Although population has not been the only criterion used to identify urban centres in the Near East, several modern surveys in the hill country of Israel and in central Jordan have operated in a similar mode, using site size as a principal criterion of site classification. In some cases, this criterion groups various types of settlements together regardless of their individuating characteristics. While this may not be a problem for a particular limited area where sites of comparable size were in fact similar in their makeup, this same categorization may obscure certain features that are important for site classification, especially in terms of the rise of urbanism in Jordan.

Early surveyors in and around Amman were fascinated by the presence of towers or *rujms*, which were interpreted as fortresses protecting the Ammonite capital of Rabbath-Ammon (Glueck 1939: 162-63; Kletter 1991: 43-44). Such towers were round, such as Rujm al-Malfuf (N = Boraas 1971: fig. 1; S = Thompson 1973: fig. 1); rectilinear (MPP Site 22 = Rufeisa, Boling 1989: 134, fig. 8.46; Franken and Abujaber 1989: fig. C23a); or a combination of both a round structure with an attached rectilinear unit as seen at Khilda (Najjar 1992: fig. 3) west of Amman. More recently, these structures have been studied in relation to the agricultural lands that they served both as lookout posts and food processing centres (Najjar 1992; Younker 1989: 195). Regional survey projects in the Beq'ah Valley (McGovern 1986), the Hesban area (Ibach 1987), and the Madaba Plains (Boling

1989) have not only added innumerable sites to the roster of Ammonite settlements but have undertaken excavation of certain sites to determine their character and function in relation to both Rabbath-Ammon and the towers scattered across the landscape of central Jordan.

Site Size

In both Cisjordan and Transjordan, each regional survey has variously characterized site size using its own recording system.[1] For the hill country of Ephraim, Finkelstein (1988–89: 146) categorized Iron Age I sites as large villages (5–6+ dunams = 0.5–0.6 ha), small villages (3–4 dunams = 0.3–0.4 ha), and sites with only a few houses or a farmstead, while the Iron Age II sites fell into the range of large sites (20+ dunams = 2.0 ha), medium sites (more than 10 dunams = 1.0 + ha), and small sites (3–9 dunams = 0.3–0.9 ha) and single structures that covered only 1–2 dunams (Finkelstein 1988–89: 152). This is in contrast to Baumgarten's (1992) classification of Late Bronze Age sites, where a small town was defined in the range of 1.5–5.0 ha and medium-size towns were between 5.0–10.0 ha. Only sites that covered more than 10.0 ha were considered cities.[2] In Finkelstein's system, Tell Jawa at 2.0 ha would fall into the class of large sites, whereas under Baumgarten's categories the same site would be considered a small town comparable to Tell Beit Mirsim or Beth-shemesh (Baumgarten 1992: 145).[3]

The Hesban survey identified sites with a single feature as 'very small', those with one or more features as 'small', a site of several acres with a 'considerable' amount of architectural remains as

1. Pre-assigned categories of site size do not appear to have been used in the survey of central Moab (Miller 1991) or Wadi el-Hasa (MacDonald 1988: 389). Whether this was a deliberate decision based on the nature of the sites encountered is not explained, although it is clear that MacDonald's recording system required information on all possible dimensions.

2. The sizes of Iron Age sites in the Levant are in sharp contrast to those in Mesopotamia where an urban site is one of 10 ha or more and functions as a central place within the urban landscape (Kühne 1994: 55).

3. Baumgarten (1992: 145, 19) has pointed out that few sites have been sufficiently excavated to determine the total occupied area, and, as a result, site size is usually an estimate based on the excavator's information (see also Beaudry 1994: 33).

'medium', tells with a recognizable depth of occupational deposits as 'large' sites and sites in the range of 10–20 acres (4–8 ha) as 'major' sites (Ibach 1987: 9) with no immediate judgment as to the degree of urbanism present.

Although site size alone is not sufficient for distinguishing types of settlement, there appears to be a certain significance to the amount of settled area enclosed within walled towns and the type of fortification system that surrounded them. Other criteria, especially the diversity of building types and the range of activities carried on within the town, will need to be analyzed before determining the identification of a given site. This applies especially to the site of Tell Jawa, since there are few comparable sites excavated to date in Transjordan.

Characteristics of Urbanism

Among 16 Iron Age II sites excavated in Cisjordan and Transjordan in the range of 1–5 ha (table 1),[4] Tell Jawa fits comfortably between Beer-sheba, Tel Halif and Tell el-'Umeiri (all in the range of 1.1–1.5 ha), and Beth-shemesh, Tell Beit Mirsim, Tell en-Nasbeh and Dibon (all in the range of 3 ha).[5] Although Beer-sheba is the smallest site whose total perimeter is known, Shiloh (1978: 41) identified the Stratum II settlement as an administrative centre because of its 'well organized plan' that appears to have been constructed as an integrated unit. In view of its small size, by contrast with first-rank administrative

---

4.   The site of Shechem at 6.0+ ha falls outside the range of the sites in table 1. Its identification as a capital city is not yet certain. Indeed, Olivier (1983) has argued convincingly that Shechem appeared to have the characteristics of a royal or administrative city rather than those of a 'capital' city.

5.   Site size is not consistently reported due to the change in size of occupied areas over time. Lehun in Moab has a very different settlement pattern from other sites mentioned in this study in that it was spread out along the wadi cliff and did not form a traditional tell. For sizes of sites listed in table 1, see: Beer-sheba (Herzog 1992: 258), Bethel (Kelso 1993: 192), Beth Shan (Mazar 1993: 214), Beth Shemesh (Herzog 1992: 237), Dothan (Ussishkin 1993: 372), Shechem (Wright 1965: 23), Tell Beit Mirsim (Greenberg 1993: 177), Tell el-Far'ah (N) (Chambon 1984: pl. 4), Tel Halif (Seger 1993: 553), Tell en-Nasbeh (Herzog 1992: 263), Tel Yokne'am (Ben-Tor 1992: 805), Tell Deir 'Alla (Franken 1989: 201), Dibon (Winnett 1964: 5), Safut (Wimmer 1987: 159), Lehun (Homès-Fredericq 1992: 188), Tell el-'Umeiri (Herr in press), Tell Jawa (Daviau 1992: 145).

centres that were in the range of 5–20 ha,[6] Herzog (1992: 261) saw the importance of comparing Beer-sheba to other small sites, in order to determine the degree to which it was different from mere 'provincial towns'. At Beer-sheba, Herzog distinguished the planning evident in the casemate wall, with its adjacent housing, and in the public store buildings. Clearly, size alone cannot be used as a satisfactory criterion to identify small urban centres; the evidence for planning in the construction of fortifications, houses and public buildings must be included.[7]

Site	1	1.5	2	2.5	3	4	5	6–10
Beer-sheba	1.1							
Bethel		1.4+						
Beth-shan						4		
Beth-shemesh				2.6				
Dothan						4		
Tell Beit Mirsim					3			
Tell el-Far'ah (N)							5+	
Tel Halif (Lahav)	1.2							
Tell en-Nasbeh					3			
Tel Yokneam						4		
Tell Deir 'Alla	0.5?							
Dibon					3			
Lehun (Iron II)	0.8+							
Safut	0.5?							
Tell el-'Umeiri		1.5						
Tell Jawa			2					

Table 1. Site size of Iron Age fortified residential towns/cities.

Since little is known archaeologically of Iron Age Dibon, Tell Beit Mirsim and Tell en-Nasbeh are the best excavated and published examples of town sites within the size range of Tell Jawa. Because no public buildings were exposed at Tell Beit Mirsim, Herzog (1992:

6. Sites generally considered to be first-rank administrative centres include Megiddo = 5.3 ha (Herzog 1992: 251), Gezer = 13.3 ha, Lachish = 7.0 ha (Herzog 1992: 258), Hazor = 12.0 ha, and Dan = 20.2 ha. On the basis of Olivier's study (1983), we can now add Shechem = 6.0+ ha. For the most recent study dealing with the royal cities in Israel and Judah, see Holladay (1995). Herzog (1992: 264) pointed out that few of these sites have been sufficiently excavated, at least in horizontal exposure, to determine the pattern and density of occupation during the Iron Age.

7. Such small centres are in sharp contrast to urban sites in Mesopotamia as shown by Redman (1978).

261) classified it as a 'provincial town', comparable to Beth-shemesh. The case of Tell en-Nasbeh is somewhat different because it began as a provincial town that was later transformed into a 'secondary adminis-trative centre' with the addition of an offset-inset wall, three four-room houses, water storage facilities and food storage areas in the form of silos (Herzog 1992: 262). The essential residential nature of this new 'city' was maintained with no recognizable palace or govern-ment residence. However, Herzog attributes direct government plan-ning to the construction of the wall system, storage facilities and the four-room houses which are orthogonal structures independent of the defensive wall.[8]

Beaudry (1994: 33) has included as indicators of city status the presence of public buildings, such as palaces, temples, markets and central plazas,[9] along with storehouses, major water systems and roads. Such diversity reflects specialization, economic exchange, social distinction and government administration (Kühne 1994: 55). Fortifi-cations and gateways were not included as indicators by Beaudry, because these features appear at a variety of sites, not all of which can be classed as urban. On the other hand, Kühne (1994: 55) includes as criteria the topographical integrity of urban sites, their fortification by a surrounding wall and a significant degree of settlement density.[10] In view of the limited exposure of most Iron Age II occupation levels at sites in Cisjordan, there are only a handful of urban centres in whose archaeological record some but not all of these features are present. Megiddo Strata VA–IVB and IVA appear to be the most fully exposed examples of an urban centre with the greatest variety of public and private structures (Shiloh 1978: fig. 9).

Urbanism at Tell Jawa

In order to test the suitability of these criteria for determining the degree of urbanization during Iron Age II in Transjordan, Tell Jawa will be used as a test case. During six seasons of excavations between

---

8. Unfortunately, this well-known building type is poorly represented in Jordan and cannot serve at this time as an indicator of administrative stature.

9. Streets and plazas may have been the locale of commercial transactions along with the street near the city gate (Baumgarten 1992: 147).

10. Kühne also includes central place as a criterion for urban settlements although this may not function in the same way in Transjordan as it did in greater Assyria.

1989 and 1995, c. 12 per cent of this Iron Age town was exposed (Daviau 1992, 1993, 1994, in press).

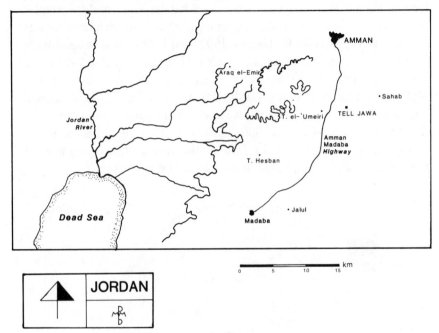

Figure 1.   Central Jordan, showing the location of Tell Jawa.

Topographical Integrity and Site Fortification
During the Iron II Period, the site of Tell Jawa was occupied during two distinct phases between the ninth and seventh centuries BCE (Daviau in press). The earlier of these phases (Stratum VIII) appears to have been associated with the construction of the casemate wall system that surrounded the entire 2.0 ha tell. Evidence limited to the southwest quarter of the site suggests that there was an earlier Iron Age I settlement that suffered severe damage. Unfortunately, its relationship to the two phases of the casemate wall remains unclear. At the same time, this evidence suggests that the later settlement was one of those refashionings of an existing town described by Mazzoni (1995).

The casemate wall was constructed of field stones that typically consisted of 90 per cent limestone boulders and 10 per cent chert slabs. These stones ranged in size from medium to large boulders (c. 0.50–0.75 × 0.75–1.00 m), with occasional examples of very large boulders (1.00–1.50 m). Such large stones were most common in the flanking towers on the west (B16) and southeast (C61–71) sides of the tell. The fortification of Tell Jawa appears to reflect deliberate choice of a site located on a hill with a view over the Madaba Plain and the implementation of a total town plan beginning with the fortifications, as was the case at Beer-sheba II (Herzog 1992: 261). This plan is seen most clearly in the incorporation of a stone-built drain (B24: 24) in the southwest corner of the wall system and a possible postern, Corridor 309, through the wall on the north (Daviau 1994: figs. 2, 4). A second indicator that the casemate wall was built as a planned unit is the continuity of its inner wall (W3000) in Field E where no adjacent house walls bonded with the inner face of the fortification system even though the floors of individual rooms sealed up against it.

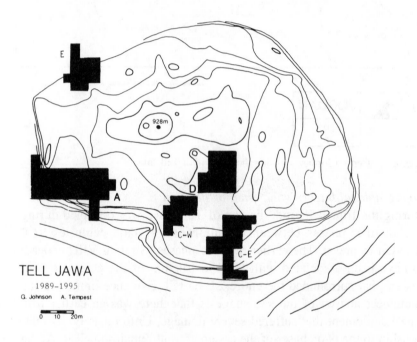

Figure 2. Tell Jawa with excavation Fields A-B, C (east and west).

A second feature of this wall is a series of offsets and insets along its outer face. At the points where the outer wall face was offset, the thickness of the wall was increased since there was no corresponding inset in the inner face of the outer wall. Such a fortification system was probably not the work of a few local farmers. In fact, we may have here an example of the type of central government planning that was used in the ninth century in central Transjordan. The evidence from Tell Jawa would thus tie in well with Mesha's claim to have built the site of Bezer with 50 men from Dibon, if only this reading of line 28 on the Mesha Inscription were beyond dispute (Jackson and Dearman 1989: 95, 120).[11]

Figure 3.   Stone built drain B24: 24 with plaster liner. The drain ran along the inside of the casemate wall and then cut through the fortification system in the southwest corner.

11. Jackson and Dearman admit that the reading of *b'š* is conjectural. Unfortunately, they assume that the *b* is preserved when it is far from clear on the stone.

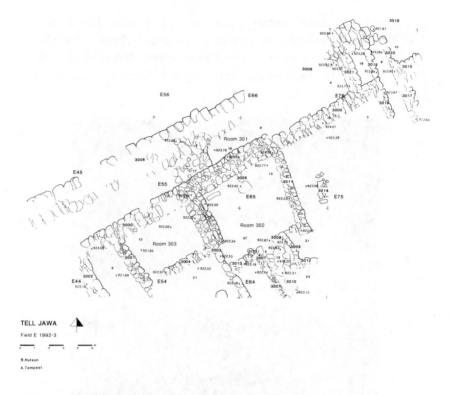

Figure 4.   Casemate Wall 3006 in Field E with offsets and insets along its outer
            face. The walls of Building 300 abut the south, inner face of Wall 3000.

Settlement Density

The extension of the casemate wall around the entire hill and the
foundation on bedrock of structures inside the wall indicate an expansion and intensification of occupation subsequent to Iron Age I.[12] This
intensification is most clearly seen in Building complex 300 that surrounded a central cistern. Eight walls of this complex ran perpendicu-
lar to and abutted the inner casemate wall, leaving no space for a road
or alley between the fortification system and the settled area. Building
300 contained at least 11 rooms and several corridors without any
evidence of streets. Apart from Corridor 309 on the east, which may
have served as a postern, the outer walls of this complex were not
reached on the west and south.

---

12. In every instance, test pits dug at various locations on the tell encountered
stone walls comparable to those in the excavation areas, and the tell itself was strewn
with Iron Age II pottery and artifacts.

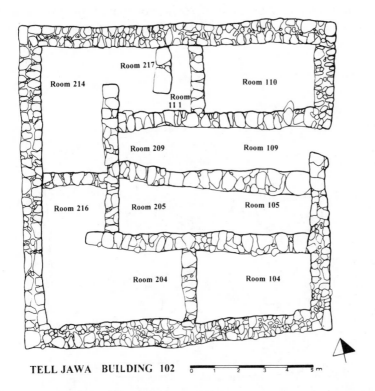

TELL JAWA BUILDING 102   0   1   2   3   4   5 m

Figure 5.   Building 102 in Fields A–B; an orthogonal building constructed adjacent
to the casemate wall system but not integrated with it.

Orthogonal Structures

By contrast to Complex 300, Building 102 in Fields A–B in the southwest had an orthogonal plan with very clearly defined outer walls.
This building measured 12.5 × 12.6 m and its outer walls were built
of boulder-and-chink construction. The southernmost wall (W1011 =
2020) was 3 m north of the casemate system and ran almost parallel to
it, comparable to the four-room houses at Tell en-Nasbeh (McCowan:
Survey Map). Building 102 had a long room plan with four parallel
units and several square rooms along the back similar to Building 32
at Beer-sheba (Herzog 1992: fig. 19). In both phases of Building 102,
the interior walls were formed of stacked boulder pillars. While this
feature is not unique to this structure, the interior plan and position of
Building 102 in relation to the fortification system suggests a different
planning than that employed in the construction of Building 300. Also,
the presence of Building 102 adds to the diversity of building types at

Tell Jawa, a feature indicative of social complexity or government administration, both indicators of a certain degree of urbanism.[13]

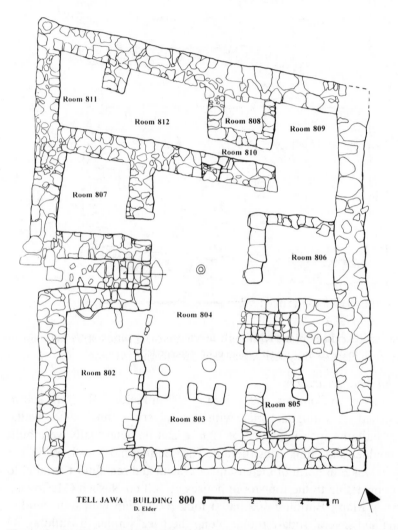

Figure 6. Building 800 in Field C-west; a late Iron II orthogonal building with two stories. Similarities with Building 600 in Field D suggest a preconceived architectural plan.

13. Immediately west of Building 102 was Courtyard 211 in B55, an area that contained more than 100 broken basalt millstones, chert pecking stones and newly fashioned hand grinders, evidence of intensive industrial activity.

The construction in Stratum VII (late eighth–seventh centuries BCE) of two orthogonal buildings (B600, B800) on the southeast terrace suggests that town planning continued through the Iron II Period. Like Building 102, these new structures were not integrated into the wall system but were located adjacent to the gate area north of a solid wall (W9000) that appears to have protected the terrace. Both Buildings show evidence of extensive domestic activity but appear to be larger than what might be expected for modest housing. Building 800 measured 13.5 × 16.5 m[14] and Building 600 was at least 12.2 × 16.0 m. In both cases, there were monolithic stone pillars standing 1.8 m tall[15] and stone-built staircases that led up to the second storey (Daviau 1994: fig. 13). In Building 800, there would have been approximately 22 rooms, while in Building 600 there could have been as many as 18. Clearly, Tell Jawa was not in the same class of settlement as Tell Beit Mirsim with its three-or four-room houses stuffed into whatever space was available within the walled town. Both Stratum VII buildings at Tell Jawa produced seals while Building 800 contained an ostracon suggesting economic and administrative activities.

Gate Complex
Another indicator in Cisjordan of a planned or administrative centre is a chambered gate complex comparable to those at Hazor, Gezer, Megiddo and Lachish. Although there are difficulties with uncovering the full plan of the Tell Jawa gate due to the presence of a modern cemetery, the western half was well preserved (Daviau in press). The walls of the gate complex were formed of large and extra-large boulders (1.00+ m). In the western half, there were three small rooms that originally opened into the central road that ran through the gate. Only the north end of the eastern half was able to be excavated, but it revealed the outer dimensions of the complex that measured 12.8 × 16.0 m, not counting the foundation of a tower built up against the outer wall. The central road was 4.1 m wide, making the Tell Jawa complex similar to that of Gezer in this respect. By comparison with the six-chambered gates at Cisjordanian sites that average 18.0 × 19.0 m (Herzog 1992: table 2), Tell Jawa is somewhat smaller. Although we cannot yet posit that this was a plan utilized at other sites in the

14. Building 800 is irregular in shape with a maximum length of 18.00 m.
15. The largest single stone, c. 4.00 m in length, was part of Wall 8011, the southern, outer wall of Building 800.

Amman region, it appears that the builders employed a known plan that included two units of chambers with protruding towers that flanked a central roadway and not just a simple overlapping of the defensive wall as at Tell en-Nasbeh (McCowan 1947: fig. 47).

Central Place

The position of Tell Jawa on the southernmost ridge of the Belqa hills overlooking the Madaba Plain was at once strategic and central in that it was equidistant between Tell el-'Umeiri and Sahab, each c. 5 km apart and 10 km south of Rabbath-Ammon.[16] Whether there were smaller Iron Age sites dependent on Tell Jawa is not clear due to the extent of modern settlement in the immediate area. Due south of Tell Jawa, 2.5 km away, is the prominent tower near er-Rufeisa (Boling 1989: fig. 8.46) that appears to have served as a lookout post. Surface sherding of this site identified Iron I and Iron II pottery along with Roman and later material. No other tell inhabited during the Iron Age is in the immediate neighbourhood.

Conclusions

This brief analysis of the excavated remains of Tell Jawa suggests that it incorporates several major features that are criteria for an administrative centre constructed at a strategic location according to a pre-conceived plan with government assistance. First, the casemate wall and gate complex were free-standing structures[17] that fortified the settlement area and preceded the construction of housing within the town. Secondly, a variety of types of buildings were constructed within the settlement, including ordinary housing, craft areas and orthogonal long room structures that were independent of the casemate wall (Shiloh 1978: 43 n. 11). Thirdly, several extra-large orthogonal buildings with two stories contained evidence of administrative and economic activities, suggesting that Tell Jawa functioned as a central place in the distribution of sites in the kingdom of Ammon.

16. On the north side of Rabbath-Ammon is the site of Safut, a prominent mound at the south end of the Baq'ah Valley. Unfortunately, Safut cannot be used for comparative purposes because it was partially cut through during road building activities that left the acropolis (?) intact but damaged the lower town (Wimmer 1987: 159).

17. Certain sections of Casemate Wall 2007, probably rebuilt after damage by earthquake, incorporated cross walls that extended into the town and became part of adjoining rooms (R203, 206).

BIBLIOGRAPHY

Baumgarten, J.J.
1992   'Urbanism in the Late Bronze Age', in The *Architecture of Ancient Israel* (ed. A. Kempinski and R. Reich; Jerusalem: Israel Exploration Society): 143-50.

Beaudry, M.
1994   'L'urbanisme à l'époque du Fer', in *'Où demeures-tu?' (Jn 1,38): La maison depuis le monde biblique en hommage au professor Guy Couturier à l'occasion de ses soixante-cinq ans* (ed. J.-C. Petit *et al.*; Québec: Fides): 31-51.

Ben-Tor, A.
1993   'Jokneam', in *NEAEHL*: 805-11.

Boling, R.G.
1989   'Site Survey in the Tell el-'Umeiri Region', in *Madaba Plains Project I: The 1984 Season at Tell el-'Umeiri and Vicinity and Subsequent Studies* (ed. L.T. Geraty *et al.*; Berrien Springs, MI: Andrews University): 98-188.

Boraas, R.S.
1971   'A Preliminary Sounding at Rujm el-Malfuf, 1969', *ADAJ* 16: 31-45.

Chambon, A.
1984   *Tell el-Far'ah I: L'Age du Fer* (Paris: Editions Recherche sur les Civilisations).

Daviau, P.M.M.
1992   'Preliminary Report of the Excavations at Tell Jawa in the Madaba Plains (1991)', *ADAJ* 36: 145-62.

1993   'Preliminary Report of the Third Season of Excavations at Tell Jawa, Jordan (1992)', *ADAJ* 37: 325-40.

1994   'Excavations at Tell Jawa, Jordan (1993): Preliminary Report', *ADAJ* 8: 173-93.

in press   'The Fifth Season of Excavations at Tell Jawa (1994): Preliminary Report', *ADAJ* 40.

Finkelstein, I.
1988–89   'The Land of Ephraim Survey 1980–1987: Preliminary Report', *TA* 15–16: 117-83.

Franken, H.J.
1989   'Deir 'Alla', in *Archaeology of Jordan II.I: Field Reports* (ed. D. Homès-Fredericq and J.B. Hennessy; Leuven: Peeters): 201-205.

Franken, H.J., and R.S. Abujaber
1989   'Yadoudeh: The History of a Land', *Madaba Plains Project I: The 1984 Season at Tell el-'Umeiri and Vicinity and Subsequent Studies* (ed. L.T. Geraty *et al.*; Berrien Springs, MI: Andrews University): 407-41.

Glueck, N.
1939   *Explorations in Eastern Palestine, III*, AASOR 18–19 (New Haven: ASOR).

Greenberg, R.
1993   'Tell Beit Mirsim', in *NEAEHL*: 177-80.
Herr, L.G.
in press   'Tell el-'Umeiri and the Madaba Plains Region during the Late
            Bronze–Iron I Transition'.
Herzog, Z.
1992   Settlement and Fortification Planning in the Iron Age', in *The
            Architecture of Ancient Israel* (ed. A. Kempinski and R. Reich;
            Jerusalem: Israel Exploration Society): 231-74.
Holladay, J.S.
1995   'The Kingdoms of Israel and Judah: Political and Economic
            Centralization in the Iron IIA–B (*ca.* 1000–750 BCE)', in *ASHL*: 368-
            98.
Homès-Fredericq, D.
1992   'Late Bronze and Iron Age Evidence from Lehun in Moab', in *Early
            Edom and Moab: The Beginning of the Iron Age in Southern Jordan*
            (ed. P. Bienkowski; Sheffield: J.R. Collis): 187-202.
Ibach, R.
1987   *Archaeological Survey of the Hesban Region: Catalogue of Sites and
            Characterization of Periods. Hesban 5* (ed. Ø.S. LaBianca; Berrien
            Springs, MI: Andrews University).
Jackson, K.P., and J.A. Dearman
1989   'The Text of the Mesha' Inscription', in *Studies in the Mesha
            Inscription and Moab* (ed. J.A. Dearman; Atlanta: Scholars Press): 91-
            130.
Kelso, J.L.
1993   'Bethel', in *NEAEHL*: 192-94.
Kletter, R.
1991   'The Rujm el-Malfuf Buildings', *BASOR* 284: 33-50.
Kühne, H.
1994   'The Urbanization of the Assyrian Provinces', in *Nuove fondazioni nel
            Vincino Oriente Antico: Realtà e ideologia* (ed. S. Mazzoni; Pisa:
            Giardini Editori e Stampatori): 55-84.
MacDonald, B.
1988   *The Wadi el Hasa Archaeological Survey 1979–1983: West-Central
            Jordan* (Waterloo, ON: Wilfrid Laurier University).
Mazar, A.
1993   'Beth-Shean', in *NEAEHL*: 214-23.
Mazzoni, S.
1995   'Settlement Pattern and New Urbanization in Syria at the Time of the
            Assyrian Conquest', in *Neo-Assyrian Geography: Convegno Inter-
            nazionale* (ed. M. Liverani; Quaderi di Geografia Storicas, 5; Rome:
            La Sapienza): 181-91.
McCowan, C.C.
1947   *Tell en-Nasbeh. I. Archaeological and Historical Results* (Berkeley:
            Palestine Institute of the Pacific School of Religion; New Haven:
            ASOR).

McGovern, P.E.
    1986   *The Late Bronze and Early Iron Ages of Central Transjordan: The Baq'ah Valley Project, 1977–1981* (Philadelphia: University Museum).

Miller, J.M. (ed.)
    1991   *Archaeological Survey of the Kerak Plateau* (Atlanta: Scholars Press).

Najjar, M.
    1992   'The Excavations at Khilda', *ADAJ* 36: 420-27 (Arabic).

Olivier, J.P.J.
    1983   'In Search of a Capital for the Northern Kingdom', *JNSL* 11: 117-32.

Redman, C.L.
    1978   *The Rise of Urbanism* (San Francisco: W.H. Freeman).

Seger, J.D.
    1993   'Tel Halif', in *NEAEHL*: 553-59.

Shiloh, Y.
    1978   'Development of Town Planning in the Israelite City', *IEJ* 28: 36-51.

Thompson, H.O.
    1973   'Rujm al-Malfuf (South)', ADAJ 17: 47-72.

Ussishkin, D.
    1993   'Dothan', in *NEAEHL*: 372-73.

Wimmer, D.
    1987   'Tell Safut Excavations, 1982–1985: A Preliminary Report', ADAJ 31: 159-74.

Winnett, F.V.
    1964   *Excavations at Dibon (Dhībān) in Moab I: The First Campaign, 1950–51*, AASOR: 36-37.

Wright, G.E.
    1965   *Shechem: The Biography of a Biblical City* (New York: McGraw–Hill).

Younker, R.W.
    1989   ' "Towers" in the Region Surrounding Tell el-'Umeiri', in *Madaba Plains Project I: The 1984 Season at Tell el-'Umeiri and Vicinity and Subsequent Studies* (ed. L.T. Geraty *et al.*; Berrien Springs, MI: Andrews University): 195-98.

ARCHAEOLOGY, URBANISM, AND THE RISE OF THE ISRAELITE STATE

William G. Dever

In the English-speaking world, scholarly interest has been focussed on 'state formation processes' since Morton Fried's *The Evolution of Political Society: An Essay in Political Anthropology* (1967), and Elman R. Service's *Origins of the State and Civilization: the Process of Cultural Evolution* (1975). Service proposed an evolutionary sequence that envisioned all social organizations as moving inevitably through progressive stages, from 'band' to 'tribe' to 'chiefdom' to 'state'. Since then, more than 20 other major analyses have been published, many advancing rival theories of the state and state formation (see the following major works: Renfrew 1972; Flannery 1972; Carneiro 1970; Friedman and Rowlands 1977; Cohen and Service 1978; Haas 1982; Tainter 1988).

Meanwhile, biblical scholars in the last two decades began to borrow socio-anthropological models for elucidating biblical texts, in this case specifically the notions of (1) 'tribe', (2) 'chiefdom' and (3) 'state'. These models were used to explain, in modern terms, the evolution of early Israel from a supposed 'tribal confederation' in the twelfth–eleventh centuries BCE, to a 'chiefdom' under Saul in the late eleventh century BCE, and finally to a fully developed nation-state under David and Solomon during the United Monarchy in the tenth century BCE. Representative works in this genre would include those of de Geus (1975); Gottwald (1979); Frick (1985); Lemche (1985) and Flanagan (1988). There were also published in the 1970s and 1980s a dozen or more other major works on 'the emergence of early Israel', using more traditional literary-critical methods. In this paper, only the latter period, the tenth century BCE, which sees the formation of the Israelite state, will be discussed.

Recent Discussions on the Rise of the Israelite State

Some of the models suggested in the recent proliferation of theoretical literature on state formation processes have been borrowed by a few historians of early Israel (e.g. Frick 1985; Coote and Whitelam 1987; Flanagan 1988; Fritz 1995). In all these works, definitions of the 'state' vary widely, but there is a common denominator in the stress on centralization of decision-making and administration that denotes, practically speaking, kingship. Thus, the state is 'bureaucratic governance by legal force' (Service 1962: 175). Or, 'the State is a society in which there is a set of offices of the society at large, conferring governance over the society at large' (Sahlins 1968: 6). A further distinction is often made between (1) 'pristine states' that developed independently, of which only six are known (Service's 'precocious' states): Egypt; Mesopotamia; the Indus Valley; the Han Dynasty in China; the Mesoamerican Maya–Aztec; and the Inca in Peru; and (2) 'secondary' states, which are usually imposed by force on neighboring peoples, of which there are many examples. In addition, other scholars have sought to identify primitive states by the terms 'inchoate early state' (Claessen and Skalnik 1978); or 'conditional state' (Webb 1975).[1] More recent works, focussing specifically on the Near/Middle East (Khoury and Kostiner 1990), develop the model of 'tribal state', which refers specifically to indigenous Levantine societies that have remained tribal, or 'segmentary', and characteristically non-urban, yet have developed sufficient centralized authority to qualify them as states as, for example, in Transjordan. Despite this typology of early states, Tapper (1990) has cautioned that such categories may be too rigid, that most early states are in fact 'hybrids'.

But why did states form at all? In his seminal work *The Collapse of Societies* (1988), Joseph Tainter, following Henry Wright (1977), has arranged the various hypotheses into four general categories: (1) managerial, (2) internal conflict, (3) external conflict, and (4) synthetic. These can be further reduced to just two main schools of thought, that is, conflict and integration. Here, only Tainter's managerial and synthetic scenarios will be examined, with reference to the case of ancient Israel.[2]

---

1. For further discussion, see the convenient summary and bibliography in Tainter (1988: 26-38), Khoury and Kostiner (1990), and especially Tapper (1990).

2. Marxist 'class-conflict' theories such as Fried (1967) have too much excess

The managerial model holds that as populations increase and societies come under socio-economic stress, managerial hierarchies inevitably emerge to meet the challenge. This model is perhaps most useful in explaining 'pristine' states; but there is no inherent reason why it cannot also be applied to what one could call 'peripheral' states like ancient Israel. But how well does such a model fit, either with the textual or the archaeological data?

The biblical texts are not unanimous in their explanation of the rise of kingship. The Deuteronomistic writers and editors of Samuel–Kings belonged to ultra-orthodox theocratic parties and were thus quite naturally anti-statist in outlook. Indeed, in the annalistic accounts in Kings, the writers really approve of only three kings in the 400-year history of Israel and Judah: David, always the ideal (and idealized) prototype; and Hezekiah and Josiah, late reform kings of Judah, who had obviously been co-opted by the extremist religious parties. Thus, in the final redaction of the biblical tradition, the prophet Samuel, who represents the antimonarchic ideal *par excellence*, is confronted by the people's demands for a king 'like all the nations', presumably to meet the growing Philistine military threat (1 Sam. 8.5). Samuel warns them of the dire consequences of setting up any sovereign but Yahweh, but nonetheless he is forced to acquiesce. Samuel thus anoints Saul, who is then acclaimed king by a sort of 'popular election', that is, a widespread recognition of his charismatic powers, which are seen as signs of divine approval. In other strands of the literary tradition, however, Saul's rise to kingship is looked upon in a more favorable light, as a beneficial and even necessary adaptation to the changing needs of an increasingly complex society. This 'biblical' explanation would conform to elements of both Tainter's managerial and synthetic models.

Although all the literary materials have been later woven into the fabric of Deuteronomistic anti-royalist propaganda in the Bible, it is striking that the contradictions have not been edited out. This fact suggests an ambivalence about kingship that was genuine, indeed native, to early and even to later Israel. In any case, however, the textual tradition in the Hebrew Bible cannot yield for us today a satisfactory historical 'explanation' of the state when taken at face value, for these texts are late, tendentious and elitist. Several recent studies

Hegelian baggage; and external conflict theories such as Carneiro's (1970) 'circumscription' model are not wholly applicable to early Israel.

by biblical scholars, however, outline a more radical approach; and it is interesting that all agree in suggesting that archaeological data may provide a corrective to the texts.[3]

For example, Frick's (1985) study on the rise of the Israelite state begins with the evolutionary sequence of 'tribe' to 'chiefdom' to 'state', following Fried, Service and others. Rather than invoking any sort of determinism, however, Frick stresses the many factors that led to statehood, using a General Systems Theory approach. He attempts a survey of the archaeological and especially the ecological data, in portraying earliest Israel as a highland agricultural society. He sees growth toward centralization, and ultimately the Monarchy, largely as an overall 'adaptive transformation', although the Philistine threat may have been one factor. Frick's approach is refreshing, but his use of the strictly archaeological data, mostly of the twelfth–eleventh centuries BCE, is much too limited to achieve his stated goal of socio-anthropological explanation.

Coote and Whitelam's (1987) attempt to explain the rise of Israel as a natural development within the context of the long settlement history of the southern Levant is a laudable departure, and they make much more (though not always expert) use of archaeological evidence. For them, the rise of the Monarchy is part of a cultural continuum, a matter of internal dynamics rather than either external threat or dialectical conflict. The Monarchy was thus, in contrast to the later biblical tradition, not an alien and hostile institution at all. As for further explanation, Coote and Whitelam are inclined toward Carneiro's 'conscription' theory, but interpreted somewhat more broadly. Thus, 'It is the combination of environmental and social circumscription with other internal and external factors that provide the impetus to the formation of the Israelite state' (1987: 147).

The most ambitious recent attempt to apply socio-anthropological models to early Israel is that of Flanagan (1988). Unfortunately, sociological jargon tends to obscure any value his novel 'hologram' of early Israel might have. Take this quotation, for example:

> If we follow the biblical precedent and read the information sources together but without the restraints of the narrative sequence and rigid

3.   For orientation to the burgeoning literature, see Davies (1992, 1995), Lemche and Thompson (1994), Finkelstein and Na'aman (1994), Lemche (1996), Thompson (1995), Provan (1995) and cf. Dever (1991, 1992, 1994b, 1995, 1996a, 1996b, in press).

archaeological space-time systemics, the archaeological and literary models suggest simultaneous processes of devolution and evolution similar to the symbioses among sedentary, semi-nomadic and nomadic peoples documented in comparative sociology (1988: 288).

Apparently, this means that (1) societies are complex and (2) things change. To his credit, however, Flanagan does attempt to use archaeological, ecological and even ethnographic data, as well as various systemic and holistic approaches. Nevertheless, in the end all Flanagan really seems to say is that the rise of the Israelite state was due to a process of centralization and adaptation. The major weakness is the book's pretentious, but amateur and idiosyncratic, archaeological reconstruction of the Iron I Period (Dever 1994a).

The 'Revisionist' Paradigm and Early Israel

Subsequent to an earlier survey of the literature on the rise of the Israelite state (Dever 1994a), the discussion has mushroomed, largely because the question of 'statehood' has now become part of the issue of whether it is possible to write a history of biblical (i.e. 'monarchical' or Iron Age) Israel at all (Lemche and Thompson 1994: 18-19, cf. Dever in 1996a, 1996b).[4]

These 'revisionist historians', as they call themselves (Lemche and Thompson 1994: 14), might well be called the 'new nihilists' (Dever 1995), recalling of course the clash in the 1950s between the American Albright–Wright–Bright school and the German school of Alt–Noth–von Rad and others over the 'historicity' of the Patriarchs. The

---

4. Several recent papers (Dever 1996a, 1996b, in press a, in press b, in press c) have included comments on the historiographical crisis that many biblical scholars now acknowledge because of the nature of the texts. Archaeologists must be involved in this crisis because most participants are oblivious to or deliberately ignore the proliferating archaeological data that could prove decisive; or worse, misrepresent the proper relationship between archaeology and biblical studies (e.g. Whitelam 1994). Furthermore, in the last two years or so, historiographic views aired by biblical scholars in the annual meetings, in journals, in popular magazines, even on the Internet, have become increasingly dogmatic, raucous and even vindictive (Lemche and Thompson 1994: 3-4; Thompson 1995; Davies 1995: 700; Whitelam 1994). The few who have attempted to introduce archaeological data into the discussion are dismissed as 'positivists', 'maximalists', old-fashioned 'Biblical Archaeologists' or even, astonishingly (in the case of the writer) as 'Fundamentalists', despite the 25-year long battle against traditional-style 'Biblical Archaeology' (Dever 1985 and references; Dever 1993).

principal full-scale works of the 'new nihilists' are by Jamieson-Drake (1991); Davies (1992); Thompson (1992) and Whitelam (1994 and 1996). A review of the historiographical and methodological issues will be found in Edelman (1991), which is already dated. All these discussions imply certain notions of 'urbanism' and 'statehood', so they need to be analyzed here.

The most recent, and most extreme, pronouncement of the 'revisionists' is that of Lemche and Thompson (1994: 18-20):

> That is the issue we have today: namely, the question of whether the Bible in its stories is talking about history and the past at all. Our argument is not that the Bible exaggerates the exploits of David, nor is it that Solomon was never as rich as the Bible makes him out to be. We are not dealing with issues of skepticism here. Rather, we are trying to argue that the Bible's stories of Saul, David and Solomon are not about history at all. History writing is a very different thing from what the Bible's authors were doing...
>
> To compare the Bible's tales about David with early Iron Age Palestine is like comparing the story of Gilgamesh with Bronze Age Uruk, Homer with ancient Mycenae, or, indeed, Arthur with early mediaeval England, or even Wagner's Siegfried with a Germany of the early Middle Ages.

They go on to say,

> In the history of Palestine that we have presented, there is no room for a historical United Monarchy, or for such kings as those presented in the biblical stories of Saul, David or Solomon. The early period in which the traditions have set their narratives is an imaginary world of long ago that never existed as such. In the real world of that time, for instance, only a few dozen villagers lived as farmers in all of the Judaean highlands. Timber, grazing lands and steppe were all marginal possibilities. There could not have been a kingdom for any Saul or David to be king of, simply because there were not enough people. Not only did a state of Judah not yet exist, but we have no evidence of there having been any political force anywhere in Palestine that was large enough or developed enough to have been even conceivably capable of unifying the many different economies and regions of this land, given the near political vacuum of the tenth century BCE. Rather, at this time, Palestine was far less unified than it had been for more than a thousand years. Jerusalem at this time can hardly be spoken of as a city... Its relationship to Judah was marginal. It first took on the form and acquired the status of a city, capable of being understood as a state capital, sometime in the middle of the seventh century.

Such *obiter dicta* of these revisionist historians reveal how oblivious they are to the mass of archaeological data now known. The latest

absurdity is the unanimous rejection by the revisionists of the Tel Dan
inscription found in 1993, a monumental Aramaic victory stela men-
tioning 'kings of Israel' and specifically the 'house of David' (Biran
and Naveh 1993). Additional fragments found in 1994 (Biran and
Naveh 1995) enable us to reconstruct the name of 'Jehoram' (or
Joram), who ruled in 849–842 BCE, making the Aramaean king in
question Hazael of Damascus. Now for many years, biblicists have
been chiding archaeologists for failure to turn up more written evidence. But when by chance a stunning early monumental inscription
does turn up, and it can be dated almost precisely to the year, what do
they do? They explain it away as being out of context and a century
and a half later, torturing the paleographic arguments; or they read
the crux, the phrase *btdwd*, as a place-name rather than a personal
name, on the pretext that a word-divider is missing; and they even
imply that the inscription may be a forgery, planted on the excavator,
the venerable Abraham Biran (see Lemche and Thompson 1994, and
references there to the burgeoning literature). The careful and unbi-
ased observer, however, who knows archaeology, epigraphy and a bit
of biblical criticism cannot escape the suspicion that Lemche, Thompson
and Whitelam (especially) cannot admit any evidence for an early
Israel, much less a state, because they have gone too far out on a limb
previously, declaring that on principle there cannot have been a real
'biblical' Israel in the Iron Age; it is all a literary construct, a
Persian–Hellenistic phantasmagoria. Yet the dogmatism of the revisionists is rather like that of the Fundamentalists whom they decry so
furiously. Their mind is made up; do not confuse them with facts.[5]

The 'revisionists' flawed historiographical (and theological?) presuppositions, as well as their neglect or abuse of the rich archaeological

5.   The 'European School' would no doubt charge in return that those who have
the 'Biblical archaeological–harmonistic presuppositions common to much American
reading' (Thompson 1995: 606) presume that there *must* have been an Iron Age
'Israel'. That, however, is not true: most simply presume that sound historical
method must allow for the possibility that there *can* have been such an Israel; and that
one must sift carefully through both biblical texts and archaeological evidence to sort
out reliable data, willing to recognize that when they do happen to converge (as
often) it is the best witness to the reality of ancient Israel. One might recall the wise
caution of a now-dismissed 'positivist' biblical historian, John Bright, who reminded
us that the historian *always* works with 'the balance of probability'. Both Funda-
mentalism and liberal revisionism transgress that rule when they take dogmatic,
extremist positions.

data that are now available have been dealt with elsewhere.[6] Here one can only take up the challenge that they pose for the theme of this volume, namely their assertion that there was no early Israelite state. It would be tempting, of course, to ignore the 'revisionists', because they have so discredited themselves. But, since many biblicists have ceased to be interested in history and are pursuing ever-more exotic literary theories, we undeconstructed archaeologists (who have always been historians) must come forward in the defense of ancient Israel. It really *did* exist, in spite of all the post-modernist piffle that one reads today. It is archaeology that resurrects those who, in the Bible's words, 'sleep in the dust'; that gives back to the people of the past their own long-lost voice. To argue that this Israel is not the ideal 'Israel' of the reactionary orthodox writers of the Bible, is completely irrelevant. Of course, one must reject the *Heilsgeschichte* as history: but there is another, 'secular' history of Israel, a socio-economic rather than political history, waiting to be written. And it will be written largely by Syro-Palestinian archaeologists, who now master a mature, independent discipline, and who in today's climate of 'post-processual archaeology' will find history writing once again a respectable profession (cf. Hodder 1986; Dever 1995, in press a).

On Defining the Terms of the Discussion

From its beginning, the present discussion on urbanization and state-hood has been plagued by a general lack of definition of the basic terms, reflecting the unfamiliarity of most biblicists and Syro-Palestinian archaeologists with what is a considerable and sophisticated ethnographic and anthropological literature.

The older term 'civilization', which implied but rarely defined 'urbanization', has largely been replaced by the term 'complex society'. By this latter term most socio-anthropologists and other commentators

6. See Halpern (1995), Dever (1995, 1996a, 1996b, in press b), and the mass of Iron Age archaeological data summarized in such standard reference works as Weippert (1988), Mazar (1990), and Ben-Tor (1992), to name only a few. Davies (1992: 24) dismisses Mazar's 160 pages on the Iron Age in a single footnote, as 'irrelevant' for a reconstruction of ancient Israel, because Davies's own 'Israel' is only a literary construct of the Persian Period. This alone would illustrate why many of the 'revisionist' statements are *presuppositions*, not conclusions. The point is that the 'revisionists' assay to do archaeology, but appear not to have even a minimal grasp of the methods and aim of today's archaeology or its potential for history writing.

refer to social configurations that are not only large, multi-faceted, and often independent, but are also marked by inequalities, that is, are hierarchically ordered, with individuals having differential access to goods and services based on inherited or acquired rank. Such differentiation is, indeed, more likely to take place in large urban settings, where administration is centralized. The term 'complex society' is perhaps less ambiguous and thus better than 'civilization'.

The term 'urban' had been notoriously ambiguous, often among archaeologists denoting little more than a 'large' or 'walled' town. Childe (1950), who like Adams (1966) virtually assumed that 'urban' was synonymous with 'civilization', developed a 'trait-list' that today is often forgotten. Among Childe's criteria were such variables as size, socio-economic stratification, institutionalized political administration, ability to produce surplus and sustain long-distance trade, monumental art and architecture and the use of writing. The frustration with such trait-lists, however, is that many of the variables in urbanization (such as the term 'chiefdoms' mentioned above), are difficult or impossible to measure archaeologically; and, furthermore, any such list is bound to be somewhat subjective, even arbitrary.

A more objective, quantifiable model of urbanism for the southern Levant has been developed by Steven Falconer in his 1987 dissertation entitled 'Heartland of Villages: Reconsidering Early Urbanism in the Southern Levant', obviously a takeoff from Adams's (1981) classic work on settlement patterns. Falconer basically argues that a population agglomerate may be defined as 'urban' when it outgrows its capacity to feed and sustain itself on immediately available resources, and so must organize and control the surrounding agricultural hinterland, that is, must become essentially a 'market-town' in Central-Place Theory terminology. On the rich alluvial plains of southern Mesopotamia, agricultural yields can easily be calculated. The 'threshold' at which the transition to an urban center took place can be fixed at about 85 acres, or a population of some 8000–9000. Of course, the southern Levant is characterized by a much smaller-scale landscape, not only fragmented but much less productive, because of poor soil and water sources. Thus, in the southern Levant, the threshold for truly urban configurations must be placed at about 15 acres and some 1500 population. Kolb (1984) proposed an even smaller criterion, 25 acres and 1000 population (although if his 100 persons per hectare is raised to the more typical figure of 250, one arrives at a population estimate of 2500). These widely accepted 'rules of thumb' will be returned to when asking whether or not Israel in the Iron Age constituted an urban society.

On the Relations between 'State', 'Civilization', and 'Urbanization': Toward a Working Methodology

A working model for identifying any state-formation process in early Israel may stem more from analysis of the relations between the concepts and terms defined above, than from the definition themselves. For most earlier scholars, 'civilization' was usually synonymous with 'state' (Service 1975: 280-82), and that may still be presumed. The more difficult question is the relation of 'urbanization' to both. That is to say, can one have a true state without a high degree of urbanization? Or, to put it another way, is urbanization a prerequisite of the state, even the 'cause' of state-formation processes? As noted above, two distinguished scholars, Adams (1966) and Childe (1950), have argued that urbanization does not cause the state, but that it is the other way around: urbanization presumes the prior existence of the state. Service (1975: 280-82), however, disagrees; and one is inclined to side with him. For example, all authorities would agree that the southern Levant in the Early and Middle Bronze Ages was highly urbanized, but no one supposes that a state yet existed, only the characteristic pattern of south Levantine city-states.

However the problem is approached, two things seem clear. On the one hand, there are early states that are predominantly non-urban, like Han Dynasty China and several of the Mesoamerican states. On the other hand, urbanization does ordinarily precede the development of the state; and although the development of cities does not necessarily 'cause' the emergence of state level organization, often it is a contributing factor. Thus, for methodological purposes, it may be assumed that a high degree of urbanization is the best criterion for recognizing at least incipient or 'peripheral' states. Such an assumption underlies the following argument vis-à-vis early Israel. The justification for the argument is simply that both urbanization and the formation of states require and presuppose centralization of authority. And it is that phenomenon that archaeology, not texts, is often in the best position to analyze.

Archaeological Evidence for Centralization and Urbanization in Tenth-Century BCE Israel

Demography

Earlier scholars like Albright had estimated the population of Iron II Israel (i.e. the period of the Divided Monarchy) to be as high as 900,000. Much more sophisticated recent demographic estimates, based on ethno-archaeology, extensive surface surveys and settlement pattern studies, yield more realistic figures, broken down by sub-phases. Thus Finkelstein (1988) and others arrive at a population of some 50,000–65,000 for the 'Proto-Israelite' Period of the twelfth–eleventh centuries BCE. By the ninth–eighth centuries BCE, Shiloh (1980) estimates growth to about 150,000. Thus the population in the tenth century BCE may have been about 100,000 (Dever 1996b).

Compare these carefully researched figures of archaeologists with Lemche and Thompson's absurd 'few dozen villages... in all the Judaean highlands' (1994: 19) in the tenth century BCE. For better comparisons, note that the lowland Maya state of Tikal had only perhaps 25,000–40,000 people; and several of the multi-valley Andean states had populations of only 75,000–160,000 (Service 1975: 186-202). Thus, on the basis of gross population size alone, Lemche and Thompson's attempt to deny early Israel state status can easily be dismissed.

Of course, even dramatic population increases from the twelfth to the tenth centuries BCE do not in themselves give evidence of urbanization or statehood; but there are other data to examine.

Settlement Type and Distribution

A better indication is the phenomenon of the concentration of the population in a relatively few large central cities, with the shrinkage or abandonment of many smaller rural sites, or what archaeologists call a classic 'three-tiered', hierarchically ordered settlement pattern. The southern Levant certainly reflects such a shift from the twelfth to the tenth centuries BCE. Most of the 300 or so twelfth–eleventh centuries BCE 'Proto-Israelite villages' that are known are abandoned by the mid-late tenth century BCE, with relatively few developing continuously into major Iron II *tells*. On the other hand, several sites, perhaps as many as 11, do develop into what may legitimately be called 'cities' by the above criteria (i.e. roughly 100 persons per acre of built-up area).

These are (table 1): Dan, Hazor, Megiddo, Ta'anach, Beth-shan, Tell el-Far'ah (N), Shechem, Aphek, Gezer, Jerusalem and Lachish.

Rank	Sites/stratum	Size (acres)	Population	9th cent. BCE	Source
'Tier 1':	Dan IVB-A	25.0	2500	III	
cities	Hazor IX	15.0	1500	VIII–VII	
(c. 20,000)	Megiddo VA/IVB	13.5 (15–25)	1300 (500)	IVA	YS; H
	Ta'anach IIA-B	16.0	1600	III	
	Beth-shan Upper	10.0	1000	IV	
	Tell el-Far'ah (N) VIIb	15.01(?)	1500	VIIc–d	
	Shechem X	13.0	1300	IX	
	Aphek Xδ	15.0	1500	X7	
	Gezer IX–VIII	33.0	3300	VII	
	Jerusalem 14	32.0	2500	13	YS
	Lachish V	18.01 (38)	1800 (500)	IV	YS; H
'Tier 2':	Tel Kinrot V–IV	1.25	1250	III	
towns	Tel Amal III	0.75	75		
	Yoqneam XVI–XIV	10.0	1000	XIII	
	Tel Qiri VIIA	2.5	250	VIIB–C	
	Dothan 4 (?)	10.0 (15)	1000		YS
	Tel Mevorakh VIII–VII	1.5	150		
	Tell Michal XIV–XIII	0.3	30		
	Tell Qasile IX–VIII	4.0	400	VII	
	Azekah	14 (?)	1400 (?)		
	Tel Batash IV	6.5	650	III	
	Beth -Shemesh IIa	10.0	1000	IIb	
	Tell el-Ful II	?	?		
	Tell Hama	1.0	100		
	Tell Mazar XII	?	?		
	Tell Beit Misrim B3	7.5	750 (1300)	A2	H
	Tel Halif VII	3.0	300	VIA	
	Tel Ser'a VII	5.0	500	VI	
	Beersheba VI (V?)	2.5	250 (600)	(V)IV	H
	Arad XII	?	?	XI–X	
'Tier 3':	Tell el-Kheleifeh I			II?	
villages,	Qadesh-barnea I			2	
hamlets,	Negev forts				
camps etc.					

Table 1. 'Three-tier' hierarchy of major tenth-century BCE sites in Iron II Israel with population estimates.[7]

Together, these 11 'tier 1' cities may have had a total population of 20,000 or more, about 20 per cent of the total population of some

7. Some coastal and Jordan Valley sites are eliminated since they are probably 'non-Israelite'. YS = Shiloh 1980; H = Herzog 1992.

100,000 that can be projected for the tenth century BCE. The relatively larger number of middle-tier sites required by the 'three-tier' model of urbanization adopted by nearly all archaeologists would number at least 20 other towns, as Mazar and Fritz have shown, most in the 300–1,000 range. The remaining two-thirds of the population would then have lived in dozens of smaller towns and villages in the rural areas, and in hamlets, farmsteads and pastoral encampments in the hinterland.[8]

Regional Administrative Centers
Not only is the emergent pattern of urbanism clear in tenth-century BCE Israel, but it is precisely the few larger 'central places' or market towns and administrative centers—like Hazor, Megiddo and Gezer—that exhibit nearly identical casemate city walls and four-entryway gates, as well as 'palaces' or citadels adjacent to the fortifications (perhaps Lachish as well). As Yadin (1958) long ago pointed out, these similarities in design and engineering can hardly be coincidence. They are obviously the result of centralized planning, not simply at one site, but countrywide, or we may say nation-wide. Another indication of centralized planning is the construction of as many as 50 'fortresses' or enclosed settlements in the southern Negev desert (rarely heavily populated in any period), most of them dated to the tenth century BCE (Mazar 1990: 390-97). What do these fortify, unless the borders of a self-conscious, independent state? The crucial data for attributing the above sites, together with a considerable archaeological assemblage, to the mid-late tenth century BCE, (i.e. to the time of Solomon) is (1) the distinctive red-slipped and hand- (i.e. not yet wheel-) burnished ceramics, dated since the 1930s to the tenth century BCE; and (2) the fact that a terminal date for these diagnostic wares can apparently be historically fixed by destruction layers at several sites, probably related to Egyptian texts describing a Palestinian raid by Pharaoh Shishak c. 930 BCE (i.e. the biblical 'Sheshonq'), which is said in 2 Kgs 14.25 to have taken place five years after Solomon's

---

8. For more detailed surveys of the data, see Weippert (1988: 471-781), Mazar (1990: 368-402), Fritz (1995: 76-120), Barkay (1992: 305-27), Holladay (1995) and Dever (in press b). On demography, see Shiloh (1980), Finkelstein (1988: 330-35) and Broshi and Finkelstein (1992). On 'rank-size' and 'three-tier hierarchy' models, see Hodder and Orton (1976: 55-73).

death. That correlation yields a late tenth century BCE date for the archaeological materials in question.[9]

Of course, a number of archaeologists of the 'Tel Aviv school' now attempt to date some of the fortifications at Hazor, Megiddo and elsewhere down into the ninth century BCE. But their arguments are based on faulty stratigraphy and ceramic typology.[10] Even if a ninth-century BCE date be conceded, however, one would still have to posit state-level organization at that time, which the 'revisionists' deny for Judah until the late seventh century BCE (Lemche and Thompson 1994: 19). The 'revisionists' simply do not understand that a state, like an urban settlement plan, is defined not by the absolute size of the population aggregate, but rather by settlement hierarchy and above all by centralization.

One useful model for understanding the emergence of urban centers is that of 'disembedded capitals'. These are administrative centers that develop as relatively compact sites, often established *de novo*, or are refounded deliberately, and are built up of largely public buildings and facilities, but contain relatively few domestic structures. From what we know of tenth-century BCE (or 'Solomonic') Jerusalem, it is a classic example of a 'disembedded capital' (which, it happens, fits the biblical description almost precisely); as is Samaria in the ninth–eighth centuries BCE. In the comparative literature, these Israelite and Judean cities would certainly be considered 'capitals' of states (Joffee, personal communication).

Socio-Economic Structure
But the late tenth century BCE, Israelite society and economy were stratified and highly specialized. The gradual shift from a simple village-based, agrarian, 'acephalous' kinship structure to an urban 'industrialized' and entrepreneurial society is complete. A class of elites is clear in the archeological record, although luxury goods are still relatively rare. On the basis of our present evidence, it appears

9. On the hand-burnished pottery and the *terminus ante quem* that the Shishak raid supplies, see Holladay (1995: 372, 377-86). For alternate views, see below and n. 10.

10. See Dever 1986, and full references there. The issues were aired in 1990 in an entire issue (no. 277/278) of *BASOR*, with arguments on the 'maximalist' side by Holladay, Stager and Dever; and on the 'minimalist' side by Finkelstein, Ussishkin, and Wightman. For the next round, see Holladay (1995), and especially Dever (in press b, in reply to Herzog in the same volume).

that literacy was probably not very widespread: the twelfth-century BCE 'Izbet Sarteh abecedary and the tenth-century BCE Gezer schoolboy's exercise tablet being an indication of at least 'functional literacy'.

Material Culture
It is the overall material culture, domestic architecture, burial customs and especially ceramics, that attest to a changeover from the 'formative' period of the twelfth–eleventh centuries BCE to the 'florescent' period that begins in the tenth century BCE and lasts until the early sixth century BCE, that is, the Monarchical Period. The pottery repertoire in particular exhibits a high degree of standardization of cultural norms, but the dominance of the so-called four-room house is no less indicative of cultural homogeneity. The emergence of a 'generic Iron II Israelite material culture' is not fortuitous, but reflects now a much more unified 'national' ideology and ethnic solidarity. Even if the biblical label 'Israelite–Judean' was unknown, one would recognize in the archaeological remains alone a 'national culture', that is, a true state.[11]

Internationalism
Finally, this growing sense of national identity expresses itself in Israel's emergence from relative isolation in the twelfth–eleventh centuries BCE into international trade and competition by the tenth century BCE. On the one hand, Phoenician and Cypriot arts and crafts are imported. On the other hand, decisive battles with the local Philistines take place; and the first sharp rivalries occur with other regional states, such as Ammon, Moab and Edom in Transjordan, and (before long) with the incipient Aramaean and Syro–Hittite states to the north.

Not only are these typical state-level processes of development clear in the archaeological record, they also accord quite well with detailed reports in the Bible in Samuel–Kings of the reigns of David and Solomon. Some biblical scholars are inclined to doubt the historical trustworthiness of the biblical version (above). Others, however, rightly regard the literary tradition as based, at least in part, on eyewitness accounts, archival records and other quite reliable sources (although, of course, somewhat exaggerated in the final interpretation

11. See the material cited in n. 10 (above). On the *continuity* of material culture from Iron I through Iron II, see Dever (in press c).

given in the Hebrew Bible). Indeed, few scholars until recently have ever questioned that by the tenth-century BCE ancient Israel did comprise a national state; it is largely the question of causation that is of concern here.

Centralization, Urbanization, and Statehood

Childe's 'trait-lists' of the characteristics of an urbanized, state-level society were noted above. It may be pertinent that of his ten characteristics, tenth-century BCE Israel exhibits at least eight; and the other two are plausible, although in the nature of the case there is scant archaeological evidence (i.e. the beginnings of 'science'; and sophisticated art). Other authorities identify a site as urban if it is (1) a topographical unit with a fortification wall, (2) densely occupied, (3) reflects social differentiation and centralized administration, (4) gives evidence of economic accumulation (surpluses) and distribution, (5) and constitutes a 'central place'. By these criteria, some 20 sites in tenth-century BCE Israel would qualify as 'urban'. The point of the foregoing analysis is that if we follow Adams's (1972: 73) view, that, in the typical evolutionary trajectory toward complex society, urbanization proceeds and presumes the development of social stratification and the state, then clearly urban Israel in the tenth century BCE was a state. The archaeological data, even when surveyed minimally, are decisive. If the name 'Israel' were not attested in the biblical or other texts, we should have to invent another term for this state; if not 'Solomon', then Solomon by another name. That our archaeologically attested 'Israel' is not the exact equivalent of the idealistic 'biblical' Israel is again evident, but irrelevant.

Why do many biblicists like the 'revisionists' not see this point? Why do they dismiss the biblical texts as 'unhistorical', but then fail to grasp the obvious implication that it is the archaeological data that are now primary? Davies, Thompson, Lemche and Whitelam have all made remarks in passing that reveal that they sense the importance of archaeology, but they continue to make declarations that fly in the face of all the archaeological evidence now available. Indeed, they appear to *ignore* the recent literature and data. For this, they cannot be forgiven, being scholars and historians, obligated to utilize all the rich data now available. Not only is early Israel now being recognized as a state, even if of the 'early inchoate' or 'peripheral' variety, but even the Transjordanian entities of Ammon, Moab and Edom are seen in the proliferating recent literature as moving toward statehood (perhaps of the 'tribal' variety) by the tenth century BCE.[12] 'Revision-ist' historians who are oblivious to these currents in scholarship are as reactionary as those theologians they so readily castigate. Neither can they any longer write a comprehensive, balanced, satisfying history of ancient Israel in the Iron Age, as Thompson (1992) attempts. Only archaeologists, and those working in dialogue with them, can. The fundamental question, long tacitly recognized, is: What kind of history of ancient Israel do we want? and what do we think is possible?

Conclusion

Presently, one can only say of the development from village to state in ancient Israel that this was a typical archaeological–cultural evolution-ary phase. It is but a single 'episode' in the long settlement history of the southern Levant, which looms larger in Western consciousness only because of the Jewish and Christian traditions. We must recall that throughout the history of this area (and indeed of the whole Middle East, whether ancient and modern), there have always been these recurring cycles of advance and abatement, specialization and de-specialization, complexity and collapse. For the most part, the basic phenomenon has been the oscillation between rural and urban styles of life. The Israelite Monarchy represents but a brief, illusory triumph of the 'Sown over the Desert'.[13]

12. See papers in this volume by Daviau, Herr and B. Routledge.

13. After this chapter was submitted, Finkelstein (1996) argued that there is at least as much evidence for dating the 'Solomonic' complex discussed here to the ninth century BCE as there is for dating it to the tenth century BCE. Since, however, he had previously (n. 10 above) argued that there was *no* evidence for a tenth-century BCE date, that would seem to leave him with no ground on which to stand. Such pure speculation does not advance the discussion.

BIBLIOGRAPHY

Adams, R. McC.
  1966   *The Evolution of Urban Society* (Chicago: Aldine).
  1972   'Patterns of Urbanization in Early Southern Mesopotamia', in *Man,
          Settlement and Urbanism* (ed. P.J. Ucko, R. Tringham and D.W.
          Dimbleby; London: Duckworth): 735-49.
  1981   *Heartland of Cities: Surveys of Ancient Settlement and Land Use on
          the Central Floodplain of the Euphrates* (Chicago: University of
          Chicago).

Barkay, G.
  1992   'The Iron Age II–III', in *The Archaeology of Ancient Israel* (ed.
          A. Ben-Tor; New Haven: Yale University Press): 302-73.

Ben-Tor, A. (ed.)
  1992   *The Archaeology of Ancient Israel* (New Haven: Yale University Press).

Biran, A., and J. Naveh
  1993   'An Aramaic Inscription of the First Temple Period from Tel Dan',
          IEJ 43: 81-98.
  1995   'The Dan Inscription: A New Fragment', *IEJ* 45: 1-18.

Broshi, M., and I. Finkelstein
  1992   'The Population of Palestine in Iron Age II', *BASOR* 287: 47-60.

Carneiro, R.L.
  1970   'A Theory of the Origin of the State', *Science* 109: 733-38.

Childe, V.G.
  1950   'The Urban Revolution', *Town Planning Review* 21.1: 3-17.

Claessen, H.J.M., and P. Skalnik
  1978   'The Early State: Theories and Hypotheses', in *The Early State* (ed.
          H.J.M. Claessen and P. Skalnik; The Hague: Mouton): 3-29.

Cohen, R., and E.R. Service (eds.)
  1978   *Origins of the State: The Anthropology of Political Evolution*
          (Philadelphia: Institute for the Study of Human Issues).

Coote, R.B., and K.W. Whitelam
  1987   *The Emergence of Early Israel in Historical Perspective* (Sheffield:
          Almond Press).

Davies, P.R.
  1992   'In Search of "Ancient Israel"' (Sheffield: JSOT Press).
  1995   'Method and Madness: Some Remarks on Doing History with the
          Bible', *JBL* 114: 669-705.

Dever, W.G.
  1985   'Syro-Palestinian and Biblical Archaeology', in *The Hebrew Bible and
          its Modern Interpreters* (ed. D.A. Knight and G.M. Tucker; Chico, CA:
          Scholars Press): 31-74.
  1986   'Late Bronze Age and Solomonic Defenses at Gezer: New Evidence',
          BASOR 262: 9-34.
  1991   'Archaeology, Material Culture and the Early Monarchical Period in
          Israel', in *The Fabric of History: Text, Artifact and Israel's Past* (ed.
          D.V. Edelman; JSOTSup, 127; Sheffield: JSOT Press): 103-15.

1992   'Unresolved Issues in the Early History of Israel: Toward a Synthesis
            of Archaeological and Textual Reconstructions', in *The Politics of
            Exegesis: Essays in Honor of Norman K. Gottwald on his Sixty-Fifth
            Birthday* (ed. D. Jobling, P.L. Day and G.T. Sheppard; Cleveland:
            Pilgrim): 195-207.

1993   'Biblical Archaeology: Death and Rebirth?', in *BATS*: 706-22.

1994a   'From Tribe to Nation: State Formation Processes in Ancient Israel',
            in *Nuove fondazioni nel Vicino Oriente Antico: Realta e ideologica*
            (ed. S. Mazzoni; Pisa: University of Pisa): 213-28.

1994b   'Archaeology, Texts, and History-Writing: Toward an Epistemology',
            in *Uncovering Ancient Stones: Essays in Memory of Neil Richardson*
            (ed. L.M. Hopf; Winona Lake, IN: Eisenbrauns): 105-17.

1995   'Will the Real Israel Please Stand Up? Archaeology and Israelite
            Historiography. Part I', *BASOR* 297: 61-80.

1996a   'The Identity of Early Israel: A Rejoinder to Keith W. Whitelam',
            JSOT 72: 3-24.

1996b   'Revisionist Israel Revisited: A Rejoinder to Niel Peter Lemche',
            CR:BS 4: 35-50.

in press a 'On listening to the Text—and the Artifacts', in *Echoes of Many
            Texts: Reflections on Jewish and Christian Traditions* (ed. W.G. Dever
            and J.E. Wright; Atlanta: Scholars Press).

in press b 'Archaeology and the "Age of Solomon": A Case-study in
            Historiography', in *The Age of Solomon: Scholarship at the Turn of
            the Millennium* (ed. L.K. Handy; Leiden: Brill).

in press c 'Israelite Origins and the "Nomadic Ideal": Can Archaeology
            Separate Fact from Fiction?', in *Mediterranean Peoples in Transition:
            Thirteenth to Tenth Centuries BCE* (ed. H. Silberman; Marbelstone,
            NY: New York University).

Edelman, D.V. (ed.)
1991   *The Fabric of History: Text, Artifact and Israel's Past* (Sheffield: JSOT
            Press).

Falconer, S.E.
1987   'Heartland of Villages: Reconsidering Early Urbanism in the Southern
            Levant' (unpublished PhD dissertation, University of Arizona).

Finkelstein, I.
1988   *The Archaeology of the Israelite Settlement* (Jerusalem: Israel
            Exploration Society).

1996   'The Archaeology of the United Monarchy: An Alternative View', *Lev*
            28: 177-87.

Finkelstein, I., and N. Na'aman (eds.)
1994   *From Nomadism to Monarchy: Archaeological and Historical Aspects
            of Early Israel* (Jerusalem: Yad Izhak Ben-zvi).

Flanagan, J.W.
1988   *David's Social Drama: A Hologram of Israel's Early Iron Age*
            (Sheffield: Almond Press).

Flannery, K.V.
1972   'The Cultural Evolution of Civilizations', *Annual Review of Ecology
            and Systematics* 3: 399-426.

Frick, F.S.
1985   *The Formation of the State in Ancient Israel: A Survey of Models and Theories* (Sheffield: JSOT Press).
Fried, M.H.
1967   *The Evolution of Political Society: An Essay in Political Anthropology* (New York: Random House).
Friedman, J., and M.J. Rowlands (eds.)
1977   *The Evolution of Social Systems* (London: Duckworth).
Fritz, V.
1995   *The City in Ancient Israel* (Sheffield: Sheffield Academic Press).
Geus, C. de
1975   *The Tribes of Israel: An Investigation into Some of the Presuppositions of Martin Noth's Amphictyonic Hypothesis* (Assen: Van Gorcum).
Gottwald, N.K.
1979   *The Tribes of Yahweh: A Sociology of the Religion of Liberated Israel, 1250–1050 BCE* (Maryknoll, NY: Orbis Books).
Haas, J.
1982   *The Evolution of the Prehistoric State* (New York: Columbia University Press).
Halpern, B.
1995   'Erasing History, The Minimalist Assault on Ancient Israel', *BRev* 11.6: 26-35, 47.
Herzog, Z.
1992   'Administrative Structures in the Iron Age; and Settlement and Fortification in the Iron Age', in *The Architecture of Ancient Israel from the Prehistoric to the Persian Periods* (ed. A. Kempinski and R. Reich; Jerusalem: Israel Exploration Society): 223-30, 231-74.
in press   *The Archaeology of the City: Architectural and Social Perspectives on City Planning in Ancient Israel.*
Hodder, I.
1986   *Reading the Past: Current Approaches to Interpretation in Archaeology* (Cambridge: Cambridge University Press).
Hodder, I., and C. Orton
1976   *Spatial Analysis in Archaeology* (Cambridge: Cambridge University Press).
Holladay, J.S.
1995   'The Kingdoms of Israel and Judah: Political and Economic Centralization in the Iron IIA–B ca. (1000–750 BCE)', in *ASHL*: 369-98.
Jamieson-Drake, D.W.
1991   *Scribes and Schools in Monarchy in Judah: A Socio-Archaeological Approach* (Sheffield: Almond Press).
Khoury, P.S., and J. Kostiner (eds.)
1990   *Tribes and State Formation in the Middle East* (Berkeley: University of California Press).
Kolb, F.
1984   *Die Stadt im Altertums* (Munich: C.H. Beck).

Lemche, N.P.
    1985   *Early Israel: Anthropological and Historical Studies on the Israelite*
                Society before the Monarchy (Leiden: Brill).
    1996   'Early Israel Revisited', *CR:BS* 4: 9-34.
Lemche, N.P., and T.L. Thompson
    1994   'Did Biran Kill David? The Bible in the Light of Archaeology', *JSOT*
                64: 3-22.
Mazar, A.
    1990   *Archaeology of the Land of the Bible, 10,000–586 BCE* (Garden City,
                NY: Doubleday).
Provan, I.W.
    1995   'Ideologies, Literary and Critical: Reflections on Recent Writing on the
                History of Israel', *JBL* 114: 585-606.
Renfrew, C.
    1972   'Beyond a Subsistence Economy: The Evolution of Social
                Organization in Prehistoric Europe', in *Reconstructing Complex*
                Societies (ed. C.B. Moore; Cambridge, MA: American Schools of
                Oriental Research): 69-85.
Sahlins, M.D.
    1968   *Tribesmen* (Englewood Cliffs, NJ: Prentice–Hall).
Service, E.R.
    1962   *Primitive Social Organization: An Evolutionary Perspective* (New
                York: Random House).
    1975   *Origins of the State and Civilization: The Process of Cultural*
                Evolution (New York: Norton).
Shiloh, Y.
    1980   'The Proto-aeolic Capital and Israelite Ashlar Masonry' (Jerusalem:
                Hebrew University).
Tainter, J.A.
    1988   *The Collapse of Societies* (Cambridge: Cambridge University Press).
Tapper, R.
    1990   'Anthropologists, Historians, and Tribespeople on Tribe and State
                Formation in the Middle East', in *Tribes and State Formation in the*
                Middle East (ed. P.S. Khoury and J. Kostiner; Berkeley: University of
                California Press): 48-73.
Thompson, T.L.
    1992   *Early History of the Israelite People from the Written and the*
                Archaeological Sources (Leiden: Brill).
    1995   'A Neo-Albrighteam School in History and Biblical Scholarship?',
                JBL 114: 683-705.
Webb, M.C.
    1975   'The Flag Follows Trade: An Essay on the Neccessary Interaction of
                Military and Commercial Factors in State Formation', in *Ancient*
                Civilizations and Trade (ed. J.A. Sabloff and C.C. Lamberg-
                Karlovsky; Albuquerque: University of New Mexico Press): 155-209.
Weippert, H.
    1988   *Palästina in vorhellenistischer Zeit* (Munich: Beck).

Whitelam, K.W.
  1994   'The Identity of Early Israel: The Realignment and Transformation of Late Bronze–Iron Age Palestine', *JSOT* 63: 57-87.
  1996   'The Invention of Ancient Israel', in *The Silencing of Palestinian History* (London: Routledge).

Wright, H.T.
  1977   'Recent Research on the Origin of the State', *ARA* 6: 379-97.

Yadin, Y.
  1958   'Solomon's City Wall and Gate at Gezer', *IEJ* 8: 80-86.

The Urban Center of Jerusalem and the Development of the Literature of the Hebrew Bible

Ehud Ben Zvi

Among the most conspicuous and perhaps the most significant tendencies in recent biblical studies,[1] three are central to the argument developed in this paper: (1) an increasing awareness of the literary aspects of biblical literature, and along with it, a widespread appreciation of the high level of the literary sophistication of its writers and of their intended audience; (2) a prevailing tendency to claim that the majority of books in the Hebrew Bible (at least in their present form) were composed in Judah (Hebrew Yehud);[2] and (3) a trend to date much of the Hebrew Bible in its present form to the postmonarchic period in general, and to the Achaemenid era in particular.[3]

Contemporary with these developments in historico-critical biblical studies, population studies concerning ancient Judah and Jerusalem began to appear (e.g. Broshi 1975; Shiloh 1980; Finkelstein 1990; Broshi and Finkelstein 1992; Zorn 1994). Since most biblical scholars prefer Achaemenid Judah and Jerusalem as the setting of the writing of most biblical books as we now know them, population studies concerning this period are the most relevant to the goals of this paper. Carter (1994) has estimated the population of Judah at 10,850 for Persian I (c. 538–450 BCE) and 17,000 for Persian II (c. 450–332 BCE)

---

1. Within the context of this paper, the term 'biblical' has the meaning of 'relating to the Hebrew Bible'. A more precise, but more cumbersome term would be 'Hebrew–biblical'.

2. See, for example, from three significantly different perspectives, Barstad (1988), Seitz (1991: 205-207) and Davies (1992: 94-112). Similar claims have, of course, been made in the past, but there is a clear tendency today to associate more and more books and texts with Judah, including so-called 'Deutero-Isaiah' and Ps. 137.

3. An alternate position that has been advanced with renewed impetus is to associate much of this literature with the Hellenistic Period (Lemche 1993; Cryer 1994). For a critique of this position, see below.

Periods. According to him, there were between 1250 and 1500 inhab-itants in Jerusalem during Persian II Period (i.e. between 7.4 per cent and 8.8 per cent of the population of Judah). Broshi (1975) more gen-erously estimated 4800 inhabitants at that time.[4]

More or less contemporaneous with, but independent from these studies, are a significant number of works which have addressed (directly or indirectly) the question of the approximate size of the social layer that enjoyed high literacy (as opposed to other levels and kinds of 'practical' literacy) in ancient Near Eastern societies, for example, Goody (1975), Baines (1983), Baines and Eyre (1983), Harris (1989) and Ray (1994).[5] Estimates concerning the different types of literacies, and especially high literacy, are highly speculative. But to illustrate the range in which discussion is conducted, one may note that Ray (1994: 64-65) has estimated that one third or one quar-ter of 1 per cent of the Egyptian population of the middle of the fourth century BCE was 'fully conversant with script and the writing of [demotic] literature' (cf. Baines 1983: 584).

The goal of this paper is not to evaluate these studies, but to explore issues and ponder heuristic questions resulting from the integration of the studies, especially issues and questions concerning the Hebrew Bible and those who produced it.

The most obvious of these issues relate to (1) the socio-political cir-cumstances involved in high literacy, and (2) the associated issue of dating. The literati were only a subgroup of the section of the popula-tion that did not produce 'tangible goods' in the agrarian society of Judah. The education and maintenance of the Judahite literati (that is, those whose reading competence included works of the complexity shown by recent studies in biblical literature), must have required a

4.   Broshi and Carter agree that the size of Jerusalem was approximately 120 dunams, but they differ concerning the population coefficient (Carter estimates c. 25 and Broshi estimates c. 40 inhabitants per dunam). The most significant difference between the two estimates, however, is that Carter excludes the public area from the area to be multiplied by the population coefficient (cf. Zorn 1994: 32, 36, 44). Such an approach results in major changes in estimates for Achaemenid Jerusalem, given its religious and administrative roles. In fact, Carter assumes that slightly more than half of the 120 dunams of Achaemenid Jerusalem were non-housing, 'public space' (Carter 1994: 134-35).

5.   For a discussion of the 'written word' in ancient Greece that is significantly different from that of Mesopotamia or Egypt, see Beard *et al.* (1991) and Thomas (1992, 1994).

significant investment of local resources, even if they numbered about the same as that in late Egypt (i.e. c. 0.25–0.33 per cent of the population[6]), and even more so if the ratio of literati to general population was higher in Judah. It might be reasonable to assume a relatively larger service sector in Achaemenid Jerusalem than one might expect for a small provincial center, especially during the Persian II Period. Given the 'restoration theology' at work in Judah, a tradition about the historical ratio of population between Jerusalem and Judah in late monarchic times (estimated to be about 1 to 3 in the late seventh century BCE, which is extremely high for an agrarian society; cf. Lenski 1966: 199-201; Lenski, Lenski and Nolan 1991: 181; Broshi and Finkelstein 1992: 54), may have had an influence on the discourse of Judah. A more significant, but related, element was the social, political and economic role of the temple in Judah. Tendencies toward commercialization and even militarization in Judah, as described by Hoglund (1991: 60-64), may have contributed to the growth of a service sector. In fact, if one assumes that the ratio of the service sector to the total population is roughly like that of Jerusalem to Judah, then one must acknowledge that the latter ratio still seems to be on the higher side of the normal parameters in agrarian societies, though not as unusual as in the late monarchic times.[7] Of course, these considerations should not blur the fact that the population of Achaemenid Jerusalem was only about 6 per cent of late monarchic Jerusalem. Yet the urban center in which most of the Hebrew Bible, as we know it, was composed was Achaemenid Jerusalem, not monarchic Jerusalem. Significant issues concerning resources and absolute numbers follow from these observations.

The presence of a group of literati, and of a number of literati that is proportionally higher than expected in relation to the total population of a small province, presupposes (1) the availability of the resources necessary for educating and continuously supporting their activities (including writing, reading, re-reading, copying, training of readers and copyists, etc.), and (2) a need for such activity in society.

The availability of resources in itself presupposes the existence of a center of power in Jerusalem able to control the resources of Judah

6.   Of course, Egypt was not a small, relatively unpopulated province with very limited resources, as Judah was.

7.   Carter (1994: 138) estimated the population of Jerusalem to be between 7.4–8.9 per cent of the population of Judah.

efficiently and channel them according to its priorities. Therefore, it is reasonable to associate most of the biblical literary activity usually assigned to the Persian Period (and, of course, its outcome, the bulk of biblical literature) with a period that follows rather then precedes: (1) the establishment of an efficient urban center controlling Judah's resources, (2) the establishment of the Jerusalemite temple (e.g. Blenkinsopp 1991: 22-26, 37-39; Davies 1992: 110-12, 116-18) and, (3) the beginning of the major increase in population and settlements in Judah that separates the Persian I and II Periods (cf. Davies 1992: 94-112). In other words, the historical circumstances of the Persian II Period were more conducive to this literary activity than those of the Persian I Period.

The ability to draw on the internal resources of Judah depended on a theology (or ideology) that legitimized the role of Jerusalem and its temple. This theology also could have contributed to the ability of Jerusalem to draw resources from non-Judahite 'Israel'. Although at times some emphasis has been placed on these 'independent', non-Judahite resources (cf. Carter 1994: 140 and bibliography), caution about their actual extent and their 'independence' is warranted. There is not much non-biblical information about the demographic and economic potential of non-Judahite 'Israel' in the Achaemenid Period (for example, there are no archaeological data comparable to that about Judahites), nor about the extent of their actual contribution to the economy of Judah. As for the biblical sources, the more the literary output of the postmonarchic period is associated with Judah, the less can be said about the potential resources of these 'exiles' (as a social group), and of their ability to support literati and 'teachers' in exile, let alone in Judah. Furthermore, given the formative character of the image of the 'exile' (and of the 'exiles') in the self-definition of Israel in Achaemenid Judah, caution advises against taking at face value the historicity of biblical references to the contributions of the 'exile' and 'exiles' to the constitution and maintenance of the center at Jerusalem, and especially its details (see, for instance, Ezra 2).[8] But even if for the sake of the argument one were to take them at face value, they would not point to a permanent flow of wealth from Judahites living outside Judah to Jerusalem, but to a single 'momentous' event in the life of the Jerusalem community. Significantly, the seemingly innocent passing reference to wealthy individuals who arrived in Jerusalem

8. On the image of the 'exile', see Ben Zvi (1995b).

from Babylon and who provided (substantially) from their own resources to the Judahite center (Zech. 6.10-14) is written in such a way that clearly implies that such a donation was considered to be exceptional (Zech. 6.14).

Of course, there are biblical texts that maintain that, on occasion, the Persian center 'encouraged' non-Judahites to donate to the temple (Ezra 1.4-6; 7.13-20). It is certainly possible that these texts reflect one of the ways used by the Persian center to channel resources to Jerusalem, or Judah to fulfill its policies, that is, to resort to 'private donations'. But if so, the latter are to be associated with, rather than disassociated from, Persian policies and their implementation. Note that these donations are usually mentioned in biblical texts together with those of the Persian king (e.g. Ezra 1.1-8; 7.13-20).[9]

Indeed, external resources and policies affecting the availability of resources in Achaemenid Judah played a *crucial role* in the development of the province and its center. In fact, the re-establishment of an efficient regional center in Jerusalem and of its temple were not only allowed by the Achaemenid center of power, but it actually provided the conditions necessary for, and allocated resources to these endeavors (Ezra 1.1-4, 5.13; Blenkinsopp 1991: 37-39; Carter 1994: 139-45). Moreover, the development of settlements, the subsequent increase of the population and the accompanying socio-economic development of Judah in the Persian II Period is likely related to Achaemenid initiative and purposes (Carter 1994: 112-27; Hoglund 1991; Hoglund 1992: 165-205; Davies 1992: 78-87; Ben Zvi 1995b: 125-29). If such was the historical background of the literary activity that resulted in the creation of biblical literature,[10] one would expect

---

9. Regarding the yearly charge of a third part of a shekel for the service of the temple (Neh. 10.33), the text (even if taken at face value) does not suggest that it was imposed over those who did not belong to the temple community, nor that it was collected from non-Judahites. Historical considerations also do not support the case for a third of a shekel from the diaspora in analogy to the half-shekel of later times.

10. This paper does not address the question of whether the resources required for this literary activity were channeled to the literati directly through the temple (which in this case, would play role of an [institutional] patron), or also, at times, through 'private' individuals ('private patrons') whose activity and resources were related, in one way or another, with the temple and the economic and political center of Jerusalem (cf. with a somewhat later figure such as a Joseph b. Tobias). The issue is significant, but (1) its study deserves a separate investigation, and (2) the possible

that such a background would be reflected not just in particular books or sections of books, but mainly in some of those features that are ubiquitous in biblical literature, because such features do not depend on a particular genre, style and theological message.

For example, the Persian empire is never mentioned in the 'oracles against the nations' found in the Latter Prophets, whereas other imperial powers, such as Assyria, Babylon and Egypt, figure prominently there. This feature is consistent with historical circumstances.[11] Such issues as the role of the Persian ruler in God's economy in books as distant as Isaiah and Chronicles may also be addressed from this perspective.[12]

Since Jerusalemite control of the resources of Judah was a *sine qua non* for the literati, it is easily understandable why a Jerusalemocentric tendency permeates the Hebrew Bible (Ben Zvi 1995b). The fact that the province of Judah could not have existed without a theological basis legitimizing its social and political structures, nor could the temple have held any of its (systemic) roles without an accepted theological basis explains, at least in part, the need for such a literature from the perspective of the center and of those who had a vested interest in its stability. Furthermore, this Jerusalemo-centrism was not only necessary for the existence of Judah and Jerusalem with the temple at their center, but also provided the literati who inscribed this theology, as well as all who accepted this Jerusalemo-centered approach, with a sense of self-identity as part of 'Israel'. At the same time, the work of these literati strongly contributed to the particular shaping of the socio-theological concept of 'Israel' conveyed by biblical literature. Thus, these literati shaped the theology of their center and were, along with other elite and non-elite Judahite groups, shaped by it.

conclusions of that investigation will not strongly affect the validity of the arguments advanced in this paper.

11. The only text in which the Persians seem to be condemned, though they are not mentioned by name, is the prayer in Neh. 9.36-37. The prayer is unusual in other regards too, and it has been dated to the Neo-Babylonian Period (see Williamson, 1990: 56-57 and bibliography).

12. See Isa. 44.28, 45.1-7, and 2 Chron. 36.22-23. See also Ben Zvi (1993: 216-49), and Japhet's (1994: 216) conclusions concerning the historical view of the author of Ezra–Nehemiah.

The work of the literati in the Judahite society could not have been accomplished if they had restricted themselves to being just writers and readers of the (traditional) divine instruction that 'Israel' was to follow. It is true that this role provided them with a theological justification for their center, for the support of their activities by their center, and with a story about themselves that legitimized their work and vested it with theological authority. It is also true that they fulfilled this role by writing and reading and rereading written texts, their work should exhibit a pervasive emphasis on the authority of the written word, and of words and language in general, as it actually shows (e.g. Exod. 31.18; Deut. 17.18; Josh. 1.8; 2 Kgs 14.6; Ezra 3.4; Neh. 8.14; 2 Chron. 30.18); significantly, it seems that there was a general trend towards an emphasis on the authority of the written word in the Achaemenid empire (see Lewis 1994: 17-32). Nevertheless, the theology that they developed had to be articulated to the general public. Communication of a text-based theology grounded on the divine authority of the written word (a common claim in biblical literature) *required* by necessity the presence of those who could read these texts competently, so they could serve as brokers of the divine knowledge to the public (cf. Neh. 8). The more highly educated the readers of these texts were required to be, the more indispensable was the role of the literati themselves, that is, those who not only re-read this literature 'day and night' (cf. Ps. 1.2; Josh. 1.8; Deut. 17.18-19) but also wrote it.

Other issues may emerge from the approach taken here. For example, the pervasive references in the Hebrew Bible (e.g. Isa. 18.7; 45.14; Hag. 2.6-8; Zech. 14.16) to an almost mythical upgrading of the resources of the center at Jerusalem, through goods coming to it from all nations, may be better understood in the light of the small size and limited resources of the actual Jerusalem and its temple (for a study of this topos from a different perspective, see Clines 1995). That Jerusalem was actually limited may explain the (relative) emphasis on the 'great' Jerusalem and its temple: both of the now idealized past as well as the future (compare and contrast Carroll 1994). Another issue is the question of the possible historical and geographical settings of the composition of books that strongly depart from the expected 'norms'. For example, there is only one book in the Hebrew Bible which, strangely enough, does not exhibit a Jerusalem-centered theology, despite the fact that a Jerusalem-centered reference is somewhat expected given the claims in the narrative. That is, in the book of Esther, the fate of Jerusalem and its temple is not mentioned at all, despite its (literary) background of the obliteration of all the Jews in the Persian empire. The fact that even a passing reference to Jerusalem and especially to its temple does not 'sneak' into the text can be contrasted with, for instance, the situation in Judith (4.2-3, 6-7, 13-14; 9.13; 16.18-20), or even in later Esther texts.[13] This fact may be seen as suggestive of a horizon of thought and perhaps of geographical and historical circumstances that were particular to the community within which Esther was composed. Significantly, the mentioned feature is only one among several 'peculiarities' in Esther (for example, the lack of direct reference to the Lord and to any dietary laws [cf. Daniel]; its characterization—and even derision—of the Persian king, the consistent use of the gentilic יהודי meaning 'Jew').

If one accepts that most of the biblical literature—at the very least in its present form—was composed in Jerusalem and during (or even around) the Persian II Period, then significant issues emerge if one focuses on the *absolute number* of the Jerusalemite literati. Whether the proportion of highly educated, potential writers was 0.25 per cent of the population of Judah, or even somewhat higher, the total number of gifted writers who could have composed the books included in the Hebrew Bible was likely not more than a handful at any point in time in Persian II Jerusalem (cf. Davies 1992: 107-108; Thompson 1992: 392; Dever 1995: 73). The number of potential readers and re-readers was probably higher, but certainly very limited too. One may assume that these writers had other professional duties in addition to writing and reading and re-reading highly sophisticated literary texts (e.g. as priests, bureaucrats and/or teachers). That means, among other things, that most of biblical literature—at least in its present form—was likely written by a small number of part-time writers in a relatively short time. How then, does one explain the diversity of the Hebrew Bible? Is it conceivable that several groups of writers, each with its own theology and particular language, could have existed simultaneously but independently of each other in the same small urban center? How many distinct literary subgroups of few part-time writers can be supported (let alone identified) within the same, relatively small socio-political framework? Not only is the potential for subgroups certainly

13. See the Greek 'A-text' 5:22b; i.e., within addition 'C'. This text was probably not an integral part of the proto–AT (Fox 1991: 136).

limited, but even if they existed, it is unlikely that they possessed the resources to build the barriers necessary for the development of their separate and distinctive (literary) in-group 'dialects'. In short, it is difficult to assume that there were separate deuteronomistic, isaianic, jeremianic, chronistic and plethora of other circles of literati in early Second Temple Jerusalem. Therefore it is difficult, if not impossible, to explain the diversity among the books of the Hebrew Bible in terms of independent, socio-cultural subgroups of highly sophisticated writers (and readers).

Of course, not all the writings of the subgroups indicated above (for example, the books of Isaiah, Jeremiah, Ezekiel, Haggai, Zechariah, Kings, Chronicles, Proverbs, Songs and Job in their present form) had to be composed, read, re-read and redacted at the same time. But any attempt to explain their diversity mainly or only by temporal separation is beset with difficulties: (1) the Persian II Period lasted little more than one hundred years; (2) there is an element of conservatism inherent in the training process of new writers within the same, traditional, ancient Near Eastern center of power; (3) neither Judah nor Jerusalem suffered the socio-political and demographic discontinuities that would have led to corresponding discontinuities in the discourse and language of the Judahite intellectual elite;[14] (4) it is more likely than not that these texts were edited and redacted for several generations, and certainly they were (re)read by subsequent audiences that transformed them in one way or another, that is, the final version of the biblical text is not likely to be the end result of only a 'fleeting' moment of composition; (5) the literary repertoire of the highly educated members of each supposedly separate circle could not have consisted only of texts that were consistent with their use of language and style and their distinctive theological approach, because if this had this been the case, their literary repertoire and educational curriculum would have been too narrow; and (6) if every circle of writers, each on its own generation, was aware of the other's literature, the assumption that they *chose* to develop distinctive linguistic and theological features to characterize their own circle as different from the others is highly unlikely, and the more so within a basically traditional society.

---

14. That is not to say that 'nothing happened' during the Achaemenid Period. But even the supposed 'rebellion' of Zerubbabel (e.g. Ahlström 1993: 820-21) could not have had such an influence. In any case what is required to provoke cultural discontinuity *is repeated,* if not extreme socio-political and demographic discontinuities.

It may be claimed that the prospects of the notion of temporal separation are much better if a significant portion of the relevant literary work can be dated to either the period preceding the establishment of the Second Temple or to the Hellenistic Period. Yet, although some post-monarchic biblical works could have been written before the establishment of the Second Temple, or the re-establishment of Jerusalem as the urban regional center, the reasons mentioned above still suggest that the conditions during that time were far less conducive to the growth and maintenance of a local, highly literate cadre than those in the period thereafter.

The main administrative center of Neo-Babylonian Judah was most likely at Mizpah (cf. Jer. 40.5-6; 2 Kgs 25.22-23) (Miller and Hayes 1986: 423-24; Ahlström 1993: 798-99). The administrative center itself was small. Zorn (1994: 48) estimates that the population of Tell en-Nasbeh (likely biblical Mizpah), Stratum 2, was about 400–500 people. Still it might be claimed that it is plausible that (1) this new regional center begun to develop some legitimizing traditions about itself, and (2) this endeavor might have included the reshaping of older accepted traditions to suit this purpose. It is possible that some of these proposed Mizpah traditions found their way into the deuteronomistic historical narrative. Yet the Jerusalemo-centrism of the mentioned narrative, its clear association with Deuteronomy, its delegitimization of non-Davidic rulers, and the minimal references to Mizpah, all converge to undermine the idea of Mizpah as the location of the composition of the deuteronomistic historical narrative.[15] The proposal of an already existing, Deuteronomistic historical narrative composed in the monarchic period but edited in Mizpah not only presupposes the existence of such a pre-existing narrative (which is in itself a much debated and debatable issue) but also does not seem consistent with the thrust of 2 Kgs 25.21-26, 30, nor with the explicit 'empty land' conception expressed in 2 Kgs 25.21 (Ben Zvi 1995b). Moreover, there are indications that significant pericopes in the deuteronomistic narrative are later than the Neo-Babylonian Period (e.g. the Elijah cycle, and the Elisha narrative) (McKenzie 1991: 81-100).

Considerations concerning the 'world system' in general and the material conditions in Judah in particular suggest (though with less *puissance* than in the Neo-Babylonian case) that the circumstances in Achaemenid Jerusalem were likely to be more conducive to the

---

15. For a different approach see McKenzie (1996), esp. 292-95.

mentioned literary activity than those in Ptolemaic Jerusalem. The
resources of Judah during the Ptolemaic era were, in fact, not larger,
but probably smaller than those in the Achaemenid Period (Smith:
1990). Moreover, there is no indication that the Ptolemaic center
invested significant resources in Judah, as the Achaemenid seem to
have done. It seems more reasonable that the *bulk* of biblical literature
was written in the Persian rather than in the Ptolemaic Period.[16] To
move back into monarchic times or forward into the second century
BCE (or any time after 200 BCE) as a period for locating the bulk of
the biblical literature is more difficult. Biblical references to events
and circumstances that existed later than 587 BCE precludes a monarchic date for—at least—the present form of many books of the
Hebrew Bible. Books such as Sirach, Jubilees, CD, the Testament of
Moses (first version), and the work of Artaphanus in Egypt—among
many others—preclude a Seleucid or Maccabean date for much of the
biblical literature not only because they assume knowledge of biblical
works, but also because (1) their style and theological stances and
(2) the social and intellectual environments reflected in many of these
works are significantly different.

Thus, in sum, whereas some biblical texts may have been composed
in the Neo-Babylonian or Persian I Period, and others in the
Ptolemaic era, it is still more reasonable to assume that the bulk of
postmonarchic biblical literature (and in fact, the bulk of biblical literature as we know it) is more likely to be associated with the Persian
II Period than with any other time in Judah. Accordingly, the issue of
how to explain the diversity of biblical literature remains, in the main,
unresolved by the approaches discussed above. Thus explanations
other than temporal and social separation must be sought to account
for the variances in style and theology.

Just as the distinctive character of books such as Isaiah, Jeremiah,
Ezekiel, Jonah, Haggai, Job, Proverbs, Kings and Chronicles cannot
be explained by means of a corresponding sociological distinctiveness,
it cannot be explained either on the grounds of genre alone. Yet if an
essentially homogeneous group of writers developed a theological and
literary discourse showing such a diversity in both forms and contents,
then there *must* be a reason or reasons whose weight corresponds to
the effort required from the writers and readers.

16. Greek or Hellenistic ideas and topoi, or traces of them, do not necessarily
point to a post-332 BCE date for the composition of a biblical book.

Regarding contents, it seems reasonable to assume that the multi-vocal theological world created by the plurality of theological approaches and claims in each of the separate texts corresponds to, and was to a large extent necessitated by, the actual theological world of these literati, which may be characterized as one in which multiple claims are intertwined and shed light on one another (cf. Newsom 1996). If this is correct, it is more likely than not that this approach to theology and to its literary expressions will 'infiltrate' in one way or another some of the works written in this period. As I pointed out elsewhere, it is the case in books as distant from one another as Obadiah and Chronicles (Ben Zvi 1995a, 1996).

Since the style of a literary work serves also communicative purposes, the question arises as to what kind of literary messages were conveyed by the selection of one style over the other. For instance, prophetic literature is characterized as either 'monarchic' or 'relatively contemporaneous', for example, Isaiah versus Haggai (cf. Ben Zvi 1996: 264-65).[17] Do style and linguistic choices convey a sense of temporal distance, and perhaps of relative authority? Outside prophetic literature, similar considerations might apply to Chronicles and Samuel–Kings. Here, the likely conclusion is that the language of Samuel–Kings serves to convey a claim for antiquity and for a more authoritative voice than that of Chronicles (cf. Ben Zvi 1988). If so, the deuteronomistic history shows deuteronomistic characteristics not because it was written or read by an 'independent' group of deuteronomistic theologians (as opposed, for instance, to priestly or Ezekielian theologians), but because these characteristics convey a linkage between these texts and Deuteronomy, and accordingly, they carry a textually inscribed claim that associates these books with the authority of Moses and of the Mosaic tradition and Torah.

There are additional issues that emerge once one focuses on the limited number of literati, on the handful of 'biblical writers' in Achaemenid Jerusalem and on their 'part-time' literary activity. First, limited resources are more conducive to and likely result in (1) the

---

17. The main exception is, of course, the book of Jonah. Its language is not what one may have expected from a prophetic book set in the monarchic period, but Jonah is different from the other prophetic books in many additional aspects. In fact, it is debatable whether Jonah was first read as a prophetic book on a par with books such as Amos, Micah, and the like, or as a comment on, and perhaps interpretative key for the other prophetic books (cf. Jones 1995: 129-69).

utilization of pre-existing literary source in new works, even in different contextual and cotextual circumstances, and (2) a preference for editing and redacting over composing from the start. The traces left by these two tendencies are easily found across the full span of genres and particular styles in biblical literature. Secondly the limited capability of the Jerusalemite literati to produce new literature, copy books, read, reread and redact biblical texts most likely resulted in a limited repertoire. This will likely have implications for understanding and evaluating (1) the strong presence of a theological discourse that claims to reflect (monarchic and pre-monarchic) events, circumstances and traditions that were centuries apart from the time of the composition of the books, (2) the proposed intertwining of multiple theological voices and the associated role of multivocality in the shaping of the theological thought of the Jerusalemite literati and its textual expressions, that is, biblical literature (cf. Newsom 1996), and (3) the development of a canon of authoritative works, issues which must be left for another occasion.

BIBLIOGRAPHY

Ahlström, G.
1993   *The History of Ancient Palestine from the Paleolithic Period to Alexander's Conquest* (Sheffield: JSOT Press).
Baines, J.
1983   'Literacy and Ancient Egyptian Society', *Man* 18: 572-99.
Baines, J., and C.J. Eyre
1983   'Four Notes on Literacy', *Göttinger Miszellen* 61: 65-96.
Barstad, H.M.
1988   'On the History and Archaeology of Judah during the Exilic Period', OLP 19: 25-36.
Beard, M. *et al.* (eds.)
1991   *Literacy in the Roman World* (Ann Arbor, MI: Journal of Roman Archaeology Supplementary Series).
Ben Zvi, E.
1988   'The Authority of 1–2 Chronicles in the Late Second Temple Period', *JSP* 3: 59-88.
1993   'A Gateway to the Chronicler's Teaching', *SJOT* 7: 216-49.
1995a   'A Sense of Proportion: An Aspect of the Theology of the Chronicler', *SJOT* 9: 37-51.
1995b   'Inclusion in and Exclusion from Israel as Conveyed by the Use of the Term "Israel" in Postmonarchic Texts', in *The Pitcher Is Broken: Memorial Essays for Gösta W. Ahlström* (ed. S.W. Holloway and L.K. Handy; Sheffield: JSOT Press): 94-149.

1996   *The Historical–Critical Study of the Book of Obadiah* (Berlin: de Gruyter).

Blenkinsopp, J.
1991   'Temple and Society in Achaemenid Judah', in *Second Temple Studies 1* (ed. P.R. Davies; Sheffield: JSOT Press): 22-53.

Broshi, M.
1975   'La population de l'ancienne Jérusalem', *RB* 82: 5-14.

Broshi, M., I. and Finkelstein
1992   'The Population of Palestine in Iron Age II', *BASOR* 295: 31-48.

Carroll, R.P.
1994   'So What Do we Know about the Temple? The Temple in the Prophets', in *Second Temple Studies 2: Temple Community in the Persian Period* (ed. T.C. Eskenazi and K.H. Richards; Sheffield: JSOT Press): 34-51.

Carter, C.E.
1994   'The Province of Yehud in the Post-Exilic Period: Sounding in Site Distribution and Demography', in *Second Temple Studies 2: Temple Community in the Persian Period* (ed. T.C. Eskenazi and K.H. Richards; Sheffield: JSOT Press): 106-45.

Clines, D.J.A.
1995   'Haggai's Temple, Constructed, Deconstructed and Reconstructed', in *Interested Parties: The Ideology of the Writers and Readers of the Hebrew Bible* (JSOTSup, 205; Sheffield Academic Press): 46-75.

Cryer, F.H.
1994   'The Problem of Dating Biblical Hebrew and the Hebrew of Daniel', in *In the Last Days: On Jewish and Christian Apocalyptic and its Period* (ed. K. Jeppesen, K. Nielsen and B. Rosenthal; Aarhus: Aarhus University Press): 185-98.

Davies, P.R.
1992   *In Search of 'Israel'* (Sheffield: JSOT Press).

Dever, W.G.
1995   'Will the Real Israel Please Stand Up? Archaeology and Israelite Historiography: Part I', *BASOR* 297: 61-80.

Finkelstein, I.
1990   'A Few Notes on Demographic Data from Recent Generations and Ethnoarchaeology', *PEQ* 122: 47-52.

Fox, V.
1991   *The Redaction of the Books of Esther* (Atlanta: Scholars Press).

Goody, J. (ed.)
1975   *Literacy in Traditional Societies* (Cambridge: Cambridge University Press).

Harris, W.V.
1989   *Ancient Literacy* (Cambridge, MA: Harvard University Press).

Hoglund, K.
1991   'The Achaemenid Context', in *Second Temple Studies 1* (ed. P.R. Davies; Sheffield: JSOT Press): 54-72.

1992   *Archaemenid Imperial Administration in Syria–Palestine and the Missions of Ezra and Nehemiah* (Atlanta: Scholars Press).

Japhet, S.
  1994   'Composition and Chronology in the Book of Ezra-Nehemiah', in
            Second Temple Studies 2: Temple Community in the Persian Period
            (ed. T.C. Eskenazi and K.H. Richards; Sheffield: JSOT Press): 189-
            216.

Jones, B.A.
  1995   *The Formation of the Book of the Twelve: A Study in Text and Canon*
            (Atlanta: Scholars Press).

Lemche, N.P.
  1993   'The Old Testament—A Hellenistic Book?', *SJOT* 7: 163-93.

Lenski, G.
  1966   *Power and Privilege* (New York: McGraw–Hill).

Lenski, G., J. Lenski and P. Nolan
  1991   *Human Societies* (New York: McGraw–Hill).

Lewis, M.
  1994   'The Persepolis Tables: Speech, Seal, and Script', in *Literacy and
            Power in the Ancient World* (ed. A.K. Bowman and G. Woolf;
            Cambridge: Cambridge University Press): 17-32.

McKenzie, S.L.
  1991   *The Trouble with Kings* (Leiden: Brill).
  1996   'Cette royauté qui fait problème', in *Israël construit son histoire* (ed.
            A. de Pury, T. Römer and J.-D. Macchi; Genève: Labor et Fides): 267-
            95.

Miller, J.M., and J.H. Hayes (eds.)
  1986   *A History of Ancient Israel and Judah* (Philadelphia: Westminster).

Moore, C.A.
  1997   *Daniel, Esther and Jeremiah: The Additions: A New Translation with
            Introduction and Commentary* (New York: Doubleday).

Newsom, C.A.
  1996   'Bakhtin, the Bible, and Dialogical Truth', *JR* 76: 290-306.

Ray, J.
  1994   'Literacy in Egypt in the Late and Persian Periods', in *Literacy and
            Power in the Ancient World* (ed. A.K. Bowman and G. Woolf;
            Cambridge: Cambridge University Press): 51-66.

Seitz, C.R.
  1991   *Zion's Final Destiny: The Development of the Book of Isaiah*
            (Philadelphia: Fortress Press).

Shiloh, Y.
  1980   'The Population of Iron Age Palestine in the Light of a Sample
            Analysis of Urban Plans, Areas, and Population Density', BASOR 239:
            25-35.

Smith, R.B.
  1990   'The Southern Levant in the Hellenistic Period', *Lev* 22: 123-20.

Thomas, R.
  1992   *Literacy and Orality in Ancient Greece* (Cambridge: Cambridge
            University Press).

1994   'Literacy and the City-State in Archaic and Classical Greece', in
            Literacy and Power in the Ancient World (ed. A.K. Bowman and G.
            Woolf; Cambridge: Cambridge University Press): 33-50.
Thompson, T.L.
    1992   *Early History of the Israelite People from the Written and the
            Archaeological Sources* (Leiden: Brill).
Williamson, H.G.M.
    1990   'Isaiah 63,7–64,11: Exilic Lament or Post-exilic Protest', *ZAW* 102:
            48-58.
Zorn, J.R.
    1994   'Estimating the Population of Ancient Settlements: Methods,
            Problems, Solutions and a Case Study', *BASOR* 395: 31-48.

THE ANCIENT EGYPTIAN 'CITY': FIGMENT OR REALITY?

Donald B. Redford

For nearly 40 years, since the published judgments of the late John
Wilson (1960), conventional wisdom has denied the term 'urban' to
ancient Egypt. And while an *a priori* definition underlies any such
denial, it is nonetheless a fact that anyone who studies Egypt in depth
would be struck by the absence of what, elsewhere in Western Asia
and the Mediterranean, we all would call a 'city'. Why should this be?
Why, when an undeniably complex society appeared (relatively suddenly) in the Nile Valley, should it have taken the form of a 'territorial state' rather than an agglomeration of metropolitan areas (Wenke
1991: 286; Trigger 1993).

Of the three basic types of what might be called 'organic' settlements (as opposed to state-sponsored, purpose-specific construction)
which appear everywhere in the ancient world, namely, metropolitan
states ('city-cum-territory'), town of parochial/agricultural purview,
and farm-centre, Egypt knows of only two. This can be stated, not so
much on the basis of taxonomic discussion, nor even on the archaeological record, but rather from the ancients' vocabulary of self-
definition. If the jargon is subjected to scrutiny, the perception of the
ancients and the reality itself will quickly emerge as one.[1]

The Egyptians had many terms for communal settlement. Most

1.   Clearly, the exponents of a culture must have their nomenclature heard first,
in whatever realm of investigation: we moderns inevitably suffer a handicap in our
estimation of the ancients, evident in our feeble attempts at categorization. Our
definitions of 'city' range from a simple 'rank-size' criterion (O'Connor 1990: 14-
15), to considerations of political power (Hoffman, 1986: 175), to density, social
stratification, and reliance on the subsistence base of a hinterland (Dever 1993: 99-
100). It is probably better to stress distance, due to social stratification, separating
power elite from subsistence base. O'Connor (1993: 570-86) rightly advises a
flexible definition.

common is the word *neywet*, often rendered 'city', though without justification.[2] The earliest examples of the hieroglyph (see fig. 3, p. 227, in this volume), which occurs already in the Archaic Period, show a cluster of round-topped or conical huts, so arranged that they can easily be misinterpreted as empty space flanking crossroads.[3] While later applied to the largest settlements in Egypt, namely Thebes, Memphis, and Heliopolis, the word in origin clearly designated a cluster of huts or farm buildings within a protective enclosure.[4] Such a generic nuance of 'human occupation' (or the potentiality of human occupation), applied to *neywet,* that the sign (or even the fully written word), was sometimes added to words denoting merely *habitable* land.[5] Scarcely less common in the vocabulary of ancient Egypt is the word *dmit*, from a root meaning 'to touch' (Erman and Grapow 1971: V, 455: 6-7; Gardiner 1947: II, 1*; Valbelle 1985: 315-19). The derived noun referred to the point on the riverbank where ships touched and whence they sailed.[6] A third word, *i3t*, 'mound', was

2.   Erman and Grapow (1971: II, 210-12) and Bietak (1979: 99). For 'urban area' see, van den Boorn (1988: 174, 326).

3.   See Kapolony (1963: 51: 189 [Den?], 73: 276A, 74: 276B, 125: 748, 77: 287, 84: 315) and Kapolony (1964: 14 no. 29). The detailed hieroglyphs at Meidum suggest wattle and daub huts.

4.   Note how, in the roster of the Wilbour Papyrus, farmers and cultivators are listed in close proximity to the major *niwt*, while the intervening tracts, far removed from the *niwt*, are given over to herdsmen and stablemasters (for pasturage) (O'Connor 1972: 695).

5.   Examples include the following: 'Upper and Lower Egypt' (Sethe 1905-1909: 1277: 10); 'Egypt (*Kmt*)' (Faulkner 1962: 286); 'township (*sp3t*)' (Erman and Grapow 1971: IV, 97); 'estate', 'district' (Faulkner 1962: 319); the *Wese*, Theban township (Sethe 1928: 82); the 'district of Min' (Sethe 1905–1909: 1136: 5; Bietak 1979: 99-100). For this reason, and because the Egyptians distinguished between 'habitable' (the 'Black Land', i.e. Egypt) and 'uninhabitable' (i.e., *ḫst*, the infertile highland), names of foreign towns are most often denied the *niwt*-sign as determinative in favor of the 'hill-country-cum-throw-stick', even though they are designated as *dmi* (Sethe 1905–1909: 650: 6, 652: 9, 654: 7, 655: 12, 1297: 15, 1303: 5). The Thutmosid toponym list, made up in the main of settlement names, is captioned 'complete list of *foreign lands* of Retenu' (Sethe 1905–1909: 780: 4). The contrast is even more striking in the formal onomastica: all Egyptian towns have the *niwt*-sign, all the foreign towns have 'hill-country' signs (Gardiner 1947: III, iii.15–v. 10).

6.   See 'The Story of Sinuhe' B 12–13, which is revealing in this regard. The 'Afterlife' (*imntt*) is also a *dmi* which one 'reaches' after a water journey: *Lebensmüde*, 38-39.

largely confined to the Old Kingdom as a term for human settlement (Erman and Grapow 1971: 26: 9-15).[7] It refers to a protuberance whereon people planted their habitations to protect themselves from the annual inundation.[8] These three words, the most ancient generic words for centres of human settlement, were followed in the Middle and New Kingdom by others equally revealing. *Dmit* is provided with *mryt*, 'harbour', and *iw* (*n m3wt*), 'gezira' (Bietak 1979: 104), makes its appearance. A very small settlement, a hamlet sufficient for a single extended family, as designated by the term *wḥyt*, which also has the meaning 'extended family' (Gardiner 1947: II, 205*; Redford 1996). At the bottom of the scale, as it were, are terms compounded with personal names, to denote centres with a single nucleus: 'the villa (*bḫn*) of so-and-so' (Gardiner 1947: II, 204-205*),[9] 'the farmstead (*iḥw*) of so-and-so' (Erman and Grapow 1971: I, 118: 5-8), the 'house (*'t*) of so-and-so' (Erman and Grapow 1971: I, 160: 1-13).

One single, unmistakable point emerges from the roster of words we have passed in review: not one denotes in origin anything more than a collection of domiciles and storehouses serving farmers directly (Trigger 1993: 9). They are all essentially rural. Greek might render *niwt* by πολις and *dmit* by κώμη (Gardiner 1947: I, 1*; Westendorf 1977: 477, 547), but these are much later developments. To the ancients living beside the Nile River, no human community could be considered apart from its agricultural base: ranking by size was meaningless (Bietak 1979: 98-99).

It would seem, then, that the metropolitan state of Western Asia and the Mediterranean, with an elite separated from the agricultural basis of their existence by many social strata, does not find a parallel on the banks of the Nile River. Even in the largest settlements in Egypt, the 'elite' are so close to the farms which support them and their way of

7. See also *i3t Ḥr i3t Stš*, 'the mounds of Horus and Seth', designating the totality of human settlement in the 'Pyramid Texts' 480b, 961b–c; and Goedicke (1967: 108[65], 141: 27 [Q33, 'hillock']). The word later took on cultic significance (Redford 1986: 10-15).

8. On *geziras*, *levées* and 'turtle-backs' as optimal locations for settlements, see Butzer (1959: 34), Butzer (1976: 22-25), van Wesemael (1988: 129), and O'Connor (1990: 693).

9. The 'Onomasticon of Amenemope' appears to rank *bḫn* over a *wḥyt*, then continue with *pr* and *'t* before delving into the parts of a domicile (Gardiner 1947: II, 204-207*).

life as to be virtually indistinguishable from farming gentry. The most populous of the centres of human habitation are described as though they were bucolic, rural communities: in the encomium on Pi-Ramesses ('Ramessesburg'), the poet waxes eloquent over the barns, the cattle, the granaries, the ponds, the fish stocks, the fowl and the foliage which, for him, constitute the real attraction and essence of the settlement (Papyrus Anastasi iv.6,1-10; Papyrus Lansing 12,1-13a, 7). At Tell el-Amarna, ancient Akhetaten ('Solar–horizon–town'), the capital of Akhenaten, the villas of the highest magnates in the land remain country farmsteads in all essentials: for example, granaries, gardens, barnyards, cattle pens and aviaries (Ricke 1932). A glance at surviving census lists from Memphis and Thebes would fail to convince, without the accompanying headings, that one was pursuing an urban, rather than a rural, survey (Kitchen 1971: I: 263-80, VI: 749-50; Peet 1930: pls. 7-8).

If the terminology thus far examined strongly suggests a rural economy underpinning ancient settlements in the Nile Valley, there remains a term which does not quite fit the pattern emerging. The word $\underline{H}nw$ was formulated in the early stages in the development of the centralized Egyptian state in clear contradistinction to all other pre-existent communities in Valley or Delta.[10] The word means 'home', 'interior', as opposed to outlying district, and at the political level the 'Centre' where the king lived. All else was periphery.[11] The $\underline{H}nw$ comprised the residences (royal, aristocratic, ancillary), the storage facilities for their upkeep, the bureaux, the administrative buildings, ateliers, work-houses, armouries and barracks required to service the head of state and his entourage, no longer a chief, not even a paramount one, but a protégé and avatar of the falcon god on earth. It is the coming of this 'Perfect God' that signals the appearance on earth of the $\underline{H}nw$, the Centre *par excellence*, the royal residence at Memphis (O'Connor 1974: 19). And for all time, the third millennium BCE would be remembered as the 'Era of the $\underline{H}nw$' (Papyrus Merikare: 10; Helck 1977: 62). And even after the Memphite regime collapsed in anarchy, the concept of a 'Centre-cum-periphery' would live on in the

10. On $\underline{H}nw$, see Erman and Grapow (1971: III, 369: 16-370: 14), Posener-Krieger (1976: 47, 263 n. c) and Meeks (1982: III, 229).
11. On the workings of Centre and Preriphery, see Yoffee and Cowgill (1988: 11-14) and Champion (1989).

term *Itj-towy*, '(Amenemhet)–is–the–Grip(per)–of–the–Two-Lands', the name of the new capital of the 12th Dynasty.[12] This is the closest ancient Egypt could come to the notion of a city in the sense we moderns might appreciate it. Significantly, when the first true European city, Alexandria, appeared in Egypt, the natives called it, not *niwt*, but 'the Residence (*Hnw*) of the Greeks which is upon the shore of the sea' (Vercoutter 1949: 179), or 'the fort of king Alexander' (Steindorff 1906-1958: II, 14: 14), or the 'Grip(per) of the Two Lands' of Ptolemy II (Steindorff 1906-1958: II, 39: 3).

Other terms for settlement beyond the parameters of agricultural reference do not antedate the appearance of the *Hnw*, but in fact presuppose what is implied by its existence (Bietak 1986: 29-35). These include fortified centres of various sorts. Concomitant with the rise of complex society and a centralized state signalled by the *Hnw*, is the sudden appearance of a number of large, rectangular enclosures of mud-brick, attested both in the archaeological record and in the lexicon (Redford 1992: 24-28, fig. 2, pl. 3). Schematized hieroglyphic renderings of such structures abound in sealings and labels of the Archaic Period, and are attached lexically to such generic terms as 'mansion' (temple), fortified farmstead, enclosure-cum-ramp and walled fort. While the last suggests a defensive purpose, these words denote much more. The phenomenon of the ramp or mud-brick wall, closely tied as it is with the emergence of the state, betrays the presence of one of the most striking capabilities of the nascent polity, namely, the ability to amass and control a workforce on a massive scale. For the enclosures are designed as much for the concentration of human beings as they are for their protection. And so the state could at will bring together hosts of individuals when required for construction, for example, agriculture, quarrying, mining and war. And if the task was something more than *ad hoc* and transitory, the state might actually invest in *niwwt m3wt*, 'New Towns', in the outlying periphery (Goedicke 1967: 143-44; Badawy 1967: 103-104).

The terms thus far mustered in this investigation suggest the relatively sudden appearance of a highly centralized state with a 'Centre' at Memphis founded on a 'Periphery', constituting a welter of small, 'organic' communities of entirely agricultural purview. The artificial

---

12. On *Itj-towy*, see Gomàa (1987: 36-38). By attraction in Ptolemaic times Thebes was also called Itj-towy (Firchow 1957: 115).

creations of the new state included the 'Centre' itself and a series of fortified settlements wherein to concentrate revenue and workforce. Most of the latter were sited in the immediate environs of the 'Centre', but a number were strategically located on the new 'national' boundaries of which the state had become abruptly and self-consciously aware.

But is this the end of the matter? Is there nothing more than a network of farm hamlets on which is imposed a series of stalag-like work camps and a royal residence? Could such a rough-hewn system have effectively controlled a reach of the Nile Valley more than 800 km long from Aswan to the sea?

Indeed, there remains one further creation (rather than a modification of a prehistoric phenomenon) for which the state was responsible: the division of the 'Periphery' into townships or 'Nomes', each with its own capital. These have been called 'major centres for the collection of annual taxes on canals, cattle and other products' (Hassan 1993: 552; O'Connor 1974: 24), and the 'key links in the chain by which Egypt was integrated' (Hassan 1993: 567), thus suggesting they represent a full-fledged second tier in the administration, by which and through which the 'Centre' indirectly controlled the countryside. The evidence, however, points to a rather different arrangement. On the nomes and their *metropoleis*, textual sources provide extensive coverage in both the Old and New Kingdoms; and close examination proves a specific function. The nome capitals were set up to accomplish three things: (1) to organize the agricultural potential of the district and to see to the maintenance of the irrigation system, (2) to provide a court of law and a juridical mechanism for settling local disputes, and (3) to promote the interest of the 'Centre'. The latter, however, in the collection of revenues and the requisitioning of goods and services, consistently *by-passed* the nome structure and went *directly* to the peasantry. (The collection boats made the rounds of each jetty and mud flat; they did *not* collect everything at the harbour of the nome capital.)

Finally, in assessing the origin and structure of human settlement in the Nile Valley, one element has yet to be mentioned. To be added to the three ancient, generic words denoting 'town' are *st, pr* and *ḥm:* words for '(cult)-seat', 'house (scil. of god so-and-so)' and 'shrine', respectively. Both texts and (now) archaeology have demonstrated conclusively the centrality of the local *numen*, the 'town-god', in the thinking and social structure of the ancients. The presence of a local 'power' and the house within which it dwelled was as much a reason for human beings to congregate and locate their domiciles as any other 'practical' considerations (Hoffman 1979: 307).[13] The parochial shrine functioned as a nucleus for the human community and retained that function to the end of ancient Egyptian history (as the late name-forms *pr* + Divine Name, and Divine Name + πολις clearly show).[14] And when, at the turn of the fourth millennium BCE, the Pharaonic state claimed sway over Valley and Delta, it quickly put the phenomenon of the shrine-centred settlement to use in its own self-interest: for at the door of the house of god stood the central government's decree-stelae,[15] and in its environs the *ku*-chapel of the reigning king and his ancestors (Goedicke 1967: 44, 208; Habachi 1957: 11-43).

The circumstances of the advent of territorial unification and complex society make Egypt a rather special case. Unification came relatively suddenly, and was effected brutally. Both the personal names of the First Dynasty rulers and motifs and heraldic devices in art prove that the paramount chief who translated himself into the new status of 'king' did so by annihilating the opposition. On the morrow of the unification he stood as a colossus without rival, able to command the loyalty and absolute obedience of all inhabitants of Valley and Delta. When Pharaoh can within days, thanks to the transit corridor of the Nile River, make his will felt, recruit labour, and transfer revenues over hundreds of miles, why cultivate and promote the idea of spontaneously developing 'cities', other than the aforesaid 'stalags'? Egyptian terminology remains somewhat fuzzy to the end: while sometimes paying lip-service to size-ranking,[16] the three basic words investigated

---

13. On the importance of the *numina* in the late Predynastic and Archaic Periods, see Helck (1987: 70-76).

14. These tend to increase in the Late Period (Redford 1963: 119-22).

15. See Koptos R, 5-7 (Goedicke 1967), 'make copies of this decree and cause that they be... set on a sandstone stela at the gate of [every temple] where your monuments are so that the sons of the sons of the people may see it' (Goedicke 1967: fig. 28); Koptos B,48 (Goedicke 1967: fig. 8); and Koptos L, 8-9 (Goedicke 1967: fig. 17).

16. On *niwwt wḥywt*, 'cities and villages', see Sethe (1905–1909: 1231: 7). On *niwwt dmiw, wḥywt*, 'cities, towns, villages', see Davies (1903–1908: VI, pl. 27: 11).

here are confusingly interchanged, especially in the New Kingdom and later.[17] The dominance of the agricultural setting, in which human society and habitation found a natural and integral place, banished a concept of urbanism such as we would be familiar with from ancient Egyptian culture.[18]

17. *Niwt* is, in fact, gradually rendered obsolete, surviving only in NH, 'Thebes' (Westendorf 1977: 477). Even Memphis is a *dmi* (Erman and Grapow 1971: IV, 1308: 16), and so is Thebes (Sethe 1905–1909: 781: 1). Despite the fact that the list encompasses the largest settlements in Egypt, the geographical section of the 'Onomasticon of Amenemope' is prefixed only by *dmi* (Gardiner 1947 : II, 1*). The same word sometimes alternates with *mnnw*, 'fort' (Valbelle 1985: 316). Similarly, Asiatic settlements are mainly designated as *dmi* in Egyptian, no matter what the size (Sethe 1905–1909: 648: 5, 649: 3, 652: 9, 658: 7, 12, 13, 660: 8, 1304: 4, 15, 1305: 15, 17, 1306: 2, 1307: 4, 1310: 11, 1312: 2, 4, 8, 10, 19; Goedicke and Wente 1962: no. 85, pl. 93; Martin 1989: pl. 115). In the Levant, interestingly enough, the New Kingdom Egyptians carefully distinguish the Canaanite *dmi* and the *whywt* belonging to the *dmi* (Sethe 1905–1909: 676: 16, 697: 7-8 (cf. 1231: 7), 1303: 15, 1305: 18, 1306: 1, 1315: 1).

18. See the apt remarks of van den Boorn (1988: 107).

BIBLIOGRAPHY

Badawy, A.
1967   'The Civic Sense of Pharaoh and Urban Development in Ancient
        Egypt', *JARCE* 6: 103-109.
Bietak, M.
1979   'Urban Archaeology and the "Town Problem in Ancient Egypt"', in
        Egyptology and the Social Sciences (ed. K. Weeks; Cairo: American
        University in Cairo): 97-144.
1986   'La naissance de la notion de ville dans l'Egypte Ancienne, un acte
        politique?', *CRIPEL* 8: 29-35.
Boorn, G.P.F. van den
1988   *The Duties of the Vizier* (London: Kegan Paul).
Butzer, K.
1959   *Die Naturlandschaft Ägyptens während der Vorgeschichte und der
        dynastischen Zeit* (Mainz: Akademie Verlag).
1976   *Early Hydraulic Civilization in Egypt: A Study in Cultural Ecology*
        (Chicago: University of Chicago Press).
Champion, T.C. (ed.)
1989   *Centre and Periphery* (London: Unwin Hyman).
Davies, N. de G.
1903–1908   *The Rock Tombs at Amarna* (6 vols.; London: Egyptian Exploration
        Society).
Dever, W.G.
1993   'The Rise of Complexity in the Land of Israel in the Early Second
        Millennium BCE', in *BATS*: 98-109.
Erman, A., and H. Grapow
1971   *Wörterbuch des ägyptischen Sprache* (5 vols.; Berlin and Leipzig:
        Akademie Verlag).
Faulkner, R.O.
1962   *Concise Dictionary of Middle Egyptian* (Oxford: Oxford University
        Press).
Firchow, O.
1957   *Thebanische Tempelinschriften* (Berlin: Akademie Verlag).
Gardiner, A.H.
1947   *Ancient Egyptian Onomastica* (3 vols.; Oxford: Oxford University
        Press).
Goedicke, H.
1967   *Königliche Dokumente aus den Alten Reich* (Wiesbaden: Otto
        Harrassowitz).
Goedicke, H., and E. Wente
1962   *Ostraka Michaelides* (Wiesbaden: Richart).
Gomàa, F.
1987   *Die Besiedlung Ägyptens wärend des Mittleren Reiches* (2 vols.;
        Wiesbaden: Routledge).

Habachi, L.
1957   *Tell Basta* (Cairo: Institut Française Archéologie Orientale).
Hassan, F.A.
1993   'Town and Village in Ancient Egypt: Ecology, Society and Urbanization', in *The Archaeology of Africa: Food, Metals and Towns* (ed. T. Shaw et al.; London: Routledge): 551-69.
Helck, W.
1977   *Die Lehre für König Merikare* (Wiesbaden: Otto Harrassowitz).
1987   *Unters zur Thinitenzeit* (Wiesbaden: Otto Harrassowitz).
Hoffman, M.A.
1979   *Egypt before the Pharaohs* (New York: Knopf).
1986   'A Model of Urban Development for the Hierakonpolis Region from Predynastic through Old Kingdom Times', *JARCE* 23: 175-87.
Kapolony, P.
1963   *Inschriften der ägyptischen Frühzeit (Ägyptologische Abhandlung herausgegeben von W. Helck und E. Otto)* (Band 8, 3 vols.; Wiesbaden: Otto Harrassowitz).
1965   'Bemerkungen zu einigen Steingafässen mit archaischen Königs-names', *MDAIK* 20: 1-46.
Kitchen, K.
1971   *Ramesside Inscriptions* (Oxford: Basil Blackwell).
Martin, G.T.
1989   *The Memphite Tomb Chapel of Horemheb* (London: Egypt Exploration Society).
Meeks, D.
1982   *Année lexicographique* (3 vols.; Paris: Meeks).
O'Connor, D.
1972   'The Geography of Settlement in Ancient Egypt', in *Man, Settlement and Urbanism* (ed. P. Ucko et al.; London: Duckworth): 681-98.
1974   'Political Systems and Archaeological Data in Egypt: 2600–1780 BC', *WA* 6: 15-38.
1990   *Ancient Egyptian Society* (Pittsburgh: Carnegie Museum of Natural History).
1993   'Urbanization in Bronze Age Egypt and Northeast Africa', in *The Archaeology of Africa: Food, Metals and Towns* (ed. T. Shaw et al.; London: Routledge): 570-86.
Peet, T.E.
1930   *The Great Tomb Robberies of the Twentieth Egyptian Dynasty* (Oxford: Egypt Exploration Society).
Posener-Krieger, P.
1976   *Les archives du temple funéraire de Néferirkarê-Kakaï* (2 vols.; Cairo: Institut Française Archéologie Orientale).
Redford, D.B.
1963   'The Pronounciation of PR in Late Toponyms', *JNES* 22: 119-22.
1986   'New Light on Temple J at Karnak', *Or* 55: 10-15.
1992   *Egypt, Canaan, and Israel in Ancient Times* (Princeton: University University Press).
1996   'Remarks on Rainey's Remarks', *BASOR* 301: 77-81.

Ricke, H.
1932   *Der Grundriss des Amarna Wohnhauses* (Leipzig: Hinrichs).
Sethe, K.
1905–1909   *Urkunden der 18. Dynastie (Urk.* IV) (4 parts; Leipzig: Hinrichs).
1928   *Aegyptische Lesestuecke zum Grebrauch im akademischen Unterricht* (Leipzig: J.-C. Hinrichs Verlag).
Steindorff, G. (ed.)
1906–1958   Urkunden des ägyptischen Altertums (Leipzig and Berlin: Hinrichs).
Trigger, B.
1993   *Early Civilizations* (Cairo: American University).
Valbelle, D.
1985   'Précisions apportées par l'iconographie à l'un des emplois du mot *dmj*', in *Mélanges Gamal eddin Mokhtar* (2 vols.; Cairo: Institut Française Archéologie Orientale): 321-26.
Vercoutter, J.
1949   'Les Haou-Nebout', *BIFAO* 48: 107-209.
Wenke, R.
1991   'The Evolution of Early Egyptian Civilization: Issues and Evidence', *Journal of World Prehistory* 5: 279-327.
Wesemael, B. van
1988   *The Archaeology of the Nile Delta: Problems and Priorities* (ed. E.C.M. van den Brink; Amsterdam: Netherlands Foundation for Achaeological Research in Egypt).
Westendorf, W.
1977   *Koptisches Handwörterbuch* (Heidelberg: Carl Winter).
Wilson, J.A.
1960   'Egypt through the New Kingdom: Civilization without Cities', in *City Invincible* (ed. C.H. Kraeling and R. McC. Adams; Chicago: Oriental Institute): 124-36.
Yoffee, N., and G.L. Cowgill (eds.)
1988   *The Collapse of Ancient States and Civilizations* (Tucson: University of Arizona Press).

TEMPLE AS THE CENTER IN ANCIENT EGYPTIAN URBANISM

Carolyn Routledge

One of the most visible elements of the ancient Egyptian city, both in the past and in the archaeological remains of today, is the temple. This visual dominance has lead some scholars to place the temple at the center of their theories of urbanism, Wilson being perhaps the most memorable (Wilson 1960). Kemp (1972: 657) does not mince words in respect to this concept: 'The relationship between these two entities, temple and town, appears to have been fundamental in the fabric of ancient Egyptian society.' Furthermore, researchers stress this leading role for the temple from the beginning of urbanism through to the development of the mature city. For example, Bietak suggests that the temple was the catalyst for the first nucleated settlements in ancient Egypt (1979: 132), the nuclei around which the first planned settlements arose (1979: 115) and, in the New Kingdom, the epitome of all urban development as represented by the 'temple town' (1979: 131).

If the temple was so central to both the development and purpose of cities, it should be expected that the temple would form part of the 'archetype' of the city in ancient Egypt (*contra* Kemp 1981: 88). Archetype here means the underlying idea, both practical and conceptual, of what constituted a city for the ancient Egyptian. Theoretically, it should be possible to reconstruct this archetype of the city by examining the positioning of the temple in relation to other public buildings and residential areas. In other words, the ideology should be 'written' on the plan.

For ancient Egypt there are significant limitations on such a study. First, there are very few sites for which the relationship between the temples and the rest of the city is clear. In fact, most sites that are identified as large urban settlements have little beyond the temple excavated (due to older excavation methodology, modern settlement and cemeteries, rising ground water levels, etc.).[1] As a result, there is a limited sample from which to draw conclusions, and it would be wise to question whether the sample can be considered representative.

A second limitation is that important urban centers in Egypt were often occupied over a long period of time. Considering the incomplete nature of the excavation of these sites, it is often difficult to establish the contemporaneity of specific remains. As a result it can be difficult to know whether particular parts of a city were active when a particular temple was in use.

A third limitation is the necessity of planning around existing monuments. Again, the problem of a city being occupied over generations might change the planning of the city away from the ideal. Until the ideal form of the city is understood, it cannot be determined when the ideal had to be modified. In a modern context this situation is common in relation to heritage buildings remaining in 'inappropriate' locations when an area of a city is replanned. Thus, one should allow for similar decisions in the planning of ancient Egyptian New Kingdom cities located upon older sites.[2]

When the sites that are available for study from ancient Egypt are considered, it appears that there is an ideal subject in the city of Amarna, ancient Akhetaten (Kemp 1985). This city was occupied for a very limited period of time, probably no more than 20 years (O'Connor 1982: 19-20). The city was planned *de novo*, having been founded by Akhenaten as his capital city on a site that had no previous occupation (Kemp 1977a: 123). Also, the site was never reoccupied to any extent until modern times, and excavation has exposed large portions of the city, enabling a relatively accurate plan to be made (Fairman 1949: 36). Finally, the city is dated to the late eighteenth Dynasty (the fourteenth century BCE), a time of great wealth and power in Egypt, and thus reflects the 'mature' Egyptian state (Kemp 1989).

However, Amarna was not representative of a normal city, if it is hypothesized that the temple was central to the archetype of the city.

---

1.   Examples of royal cities that have poor exposure, but would offer important comparative materials for our knowledge of general city planning, include Memphis, Heliopolis and Tanis.

2.   That this is a factor in the planning of ancient Egyptian cities is indicated by the example of the city of Per-Ramesses, which was planned, apparently, to include the old Seth temple, but this temple maintained an orientation at odds with the other official buildings in that city (Bietak 1979: 119).

Akhenaten is believed to have built Amarna as part of his sweeping religious reforms that brought forward a new deity, the Aten, at the cost of all other deities. Such reforms should have an effect on the role of the temple in society and thus in the planning of the city.

Therefore, Amarna cannot be used to elucidate the typical ancient Egyptian city before first establishing just how this city was, or was not, typical.[3] Fortunately, there is another royal city from just slightly later that provides an excellent companion to Amarna, but under traditional religious influence. This is the site of Per-Ramesses at modern Qantir-Tell ed-Dab'a (Bietak 1985a). This site also represents the vision of a single ruler, Ramesses II, founded almost *de novo* as a new royal capital city.[4] Unfortunately, the site has only begun to be excavated and the preservation does not approach that found at Amarna (Pusch 1989). In order to supplement the information from this site, it is also necessary to consider evidence from Thebes, modern Luxor, the royal capital prior to Akhenaten's reign (Stadelmann 1986). This site suffers from several of the limitations that were noted earlier: it is a very old site occupied over a long period of time; many pharaohs had a hand in the planning of the site, probably offering several visions of the ideal city; and the site, while more exposed than Per-Ramesses, still awaits excavation beyond the major temple complexes and the palace complex of Amenhotep III.

Analysis of City Plans at Amarna, Per-Ramesses and Thebes

Amarna

Ancient Akhetaten was located in Middle Egypt on the east bank of the Nile River (fig. 1). The long, narrow city is believed to have been limited to the east bank of the Nile.[5] One monumental road, called the

3.   The possibility that Amarna is not a 'typical' city is admitted generally, but this fact often is downplayed or denied for many specific elements. For examples, see Kemp (1977a), Fairman (1949: 41-42), Badawy (1968: 55, 82-84), Bietak (1979: 121-23), O'Connor (1982: 19, 22, 24; 1989: 83), and Smith (1981: 315).

4.   While Tell ed-Dab'a had a long history as Avaris of the Hyksos, it was abandoned after the expulsion of the Hyksos (Bietak 1981) until the New Kingdom site was planned and built at the beginning of the nineteenth Dynasty. The planning and major building seems to be primarily the work of Ramesses II (Bietak 1979: 119; Kitchen 1982: 119-21).

5.   Akhenaten claimed the west bank as part of his city, according to his boundary stelae, but settlement was limited to the east bank. It is hypothesized that the west

'Royal Road' today, runs the entire length of the city (Kemp 1976: 96). Furthermore, Akhetaten is divided into several sectors that generally are considered to have been planned when the city was founded (Kemp 1989: 276; O'Connor 1989: 83; Bietak 1985b: 1240; Uphill 1988: 61). The interrelations of some of these sectors is unclear, due to lost river frontage and the fact that relatively large areas have not been excavated. Moving north to south these sectors are: (1) the North City: administrative buildings, residential palace, elite housing, north palace, great ramp or gate; (2) the North Suburb: noble, middle-class and lower-class housing; (3) the Central City: large temple, official palace, small temple, official administration (king's house, archives, police barracks, temple support) and bridge; (4) the South Suburb:

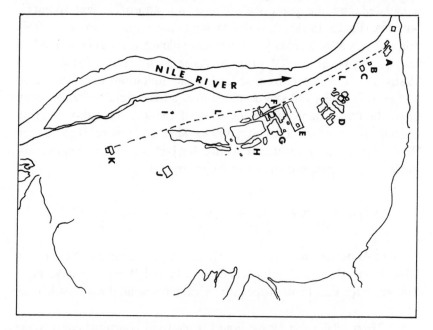

Figure 1. Sketch plan Amarna/Akhetaten (after Kemp 1985: 311-12). North City: A, residential palace; B, great ramp or gate; C, north palace. North Suburb: D, residential quarter. Central City: E, great temple to the Aten; F, official palace; G, official administration and lesser temple to the Aten. South Suburb: H, residential quarter; I, river 'temple'. South 'City': J, Kom el-Nana; K, Maru-Aten complexes. Royal Road: L, probable procession routes.

bank was used as agricultural land to supply the city (Bietak 1979: 123; Kemp 1989: 267-69).

noble and middle-class housing, and the so-called 'River Temple' (possibly a government harbour facility) (Bietak 1985b: 1241); and (5) the South 'City': the Kom el-Nana and Maru-Aten complexes.[6]

The interpretation of some of these buildings is controversial, and the loss of the river frontage may be critical to our understanding of the planning of this city. However, some generalizations can be made. It is clear that the central area of the city represents a nucleation of temples and official buildings. That this is not just a modern construct is indicated by a specific ancient name for this area, 'the island of the Sun-Disc, distinguished in Sed Festivals' (O'Connor 1989: 83). The main residential areas surround the Central City to the north and south. Beyond these residential areas lie two 'cities' centered on what is commonly identified as the royal residence, and on the Maru-complexes and the nearby Kom el-Nana buildings. Both of these areas seem to be primarily royal developments with religious undertones (cf. O'Connor 1989; O'Connor 1995: 285-86; Badawy 1956; Kemp 1989: 285).

The Royal Road seems to be the element that ties these three areas together and, as Kemp (1976: 92-94; 1989: 276-78) and O'Connor (1995: 284) note, Akhenaten's procession to and from the Central City was an important element in city planning. This fact is also supported by the centrality of the scenes of these processions in Amarna art (Kemp 1989: 274-75).

In summary, Amarna may be characterized as a city centered on a temple area (the Central City). This city was physically connected to outlying residential areas and palace complexes by the Royal Road and ideologically connected by royal processions between the two outlying royal establishments and the center.[7]

The question, then, is whether the plan at Amarna was a typical form for the royal capital cities. Unfortunately, as previously mentioned, the other capital cities from the same time period are difficult

6.   The exact nature of Kom el-Nana and Maru-Aten complexes is debated. Opinions fluctuate between interpreting the complexes as temples or palaces (Kemp 1989: 285; Badawy 1956; O'Connor 1989: 85).

7.   O'Connor suggested that the city plan should be related to the cardinal points of the compass (1995: 289-90), with the king moving north to south and the sun (god) moving east to west. This interpretation may be correct, but it is likely that there are multiple levels of meaning to be found in these processions and their relationship to the basic plan of the city.

to compare, and therefore will be examined here only from the point
of view of basic planning in relation to temples.

Per-Ramesses

The city of the Ramesside pharaohs, it was the next major capital city
to be built after Amarna (fig. 2). The site is located to the east of a
now dry eastern branch of the Nile at modern Qantir-Tell ed-Dabʿa.
A reconstruction of the area based on excavated remains and old
waterways gives some indication of the major elements of the ancient
city (Bietak 1975, 1985a: 138; 1991: 30; Kitchen 1982: 123; Uphill
1988: 63). In addition, an analysis of the textual remains conducted
some years ago by Uphill (1984) allows for a basic idea of the conceptual plan of the city.

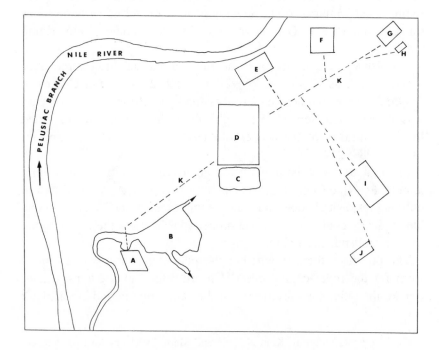

Figure 2. Conjectural sketch plan of Per-Ramesses (after Bietak 1985: 137-38;
           Kitchen 1982: 123). A, the temple of Seth; B, lake; C, lake of the resi-
           dence; D, palace; E, temple of Amun; F, jubilee halls; G, temple of Ptah;
           H, temple of Wadjet; I, temple of Re; J, temple of Astarte; K, proces-
           sional routes.

The city was generally a square shape with at least one large lake in its central area, possibly near the large palace complex. The city may have extended on both sides of the Nile (see plan in Bietak 1991: 30). Per-Ramesses, according to literary descriptions, was divided into four quarters: '...its west is the house of Amun, its south is the house of Seth, Astarte appears in its east and Wadjet in its north' (Gardiner 1937: 12, 1.4–1.5) Each of these quarters is described as belonging to a deity. When related to archaeological remains on the ground, the New Kingdom temple of Seth is located in the southern area (Tell ed-Dab'a) and would fit with the literary description. Uphill concludes from this description and the physical remains that each of the four quarters was probably centered on a temple to the deity in charge of that quarter (Uphill 1969: 30-31, 1984). A large palace was located in the center of the city. In addition to the Seth temple, a very large temple seems to have been located north of the palace, and one to the south-east, probably joined by processional ways (Bietak 1985b: 1242).

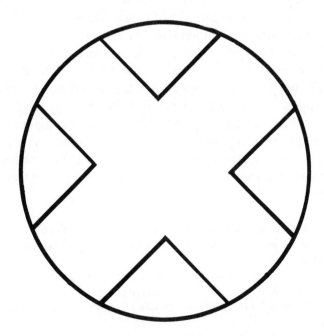

Figure 3. Hieroglyphic sign for city, *newet* (after Gardiner 1957: 498, sign-list O49).

Thus it appears that in many ways Per-Ramesses was a very different city from Amarna. It was squarish, with a central royal establishment and temples fanning out from this central point. The various quarters each had a temple as an ideologically central point rather than the temples being located in the center. The linear pattern of Amarna cannot be related to the plan of Per-Ramesses, but rather is reminiscent of the hieroglyphic sign *newet*, 'city', depicted as a circle divided into four segments (fig. 3).[8] The question then arises, did the differences between these two cities arise from geographical factors (cf. Janssen 1983: 276), or do they reflect essential differences in how the cities were conceived? Interestingly for this study, a Ramesside scribe describes Per-Ramesses as 'like the plan of Thebes' (Gardiner 1937: 12, 1.2). It is necessary, therefore, to examine Thebes in order to compare the general plans of these cities.

Thebes

Like Amarna, this city was located in the Nile valley, rather than in the Delta like Per-Ramesses (fig. 4). Thebes was similar to Amarna in terms of its geographical setting, but of course Thebes was not a *de novo* capital like Amarna.[9] Furthermore, Thebes was located on both banks of the Nile, although it is assumed that the majority of the residential areas were on the east bank (Bietak 1985b: 1239; Kitchen 1982: 116).[10] Today, the major remains on the east bank are a series of temple complexes with the Amun temple being the most prominent. The west bank had a strong funerary character, as it was the location of the cemetery for the city and the New Kingdom pharaohs (except Akhenaten), as well as the mortuary temples and their support buildings. The major exception to this characterization is the fact that the

8.   The origin of the hieroglyphic sign (see Fairman 1949: 35; Bietak 1979: 106, 1986) is not being discussed here, but only the New Kingdom understanding or re-interpretation of it.

9.   Kemp (1977b: 196) suggests that Thebes was resituated and planned at the beginning of the New Kingdom, although the position of the Amun temple and its alignment with Deir el-Bahri was maintained (see note 2 above for a similar situation in ancient Egypt).

10.   This definition should not be held too strictly. There were mayors of both the east and west banks at Thebes, suggesting the possibility of a stronger residential character in the west than current archaeological remains indicate (Uphill 1988: 52-54; O'Connor 1983: 216).

palace complex of Akhenaten's father, Amenhotep III, with its large artificial lake, is also located on the west bank.[11]

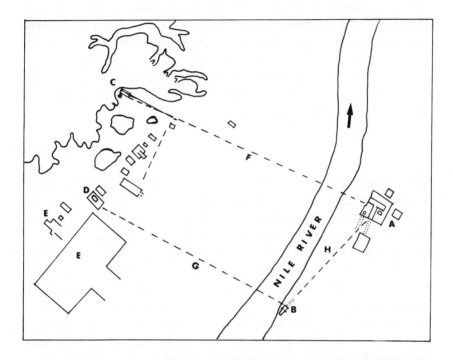

Figure 4.   Sketch plan of Thebes (after Stadelmann 1986: 469-70 and Kemp 1989: 203). A, Karnak temple; B, Luxor temple; C, Deir el-Bahri; D, Medinet Habu; E, palace complex and lake of Amenhotep III; F, processional route of Festival of the Valley; G, processional route of Amun of Opet; H, processional route of Festival of Opet.

Processional ways were certainly an important feature of this capital city, with the routes being marked by pylons, stone paved roads, sphinxes and bark rest stations (O'Connor 1989: 82). The Nile also provided a procession route. That the west bank should be included in these processional routes is indicated by the Festival of the Valley and

11.   Bietak compares this lake with the lake of the residence near the palace at Per-Ramesses (1985b: 1242). The term Maru is also applied to both this Theban lake and the Maru-Aten complex with a lake (Badawy 1956: 59-60). That such a lake is an important element in city planning also may be indicated by the possibility that a similar lake was located in Memphis beside the great Ptah temple (Uphill 1988: 50).

the Processions of Opet. As Kemp (1989: 210) notes, these processional routes form the Estate of Amun, and thus would form the official plan of the city of Thebes. What is interesting in this plan is the comparison to Per-Ramesses. Thebes is readily divided into four sectors, roughly forming a square: the Karnak temple, the Luxor temple, Deir el-Bahri and Medinet Habu (cf. Bietak 1985b: 1238; Kemp 1989: 203). Note that these sectors are centered on temples much like was described for Per-Ramesses. These features suggest that the comparison between Per-Ramesses and Thebes was not simply a poetic device of the Ramesside scribe.

Conclusions

There was an archetypal form for the royal city of the New Kingdom: a squarish-shaped city divided into four quarters centered on temples with processional routes joining the four areas. It can be suggested that this form was based consciously on the ideogram for city (fig. 3) by the New Kingdom planners, whatever the original meaning of this sign.[12] Amarna presents quite a different plan when compared with this one. Amarna had a centralized temple area with processional routes arranged in a linear pattern, connecting what might be termed 'palaces' to the center. It is difficult to partition the city into four quarters, even in a linear pattern.[13] As a result of this analysis, it may be concluded that Amarna was not a *typical* city in these aspects of planning. Therefore, it is likely that Akhenaten (or his planners) intentionally altered the plan of his city.

12. It may not be a coincidence that during the New Kingdom Thebes was known as *The City*. For example, in one hymn to Amun it is said that Thebes is 'the norm for all cities', and 'all cities are called cities after Thebes' (Barucq and Daumas 1980: 211-12), possibly indicating that the ancient Egyptians recognized Thebes's conformity to the ideal city.

13. This statement contradicts O'Connor, who divides Amarna into four zones based on use (recreational, secular, sacred and residential). The initial problem is that O'Connor's zones cannot be applied successfully to Thebes and Per-Ramesses. Also, there are problems with his division of Amarna in that he characterizes large residential areas as 'sacred' or 'secular'. For example, he includes the north suburb as part of the sacred city, but this residential area is usually characterized as middle class and business oriented, while the south suburb, which he describes as part of the secular city, contained the houses of high status individuals and priests (see Badawy 1968: 78-81; O'Connor 1989, 1995: 284-86).

The question of what drove Akhenaten to alter the planning of his city attempts to get at the idea, or archetype, behind the form of the New Kingdom royal city. In the first instance, it is obvious that the processional routes between the official buildings were a central feature of all three of the New Kingdom royal cities that have been examined. The significance of royal processions is well-known and studied in anthropological and sociological literature (e.g. Cannadine 1987: 3; Kuhrt 1987: 52; Wilentz 1985). As Geertz (1983: 125) points out, royal processions 'locate the society's center and affirm its connection with transcendent things by stamping a territory with ritual signs of dominance'.

According to the present interpretation of the organization of Amarna, Akhenaten changed the traditional focus of the processions as part of his city planning. In the standard New Kingdom city the processional routes were between temples. In Amarna the processional routes were between the one temple area and the palaces. Shifting the processional routes to give primacy to the palace suggests a change in the role of the pharaoh in Egyptian society.

In attempting to define this change more closely it is instructive to turn to an analysis of Egyptian kingship in the New Kingdom. Recently, Redford (1995) conducted such a study for the eighteenth Dynasty. He suggests that one of the most important roles of the king is the maintenance of the gods and their shrines (Redford 1995: 182). Akhenaten changed this role into a more intense relationship that Redford (1995: 179-80) describes as the 'father–son axis', in which Akhenaten stressed 'the unity of supernal and earthly kingship', and focused 'all attention on the role of himself and his father, the sun [disc]' (Redford 1995: 175). Therefore, the reason Akhenaten changed the plan of his capital city was because the plan of the Egyptian city carried a message regarding the place of the gods and the king in society (cf. Assmann 1972: 146, 152, with regard to architectural changes of a similar nature). A city with a dispersed temple pattern based on four quarters represented the world view of the Egyptians: the four quarters represented the diversity of the world and its deities. The king regularly travelled the great processional routes between the temples to serve the gods and thereby unite the cosmos and maintain the proper relationship between Egypt and the universe.[14]

14. It is a mistake to read too much significance into the four-quarters elements of city planning as described by Wheatley (1971) and Rykwert (1988) without specific

At Amarna, however, there was one deity in which everything was centralized. There no longer was a diversity to unite. The pharaoh regularly processed between his various palaces and the central temple area to serve this god, but also to stress the unique relationship and responsibility he had as the son of the Aten. Furthermore, one result of Akhenaten's reforms is a 'sacralization' of the palace structures in an attempt to reflect the change his melding of king and divinity represented, perhaps explaining the modern difficulty in labelling these buildings as palace or temple.[15]

Therefore it can be concluded that the placement of temples and palaces (in Akhenaten's case), was an integral element in the archetype of the New Kingdom city, providing through royal processions a concrete, physical representation of the conceptual relationship between society, king and divinity. Thus, the conceptual elements of religion and royalty were mapped out on the ground in New Kingdom royal cities.

Returning to the questions that originally gave rise to this study, the evidence clearly indicates that, in the mature ancient Egyptian state, the temple was a central organizational principle of the city, both conceptually and practically.

ACKNOWLEDGMENTS

I would like to thank Dr Paul-Hubert Poirier of the Université Laval, Dr Bruce Routledge of the University of Pennsylvania, and Mr Greg Mumford, University of Toronto, without whom this paper could not have been completed.

study of the situation for New Kingdom Egypt.
    15. One thinks here of the confusion over the identification of the Maru-Aten, Kom el-Nana and the palaces (Badawy 1956; Uphill 1970; Assmann 1972; Kemp 1989: 285; O'Connor 1989: 85; O'Connor 1995: 284-86).

BIBLIOGRAPHY

Assmann, J.
1972   'Palast oder Tempel? Überlegungen zur Architektur und Topographie von Amarna', *JNES* 31: 143-55.

Badawy, A.
1956   'Maru-Aten: Pleasure Resort or Temple?', *JEA* 42: 58-64.
1968   *A History of Egyptian Architecture*. III. *The Empire* (Berkeley: University of California Press).

Barucq, A., and F. Daumas
1980   *Hymnes et prieres de l'Égypte Ancienne* (Paris: Cerf).

Bietak, M.
1975   *Der Fundort im Rahmen der archäologischen-geographischen Untersuchungen über das ägyptische Ostdelta. Tel el-Dab'a II* (Vienna: Österreichischen Akademie der Wissenschaften).
1979   'Urban Archaeology and the "Town Problem" in Ancient Egypt', in *Egyptology and the Social Sciences* (ed. K. Weeks; Cairo: American University): 95-144.
1981   *Avaris and Piramesse: Archaeological Exploration in the Eastern Nile Delta* (London: Proceedings of the British Academy).
1985a   'Ramesesstadt', *LdÄ* 5: 128-43.
1985b   'Stadt(anlage)', *LdÄ* 5: 1233-49.
1986   'La Naissance de la notion de ville dans l'Egypte Ancienne, un acte politique?', *CRIPEL* 8: 29-35.
1991   'Egypt and Canaan during the Middle Bronze Age', *BASOR* 281: 27-72.

Cannadine, D.
1987   'Introduction: Divine Rites of Kings', in *Rituals of Royalty: Power and Ceremonial in Traditional Societies* (ed. D. Cannadine and S. Price; Cambridge: Cambridge University Press): 1-19.

Fairman, H.
1949   'Town Planning in Pharaonic Egypt', *Town Planning Review* 20: 32-51.

Gardiner, A.H.
1937   *Late-Egyptian Miscellanies* (Brussels: Édition de la Fondation Égyptologique Reine Élisabeth).
1957   *Egyptian Grammar* (3rd edn; Oxford: Griffith Institute).

Geertz, C.
1983   *Local Knowledge: Further Essays in Interpretive Anthropology* (New York: Torch).

Janssen, J.
1983   'El-Amarna as a Residential City', *BeO* 40: 273-88.

Kemp, B.
1972   'Temple and Town in Ancient Egypt', in *Man, Settlement and Urbanism* (ed. P. Ucko, R. Tringham and G. Dimbleby; London: Duckworth): 657-80.

1976	'The Window of Appearance at El-Amarna, and the Basic Structure of this City', *JEA* 62: 81-99.
1977a	'The City of el-Amarna as a Source for the Study of Urban Society in Ancient Egypt', *WA* 9:123-39.
1977b	'The Early Development of Towns in Egypt', *Ant* 51: 185-200.
1981	'The Character of the South Suburb at Tell el-'Amarna', MDOG 113: 81-97.
1985	'Tell el-Amarna', *LdÄ* 5: 309-19.
1989	*Ancient Egypt: Anatomy of a Civilization* (London: Routledge).

Kitchen, K.
1982	*Pharaoh Triumphant: The Life and Times of Ramesses II* (Mississauga: BenBen).

Kuhrt, A.
1987	'Usurpation, Conquest and Ceremonial: From Babylon to Persia', in *Rituals of Royalty: Power and Ceremonial in Traditional Socities* (ed. D. Cannadine and S. Price; Cambridge: Cambridge University Press): 20-55.

O'Connor, D.
1982	'Cities and Towns', in *Egypt's Golden Age: The Art of Living in the New Kingdom, 1558–1085 BC* (ed. E. Brovarski, S. Doll and R. Freed; Boston: Museum of Fine Arts): 17-25.
1983	'New Kingdom and Third Intermediate Period, 1552–664 BC', in *Ancient Egypt: A Social History* (ed. B. Trigger *et al.*; Cambridge: University Press): 183-278.
1989	'City and Palace in New Kingdom Egypt', *CRIPEL* 11: 73-87.
1995	'Beloved of Maat, the Horizon of Re. The Royal Palace in New Kingdom Egypt', in *Ancient Egyptian Kingship* (ed. D. O'Connor and D. Silverman; Leiden: Brill): 261-300.

Pusch, E.
1989	'Bericht über die sechste Hauptkampagne in Qantir/Piramesse-Nord', *Göttinger Miszellen* 112: 67-93.

Redford, D.B.
1995	'The Concept of Kingship during the Eighteenth Dynasty', in *Ancient Egyptian Kingship* (ed. D. O'Connor and D. Silverman; Leiden: Brill): 157-83.

Rykwert, J.
1988	*The Idea of a Town* (Cambridge: MIT).

Smith, W.S.
1981	*The Art and Architecture of Ancient Egypt* (Harmondsworth: Penguin Books).

Stadelmann, R.
1986	'Theben', *LdÄ* 6: 465-73.

Uphill, E.
1969	'Pithom and Raamses: Their Location and Significance II', *JNES* 28: 15-39.
1970	'The Per Aten at Amarna', *JNES* 29: 151-66.
1984	*The Temples of Per Ramesses* (Warminster: Aris & Phillips).
1988	*Egyptian Towns and Cities* (Aylesbury: Shire).

Wheatley, P.
1971   *The Pivot of the Four Quarters: A Preliminary Enquiry into the Origins and Character of the Ancient Chinese City* (Edinburgh: Edinburgh University Press).

Wilentz, S.
1985   *Rites of Power: Symbolism, Ritual and Politics since the Middle Ages* (Philadelphia: University Press).

Wilson, J.A.
1960   'Egypt through the New Kingdom: Civilization without Cities', in *City Invincible* (ed. C. Kraeling and R. McAdams; Chicago: University of Chicago Press): 124-36.

'METRO' NEA PAPHOS:
SUBURBAN SPRAWL IN SOUTHWESTERN CYPRUS
IN THE HELLENISTIC AND EARLIER ROMAN PERIODS

David W. Rupp

When one begins an archaeological survey project in a region which is not well-known archaeologically except for a few major locales, one does not know what to expect to find or the ultimate significance of these finds. The tasks facing researchers studying the spatial and the chronological distribution of data recovered by the survey crews is to identify meaningful patterns and then to interpret them plausibly within the limitations of the data sets. The extensive survey work of the Canadian Palaipaphos Survey Project (hereafter CPSP) and the Western Cyprus Project (hereafter WCP) in the Paphos District of Cyprus between 1979 and 1992 revealed many unexpected results. One of these was the distinctive spatial and chronological distribution of sites on the coastal plain to the East of Nea Paphos in the Hellenistic and Earlier Roman Periods, c. 300 BCE and 200 CE. The present paper represents an attempt to explain their presence and pattern of distribution in the context of the political and economic developments in the eastern Mediterranean in these periods.

General Background

The image that many individuals have of the ancient Greek and Roman worlds is one of mature development and permanence: Classical Greece and Imperial Rome. This superficial impression focuses on two ancient Mediterranean societies at the height of their political, economic and cultural powers. It implies a static, monolithic view of these complex societies devoid of any change. Growth and decline, in other words, change, is a constant feature of our world, present and past. To deny such possibilities to the Greeks and to the Romans by assuming a stable, unchanging society is obviously unrealistic and, therefore, unacceptable. More importantly, such a view is not supported by historical or archaeological evidence.

The following will explore the problem of documenting change in the past by examining the evidence for settlement growth in southwestern Cyprus between the late fourth century BCE and the end of the second century CE. The underlying assumptions here are that archaeological evidence from the surface can be equated with buried settlements and that the size and number of such sites are valid indicators of ancient population levels as well as changes in them. This case study will enable us to appreciate the potential and the problems inherent in any attempt to document the dynamic 'target' that ancient societies represent.

Before one can interpret properly the evidence available for this study, one must understand the typical ways in which population growth was handled in Greek and Roman cultures during the first millennium BCE. The majority of the major cities in both cultures, which had their origin in the early Iron Age, evolved in an essentially unplanned, agglutinative fashion over time within the confines of their defensive wall system (Morris 1991: 27-34). On occasion the fortification systems of some of these cities were expanded, allowing additional growth. A few existing Classical Greek *poleis* were refounded at a later date based on an orthogonal plan (Boyd 1981). In general, population growth was handled by colonization, as, in theory at least, each citizen family required sufficiently large agricultural holdings to be economically independent. Such colonial foundations were conscious, formal undertakings (Metraux 1978: 202-23; Salmon 1969). The urban focus of these colonies exhibit orthogonal planning and functional zoning (Castagnoli 1971: 10-64). Most Greek or Roman colonial foundations did not outgrow the confines of their original urban boundaries and civic physical plant. However, some did experience population growth. The challenge of dealing with increased numbers was apparently not handled by increasing significantly the population density within the omnipresent fortification walls. Rather, the new residents were allowed to build their houses and establishments immediately outside of the walls. Thus, buildings were built in a haphazard fashion along the principal roads leading from the city gates, thereby extending its 'armature' (MacDonald 1986: 5-31). There is limited evidence of formal planning control of this ongoing process either via the conscious dismantling of the city walls[1] and the systematic extension of the city's orthogonal plan or the laying out of a new, separate grid plan beyond the existing walls.[2] The resulting 'suburbs' of these cities were simply unplanned extensions to the original settlement beyond the fortification walls. This opportunistic development generally occurred along the major long distance transportation corridors passing through the city. The resulting extension of the city's armature was limited only by the presence of pre-existing tombs and cemeteries along these roads (Stambaugh 1988: 194-97). Thamugadi/Timgad (Stambaugh 1988: 285-86) and Cuicul/Djemila (MacDonald 1986: 5-14), both in modern Algeria, are good examples of this process in the Roman Empire. In each example at least a portion of the original city wall was torn down. The gate was left freestanding at Cuicul, and at Thamugadi it was replaced by a triumphal arch.[3]

During the early imperial period the Romans made two innovations that provided in some cases other strategies for handling population growth. Increased population density was one strategy. In Rome and its port city, Ostia, multi-storey apartment blocks or *insulae* were constructed (Ward-Perkins 1981: 147-48, 192-93; Stambaugh 1988: 174-48) using the structural potential of vaulting and *opus testaceum* or brick-faced concrete (Ward-Perkins 1981: 98-100). A more widespread strategy, which would have kept the urban population density

---

1.   The defensive walls of the *castrum* of Ostia founded in 349 BCE appear to have been torn down and new ones built in by the Roman dictator Sulla, c. 82–79 BCE, to enclose an area 30 times greater than before (Meiggs 1973: 34-35). The enlarged urban area was built up gradually in several episodes between the late first century BCE and the mid-second century CE (Meiggs 1973: 41-78, 128-48). As only part of the enlarged Ostian urban scape displays regularity in layout (Meiggs 1973: plan) it is difficult to suggest the extent that conscious, systematic planning played in any phase in this development.

2.   The approximately orthogonal plan of this quarter had a different orientation from that of the original city (MacDonald 1986: fig. 36).

3.   The expansion of Athens under Hadrian's patronage, c. 128–138 CE resulted in the erection of a decorative arch to mark the boundary between the 'old' Athens of Theseus and the 'new' one of Hadrian. It is not clear, however, if this expansion was planned formally in the sense of the laying out of an orthogonal grid or that the new area was allowed to evolved haphazardly outside of the public monuments situated within the line of the new fortification walls (Shear 1981: 372-77; Boatwright 1983).

within traditional limits, was the construction at the city's foundation of administrative, economic, religious and cultural facilities of sufficient size to accommodate not only the *intra muros* population of the city but also the *extra muros* (i.e. 'suburban' and rural) population in the *territorium* of that city (Duncan-Jones 1963). These non-residents would have utilized these facilities when they had cause to visit the city for them or some other reason. They would have returned to their households that day or after a short stay. Such cities had a high density of public and religious buildings and complexes, and these as well as open public spaces constituted a high portion of the area encompassed by the walls.

One can conclude from this basic review of the problem of urban population growth in the Greek and Roman worlds the following points. First, significant urban population growth after the establishment of a new city was an infrequent phenomenon. Secondly, when such growth occurred it was normally handled in a piecemeal, haphazard fashion with limited, if any, formal planning controls. Finally, the city in question, as a result of such physical expansion, simply oozed out from the city gates along the road networks, avoiding any cemetery in its path. The impression from the air would have been of an amoeba-like blob with linear features projecting from it, representing the roads.

The Cypriot Iron Age Background

With this background in mind it is possible to turn to southwestern Cyprus in order to examine the data available to document population growth around the Hellenistic and Earlier Roman city of Nea Paphos (modern Kato Paphos) (fig. 1). Once again some preliminary information is required in order to appreciate the trends visible in the data. This will necessitate a brief overview of the island's political history and the resulting system of settlement between the eighth and fourth centuries BCE.

It has been demonstrated (Rupp 1987a) that states in the form of regional hereditary monarchies emerged in Cyprus in the eighth and seventh centuries BCE. As a direct consequence of this political, economic and social transformation of Iron Age Cypriote society, a functionally stratified hierarchical system of settlement evolved. Each regional monarchy in this system had three tiers of settlement. There was a rich, urbanized central place that dominated the region and which served as the 'gateway community' for the regional and long-distance trade networks. The principal settlements of the territorial kingdoms (fig. 2) were located at strategic places along the coast and in the central and eastern plains. They were spaced in a more or less uniform fashion. The distance between them was as little as 13 km and as great as 101 km. While the average distance was 42.2 km most lay between 36 and 40 km. They were located on prominent, well-defined topographical features, that is, on distinct plateaus or on low hills. They all appear to have been fortified.

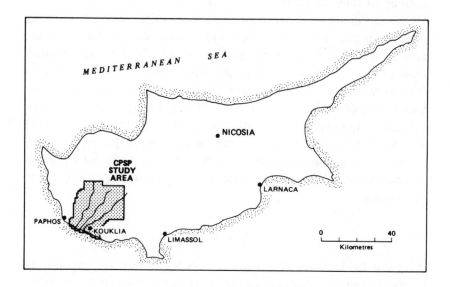

Figure 1. Map of Cyprus showing the Canadian Palaipaphos Survey Project research zone.

The secondary settlements, functioning possibly as market centers, were situated between the primary settlements in more remote areas of their rural hinterlands. Finally, strings of numerous poor, small agricultural villages emanated from them. This settlement system is a classic example of what is called a dendritic central place system (Smith 1976: 34-36; Kelley 1976). A dendritic track/road network probably developed over the centuries to connect the tertiary settlements to the secondary ones and then to the kingdom center (Bekker-Nielsen 1994: 186-88, 190 n. 4; Bekker-Nielsen 1995).

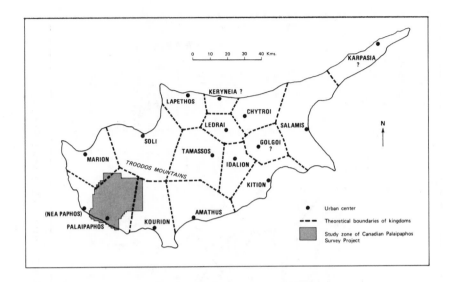

Figure 2. Theoretical reconstruction of the boundaries of the maximum possible
Cypriot kingdoms in the Cypro–Archaic II period.

Hellenistic and Earlier Roman Cyprus

The political system described above existed for the duration of the
independence of the kingdoms, through the late fourth century BCE,
when Alexander the Great's successors, Ptolemaios I Soter (306–282
BCE) and Antigonos I Monophthalmos (306–301 BCE), in their contest
for control of their island snuffed out the ruling dynasties. After 294
BCE until the annexation of Cyprus by Rome in 58 BCE, the island was
essentially a part of the Ptolemaic kingdom. During this time the
existing political system of independent regional kingdoms was transformed into a unified island-wide political system focused essentially
on the former kingdom centers. Each major city had severely circumscribed political and economic rights for it and its rural hinterland.
The *metropolis* or primary urban center on the island was the local
seat of administration for the Ptolemaic king and his bureaucracy
resident in Alexandria in Egypt. Alexandria, however, was the actual
apex or offshore imperial center of the hierarchical settlement system
(Bagnall 1976). Salamis on the eastern coast was the *metropolis* until
the early second century BCE when its functions were transferred to
Nea Paphos. As the closest city to Alexandria and the farthest from

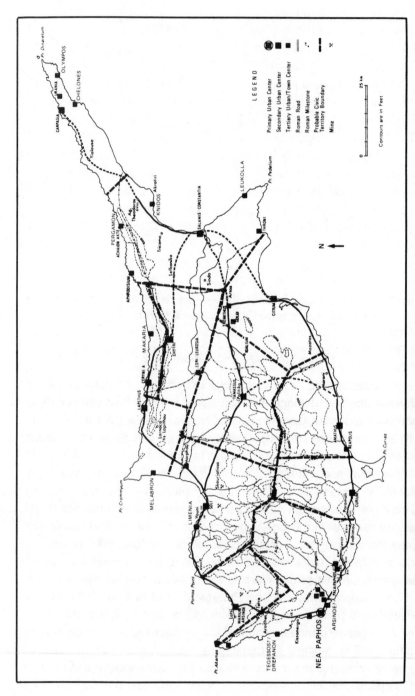

Figure 3. Reconstruction of the settlement system of Earlier Roman Cyprus (c. 50 BCE–250 CE) (after Mitford 1980: fig. 1).

the Syro-Palestinian littoral, Nea Paphos was a logical choice. Damage caused by unrecorded serious earthquakes and/or the silting up of Salamis's harbor may have been other contributing factors.

The annexation of the island to Rome in 58 BCE saw few changes in overall political setup (fig. 3). Nea Paphos continued to serve as the primary urban center or *metropolis* of the island throughout the Earlier Roman Period. In addition, it served as a *conventus* or district center for administrative and judicial functions as well as the administrative center of its civic territory. Salamis, Lapethos and Amathous also served as district centers. These political functions required permanent personnel, buildings and communication networks to maintain them. As each secondary city administered its own civic territory, a similar (although less complex) administrative setup and physical plant was present in each of them.

The basic features of the settlement system of Cyprus in the Hellenistic and Earlier Roman Periods can be inferred from a variety of sources traditionally available to classical archaeologists (table 1). These include: (1) the few historical texts as well as geographical lists and maps that refer generally to the urbanized Iron Age kingdom centers, as well as their sanctuaries and ports; (2) epigraphical texts that mention where the statue or monument was located and/or from where the dedication came, as well as milestones; (3) topographical studies of major settlements and sanctuaries; (4) the finds of systematic and rescue excavations, especially of tombs, by the Cypriote Department of Antiquities and by foreign projects; (5) chance/accidental finds of architectural members, inscribed statue bases, inscribed altars and fragments of various monuments or inscribed funerary stelae; and (6) coins, especially hoards.

These data sources reveal a three-tiered settlement system (table 2). The *metropolis* was the sole occupant of the first tier. The second tier consisted of urban centers of the Iron Age kingdoms. They all appear to have been fortified. The third tier was made up of the small tertiary cities and non-urbanized towns that were located between the principal cities in the more remote areas of their territories, as at Melabron (modern Ayia Irini) or Tegessos?/Drepanon (modern Agios Georgios) on Cape Drepanon. Despite the minor importance of the latter two tiers, a number of these settlements are referred to by name in the written sources and/or are shown on copies of ancient maps.

Table 1. Evidence for reconstructing the hierarchical pattern of cities and towns in Roman Cyprus.

SETTLEMENTS / EVIDENCE FOR RECONSTRUCTING THE HIERARCHICAL PATTERN OF CITIES AND TOWNS IN ROMAN CYPRUS	Salamis, Constantia	Knidos	Arsinoe	Leukolla	Thronoi	Karpasia/Carpasium	Ourania	Chelones	Olympos	Keryneia	Makaria	Pergamon	Aphrodision	Lapethos	Melabron	Soloi/Soloe	Morphou	Limenia	Arsinoe	Nea Paphos	Palaipaphos/Palaepaphos	Tegessos?/Drepanon	Kourion/Curium	Treta?	Boosura?	Amathous/Amathus	Neapolis/Nemessos	Kition/Citium	Tremithous/Tremithus	Golgoi/Golgoe	Idalion/Idalium?	Chytroi/Chytri	Ledra?	Tamessos/Tamasos
DOCUMENTARY EVIDENCE																																		
Pliny the Elder	x	x	x			x			?	x				x		x				x	x		x			x		x		x	x	x		x
Strabo	x	x	x	x	?	x			?	x		?	x	x		x		x	x	x	x		x			x		x	x					x
Claudios Ptolemaios	x				x	x				?	x	?	x	x	?	x			x	x	x		x			x	?	x	x			x		x
Tabula Peutingeriana	x					x				?	?	?	?	x	?	x			?	x	x		x			x	?	x	x			x		x
conventus capital	x																			x														
Emperor cult(s)	x					x								x		x				x			x			x		x						
Dedications to Emperor	x					x							x	x		x			?	x	x		x			x						x		x
Inscriptions – general	x					x			x	x		?	x	x		x	x	x	x	x	x		x			x	x	x	x			x	x	x
Games	x		?			x								x		x			x	x			x					x						
URBAN FEATURES																																		
Estimated extent in hectares	275					29								100		41			38	105	16		23			40								
Fortification walls	x	x			x	x				x				x		x				x	x		x			x		x				x		x
Harbor with moles	x				x	x				x				x		x			x	x	x		x			x								
Harbor without moles	?	?					?	?	?		?	?	?		?		?																	
Paved colonnade streets	x															x	x																	
Forum/agora	x															x					x													
Temples,sanctuaries	x			?		x		x	x	x		?	x	x	x	x	x	x	x	x	x		x			x		x		x		x	x	x
Theater	x															x			?	x	x		x			x								
Odeion	x																																	
Amphitheater	x																						x											
Stadium	x				x	x			x	x				x		x				x		x	x					x		x		x	x	
Gymnasium	x	x			x	x			x	x				x		x							x											
Aqueduct	x	x																	?	x			x			x								
Fountain(s)																				x			x			x								
Nymphaeum																x				x			x			x								
Bath(s)	x													x						x	x		x			x		x						
Governor's palace	x																			x														
Elaborate peristyle houses	x					x								x		x			?	x	x		x			x		x				x		x
Bronze stone lifesize sculpture	x																			x	x	x	x											
Mint: bronze coins	?																			x	x		x			x		x			x	x		

SYMBOL KEY: METROPOLIS ⊚ ; FIRST ORDER CITY ■ ; SECOND ORDER CITY ■ ; TOWN ■ ; LARGE VILLAGE ■ ; MEDIUM VILLAGE ■

Type of Evidence / Settlement Hierarchy	Primary Urban Center	Secondary Urban Center	Tertiary Urban/Town Center	Large Village	Medium village	Small Village	Farmstead/Villa
Primary Archaeological Data	x	x	x	x	x	x	x
Imported/High Status Artifacts	x	x	•	•			
Public Architecture	x	x	•				
Religious Architecture	x	x	•				
Artistic Remains	x	x	•				
Inscriptions	x	x	•	•			
Documentary References	x	x	•	•			
Map References	x	x	•				

x = Present
• = May be present

Table 2. Reconstruction of the settlement system of Hellenistic and Earlier Roman Cyprus based on traditional data sources.

The primary city and the secondary cities share a wide range of urban attributes and amenities (tables 1 and 2). These are the standard urban features of Greco–Roman cities in the eastern Mediterranean. What distinguishes one from another are the functions that they performed in the political and administrative systems of the island (table 3). Those cities which had more and higher functions were larger in size and had more numerous and elaborate urban features. The rich archaeological, architectural, artistic and documentary evidence from Salamis, Nea Paphos and the other cities unequivocally supports the supposition that they were the political, economic, social and cultural centers of the island where the indigenous Cypriote elite resided.

The economic functions of each tier of the settlement system were also stratified (table 3). The primary center continued to serve as the principal 'gateway community' of the long-distance exchange networks. Secondary exchange nodes were located at the secondary urban centers within their territories. The tertiary cities and the towns probably served as minor intra-regional production and distribution centers. Our understanding of the island's settlement system between c. 300 BCE and 200 CE could not progress beyond this level without a new and extensive body of evidence.

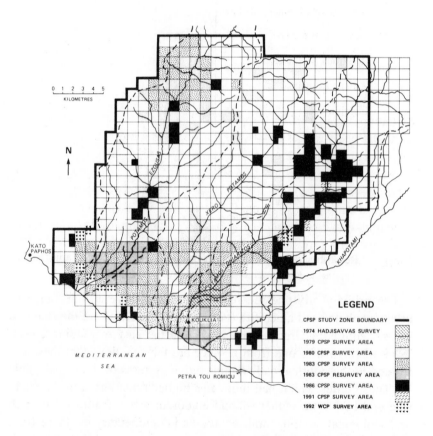

Figure 4.   Map of the Canadian Palaipaphos Survey Project research zone showing areas surveyed by the Canadian Palaipaphos Survey Project and the Western Cyprus Project.

The Results of the CPSP and the WCP Fieldwork

During the past 40 years in Cyprus another source of data on the island's changing settlement patterns has gradually emerged. This new data acquisition technique is archaeological survey. The western part of the island, corresponding to the modern Paphos District, is reasonably well investigated by this method of surface investigation. A careful study of the distribution and relative density of the artifactual material collected in this fashion can reveal surprisingly accurate information on the probable location, extent, functions and periods of occupation of a settlement. In essence archaeological survey reveals information on the totality of settlement and land use in a region, not just on the highly visible architectural and artistic remains of its largest and most important settlements.

Between 1979 and 1992 two international teams of researchers under the direction of the author engaged in an archaeological survey in a 635 km square research zone in southwestern Cyprus (figs. 1 and 4) (Rupp 1981, 1987b; Rupp et al. 1984, 1986, 1992, 1993).[4] The principal one was the CPSP and the other was the WCP. Included in this research zone were the coastal plain and adjacent uplands lying between Palaipaphos and Nea Paphos. In five field seasons approximately 45 per cent of this area was uniformly surveyed by the dedicated survey crews of the CPSP and the WCP (fig. 4). Their peregrinations produced evidence of human occupation in this area dating from the sixth millennium BCE through the earlier half of this century. A significant number of the sites had evidence of occupation from the third century BCE through the second century CE.

Based on the CPSP data (Lund 1993) it is proposed here that four more tiers existed at the bottom in the Cypriote settlement hierarchy during the Hellenistic and Earlier Roman Periods (table 3). These are based on the clustering of the areal extent of the surface artifact scatters seen at the sites. Starting at the lowest tier they are as follows. The smallest and most numerous sites, labelled here 'farmsteads' or *villae*, have scatters ranging in size from 0.1 to 1.2 ha.

4.   This fieldwork and research were made possible in part by grants from the Social Sciences and Humanities Research Council of Canada, the Institute for Aegean Prehistory, Brock University and its Archaeological Practica, and individual donors. Both the CPSP and the WCP were affiliated with the American Schools of Oriental Research.

Settlement Hierarchy	Political Function(s)	Probable Economic Function(s)
Primary Urban Center (= *metropolis* of the island) [c. 105-205 ha]	administers: — the island for Rome — a *conventus* — a civic *territorium* with possibly a *demos* and a *boule*	'gateway community' is long distance exchange network; central place of the civic *territorium* major production center
Secondary Urban Centers [c. 23-100 ha]	administers: — the island for Rome — a *conventus* — a civic *territorium* with possibly a *demos* and a *boule*	'gateway community' is long distance exchange network; central place of the civic *territorium* major production center
Tertiary Urban / Town Centers [c. 16-30 ha]	may? administer a region within a civic *territorium*	regional market center; secondary production center?
Large Villages [c. 9.5-15.5 ha]	none	local market center? minor production center?; agricultural and animal husbandry products; natural resources acquisition
Medium Villages [c. 5.2-8.5 ha]	none	agricultural and animal husbandry products; natural resources acquisition
Small Vllages [c. 1.3-5.0 ha]	none	agricultural and animal husbandry products; natural resources acquisition
Farmsteads / *'villae'* [c. 0.1-1.2 ha]	none	agricultural and animal husbandry products; natural resources acquisition

Table 3.   Reconstruction of the settlement system as well as the political and economic functions of the different tiers for Hellenistic and Earlier Roman Cyprus using all available data sources.

'Small villages' are also very frequent. Their size varies from 1.5 to 10 ha. Approximately half as many 'medium villages' exist. Their areas run from 11 to 15 ha. Much less prevalent are 'large villages' with sizes varying from 20 to 28 ha. A few 'towns' are present which range in size from 29 to 35 ha. Except for Palaipaphos, the Iron Age kingdom center in the region, none of these towns produced evidence of any of the attributes of urbanism from the remains visible on the surface. The large villages probably performed the roles of local market and minor craft production centers in the economy. The inhabitants of these villages and the others in the lowest two tiers produced the agricultural goods, animal husbandry products and natural resource materials that the entire system depended upon. Thus, in this dendritic central place system the hinterland of each civic territory was systematically exploited for the benefit of the residents of the principal city and, ultimately, for the foreign rulers offshore.

Nea Paphos: Case Study

The civic territory of Nea Paphos offers us a suitable case study to investigate more fully the changing nature of settlement and urbanism on the island between c. 300 BCE and 200 CE.

These developments must be seen, however, in their historical context. From the time of the emergence of the kingdom of Paphos in the mid-eighth century BCE until the later fourth century BCE the urban center of the territorial monarchy was located at Paphos (the modern village of Kouklia) (fig. 5). Here was the famous sanctuary of the Paphian Aphrodite. The city was located on the first major marine terrace overlooking the sea. Its 'port' settlement (CPSP 79–D–5) was situated about 2 km to the south/southeast on the shore to the east of the mouth of a small stream where there once was a natural anchorage or *hyphormos* (Strabo XIV 6.3) (Leonard 1995: 232) before it silted up. The last king of Paphos, Nikokles II, son of Timarchos, founded between 321–320 and 313–312 BCE a new political and economic center on the coast about 17 km to the northwest (Mlynarczyk 1985a; Daszewski 1987). This new city, which came to be called Nea Paphos, or 'new Paphos', was built on the site of an existing small settlement possibly called Erythra or Erythrai (fig. 5) which dated from the later fifth century BCE (Mlynarczyk 1985a: 69, 76, 1990: 74-76, 85-94). As well there may have been an earlier minor occupation in this area during the later Cypro–Archaic Period (Daszewski 1987: 171; Mlynarczyk 1990: 74). Here was located the best natural, protected harbor in all of southwestern Cyprus. An ambitious orthogonal plan comprised of two separate but related grids was laid out over the topography of the site (Mlynarczyk 1982; Daszewski 1987: 173-74). Defensive fortifications were constructed along the natural breaks in the contours of the site enclosing about 105 ha (Nicolaou 1966: 567-78, fig. 3). Public spaces were placed on the lower, level ground in the central part of the city and sanctuaries built on the low hills that enclose this main area. The initial inhabitants for this new city probably came to the existing settlement of Erythrai from a town (?) located immediately to the north on the first major marine terrace now under the modern town of Paphos (once Ktima) (fig. 5) and the former kingdom center of Paphos (Daszewski 1987: 173).

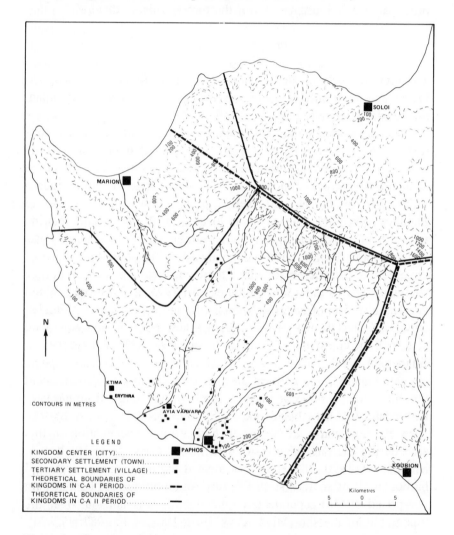

Figure 5. Western Cyprus: Cypro–Archaic settlement system.

The Polish archaeologist W.A. Daszewski (1987: 174-75) believes that Ptolemaios I Soter, the first Hellenistic king of Egypt, became interested in this new city because of his need for a forward naval base in his struggles against Antigonos I Monophthalmos for control of the eastern Mediterranean and the Levantine coast. Daszewski (1987: 175) argues that the construction of two artificial moles to enclose a c. 22 ha triple harbor, possibly a *limen kleistos*, c. 315–13 BCE (Leonard and Hohlfelder 1993: 372-79) as well as the transfer in 312 BCE of the population of the destroyed Cypriot kingdom center of Marion to the north (Diodorus Siculus 19.59.1, 62.6, 79.4, *contra* Bekker-Nielsen 1994: 183) were part of Ptolemaios's policy to create a viable naval base. These policies appear to have worked, as the city quickly became the political, economic and cultural center of the kingdom. It retained this pre-eminent position in the region after the demise of the kingdom following Nikokles II's and his family's enforced suicide in 310–309 BCE (Diodorus Siculus 20.21, *contra* Bekker-Nielsen 1994: 191 n. 4) by Menelaos for plotting with other Cypriot kings against Ptolemaios I Soter. When Demetrios Poliorketes, son and co-regent of Antigonos I Monophthalmos, controlled the island from about 306 to 294 BCE he may also have contributed to the construction of the city's defensive walls and its harbor, not to mention its prosperity (Daszewski 1987: 175). The former kingdom center Paphos, called Palaia or Palaipaphos or 'Old Paphos' by at least the second quarter of the second century BCE (Mlynarczyk 1990: 23), was stripped of all but its religious functions due to the presence of the Sanctuary of Aphrodite. The ample forests of cedar, cypress and pine in the nearby Troodos Mountains and their foothills allowed Nea Paphos to become a naval shipbuilding center (Hauben 1987). During Ptolemaios II Philadelphos's reign (285–82 to 246–45 BCE) two of the largest naval ships mentioned in the ancient texts, a *triakonteres* and an *eikoseres*, were built here by the naval architect Pyrgoteles, son of Zoes, for the admiral Kallikrates of Samos (Nicolaou 1966: 564; Daszewski 1987: 175). The designation of Nea Paphos as the *metropolis* or primate center on the island during the reign of Ptolemaios V Epiphanes (205–204 to 181–80 BCE) (Nicolaou 1966: 564-65, *contra* Bekker-Nielsen 1994: 191 n. 5) greatly stimulated its urbanism (Daszewski 1985) and the development of the region until the Rome's annexation of the island.

Archaeological rescue excavations by the Cypriot Department of Antiquities over the past two decades outside the line of the city walls in the environs of the modern resort town of Kato Paphos have revealed many things. Most importantly these finds indicate that there were extensive cemeteries immediately outside the walls along the ancient roads (Nicolalou 1966: 600-601; Mlynarczyk 1985a: 71-76; Daszewski 1987: 171-72). These were located primarily to the north-northwest and east-southeast of the city. The city, therefore, could not have expanded outward from its city gates except to the north. There is no evidence for the latter, however.

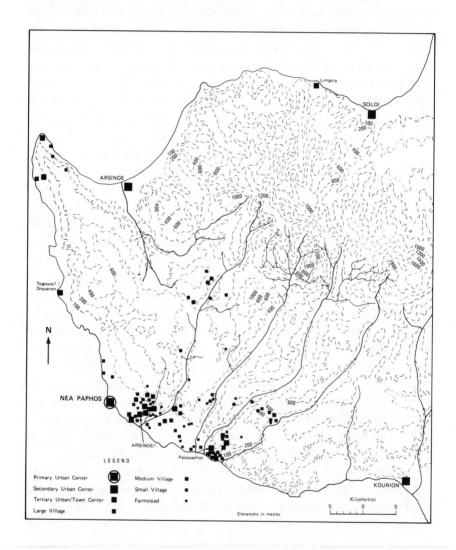

Figure 6. Western Cyprus: Hellenistic settlement pattern (c. 300–50 BCE).

The Settlement Pattern in the Immediate Environs of Nea Paphos

Although, as indicated previously, the entire region surrounding Nea Paphos has not been surveyed due to modern development and to the limits of the CPSP research zone (fig. 4) a sufficiently large percentage has been uniformly surveyed to suggest that the following settlement growth occurred: An arc of settlements emerged beginning on the shoreline and stretched for at least 6–7 km to the north–northwest to at least the first major marine terrace (figs. 6 and 7).

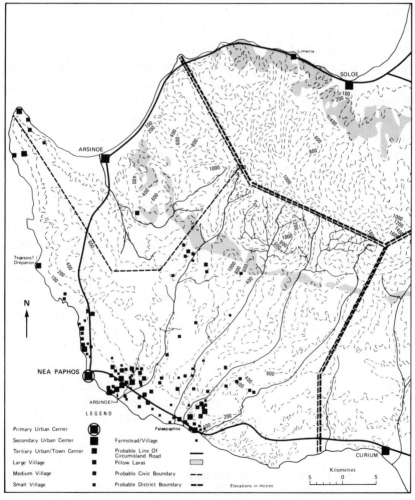

Figure 7. A reconstruction of the Earlier Roman settlement system in western Cyprus (c. 50 BCE–250 CE).

This arc is about 3–4 km wide. The formation and growth of these outlying settlements did not appear to have gained much momentum until the second quarter of the third century BCE, when Ptolemaios II Philadelphios, c. 270–265 BCE, founded a town or city on the coastal plain between Palaipaphos and Nea Paphos, which he called Arsinoe after his sister/wife, Arsinoe II.[5] This Arsinoe, as Strabo informs us in his *Geographia* (XIV 6.3), had a sanctuary with a sacred grove and a 'landing stage' nearby situated adjacent to a natural anchorage or *prosormos* (Leonard 1995: 232). Such detail on the topography of minor settlements on the island is unusual.

The largest site on the coastal plain, CPSP 83-E-126 (fig. 8), has a surface artifact scatter of over 35 ha. It is located near the western bank of the Ezousas Potamos and about 1 km from the sea. In the northwestern portion of the scatter, fragments of unfluted stone column drums and Doric capitals were found. These architectural fragments were the only ones found by the CPSP on the coastal plain. In southwestern Cyprus fragments are normally found only in association with cities or sanctuaries. In addition, on the coast in the lee of a small cape less than 1 km to the southeast is another town-sized scatter, CPSP 86-E-2. The Moulia Rocks offshore and the inshore 'reefs' would have provided some protection from the prevailing easterly winds and coastal currents for an anchorage here. These may be the remnants of the Noumenios island mentioned by the *Stadiasmus sive Periplus Maris Magni* (297–99) and Pliny the Younger's Hiera and Cepia islands (*Nat. Hist.* 5.131) (Leonard 1995: 242 n. 30). It should be noted here that there are three different-sized villages, CPSP 86-E-3 to 5, in the immediate area as well. A section of a subterranean aqueduct system is exposed here too. This region could have been served by the road which exited from Nea Paphos's eastern gate (Nicolaou 1966: fig. 3).

Since CPSP 83-E-126 is so close to Nea Paphos, c. 4 km, it should only be considered a town, that is, lacking all normal urban features except for a formal sanctuary. This is in contrast to the tertiary level urban center of Tegessos?/Drepanon located at Agios Georgios

5.   This was part of the Ptolemaic foreign colonization policy. As most were port settlements (or coastal at least in this case), the specific aim of their founding was to strengthen the Ptolemaic Thalassocracy throughout the eastern Mediterranean (Cohen 1983: 72-74).

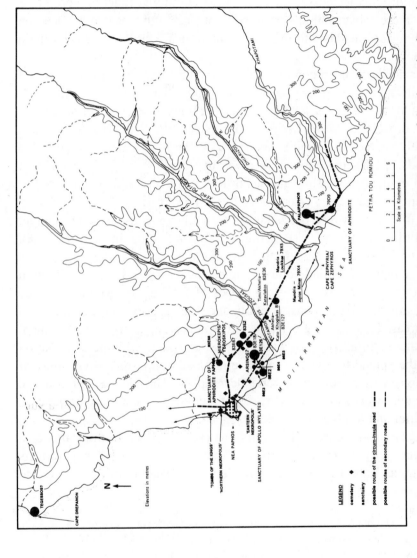

Figure 8. Map of southwestern Cyprus showing major settlements and the probable route of the circum-insula road as well as secondary routes in the Earlier Roman period.

on Cape Drepanon (fig. 6), which was founded probably in the Hellenistic Period.[6] Its position on the northwestern periphery of the Paphian civic territory permitted this settlement to have more functions than would be expected for its size. These additional functions produced the more substantial and impressive physical remains that are seen on the surface at this site than are evident at CPSP 83-E-126. Its main functions would have been that of a secondary population center for Nea Paphos and probably a secondary market center for the coastal plain and the lower Ezousas Potamos valley. The residents of this town would have used Nea Paphos as their administrative and cultural center.

Yeroskipou *Litharka/Vounimenos* (CPSP 83-E-126) is the most likely source for Strabo's Arsinoe, as its large size and position in the landscape fits the impression given by phrasing in his description. It has evidence of a sanctuary.[7] Further, there is a landing stage settlement on a protected coastal location (CPSP 86-E-2). At the beginning of this century I.K. Peristianis noted the remains of some ancient buildings in this area (Peristianis 1910: 405-406). In fact, the small natural harbor of this settlement could have been the area where Ptolemaios II Philadelphios's monstrous warships were built with timber from the southwestern slopes of the Troodos Mountains. The remainder of the coastal plain and the interior display signs of increased, though still limited, settlement.[8] The growth of settlement in the hinterland (fig. 6) was probably associated with the exploitation of the upland forests and copper mining as well as the provisioning of the growing population around Nea Paphos. The Akamas Peninsula to the northwest shows signs as well of significantly increased occupation (Fejfer and Mathiesen 1995: 56).

Palaipaphos, now only a religious center, shrank to the status of a tertiary city or town. The focus of habitation began shifting from its original Late Bronze Age location northeast of the sanctuary to

6. The main period of occupation of this tertiary level city, however, was the later Roman Period when it was called Drepanum (Bekker-Nielsen 1994: 183; Fejfer and Mathiesen 1995: 54-55). The small island of Yeronisos 500 m to the southwest off Cape Drepanon has substantial Ptolemaic Period remains (Christou 1994: 688-89).

7. This sanctuary may have been dedicated to Aphrodite Euploia, the protectress of sailors, who was associated closely with Arsinoe II (Hauben 1987).

8. The first extensive land-use of the western Akamas Peninsula to the northwest of Nea Paphos occurred during this period (Fejfer and Hayes 1995: 66).

immediately north of it. The concentration of sites that once surrounded the settlement since the seventh century BCE decreased at the
same time.

In the subsequent Earlier Roman Period, from 58 BCE to c. 200 CE,
the pattern of settlement was essentially unchanged (fig. 7). There are
indications that the area within Nea Paphos's city walls was more built
up (Maier and Karageorghis 1984: 247-97). In the earlier part of the
first century CE, the hypothetical but probable *circum-insula* or peripheral coastal road connecting the major urban centers with their own
internal road networks was formalized, most likely by the Roman
imperial administration (Mitford 1980). The line of this major road
(fig. 8) running to the south–southeast probably left the city at the
Northeast Gate ('Gate III') (Mlynarczyk 1985b: fig. 1) and headed off
in an easterly direction toward Yeroskipou.[9] It would have taken this
route because the easiest place to ascend the escarpment of the first
major marine terrace is to the southwest of Yeroskipou. There was a
sanctuary, *Hierokepis*, and probably a village near the center of the
modern town. To the north of Yeroskipou, at the base of the second
major marine terrace, there was a town-sized settlement, CPSP 83-E-
68, with the remains of a subterranean aqueduct nearby. The road
most likely followed the line of the modern road toward Limassol, as
first proposed by T.B. Mitford (1939; Mitford 1980: 1332-37). This

---

9. J. Mlynarcyzk (1985b: 286-87) has proposed a different route further south
which traverses the Eastern Necropolis with its Sanctuary of Apollo Hylates and then
weaves its way to Palaipaphos. Even though she did not have available the CPSP
data her proposed route fails to consider both the actual topography of the area and
the concept of least effort in organizing human affairs. T. Bekker-Nielsen's reconstruction (1995: 96-99, figs. 14, 16) agrees in part with the one offered here. While
his road line from east of Akhelia to Kouklia and then on the Khapotamoi is sound,
his road line from Akhelia to Nea Paphos which cuts straight across the coast plain to
Nea Paphos's East Gate is not likely the principal route but a secondary one,
connecting Arsinoe with Nea Paphos and with the main route on along the first
marine terrace. The presence of a Cypro–Archaic Period sanctuary on the eastern
edge of Yeroskipou and a long-lived settlement with cemetery under the modern
town of Paphos would suggest that the primitive predecessor of the Roman road
connected these nodes of human activity in the later Iron Age at least with Paphos. A
road down to Nea Paphos is only required after its founding. From the general
absence of evidence for settlements or cemetaries in the coastal plain between
Palaipaphos and Nea Paphos Potamos prior to the Hellenistic Period, one could
conclude that there was little or no settlement and, therefore, no road system.

road would have functioned as well as Strabo's (XIV 6.3) *iera odos* or 'sacred road' from the Sanctuary of Aphrodite Paphia on the 'Fabrika Hill' in the northeastern part of Nea Paphos (Mlynarczyk 1985b) to the Sanctuary of Aphrodite at Palaipaphos. A few settlements and cemeteries were located along or near this road to the southeast as well as on the higher second major marine terrace (CPSP 83-E-67, 2, 18, 127 and 36). The number of settlements decreased rapidly as one moved away from the Ezousas Potamos along the road.

There was a slight increase in settlements to the north of Nea Paphos and in the upper reaches of the main river valleys (fig. 7). In the northern portion of the Ezousas Potamos it may have been connected with copper mining in the Lower Pillow Lava Formation, which rings the Troodos Mountains. The appearance or enlargement of pre-existing sanctuaries in the hinterland also must attest to a greater population living there.

Conclusions

The emergence of settlements of varying sizes beyond the limits of the extra-mural cemeteries of Nea Paphos on the coastal plain and the first major marine terrace represents, in part, what we would call today the 'bedroom communities' of a metropolitan urban area. The positioning of these towns and villages in the landscape and their close proximity to each other argue that they would had more than simply an agricultural function in a subsistence economy. They are ideally suited to supply Nea Paphos with agricultural and animal husbandry products for its urban population. Various basic craft products may have been produced here too. These settlements must have housed the lower socio-economic classes of a city, that had outgrown the limits of its circumscribed physical plant for single-storey residential structures. Starting in the second century BCE, rather than increasing significantly the density of the population within the city walls by having unplanned development along the roads out of the city, or later in the Earlier Roman Period the construction of multi-storey apartment blocks for the non-elite residents, another strategy was adopted. This third strategy for urban growth outlined in this paper was what we would call today 'suburban sprawl'.[10]

10. D. Redford (personal communication) believes that the numerous low mounds formed by former settlements which once existed beyond the cemeteries

This suburban sprawl, which began in the early Hellenistic Period and persisted through the Earlier Roman Period, however, was apparently different from ours. That is, the socio-political elite associated with the island's *metropolis* from c. 200 BCE through c. 200 CE preferred to live in the city itself with all its amenities and facilities for rich, sophisticated urban life or the Roman concept of *urbanitas* (Stambaugh 1988: 198-212). In 143 CE during the reign of Antoninus Pius, Aelius Aristides, a provincial Roman rhetor from Smyrna, extolled in his *Roman Oration* (Oliver 1953) the allure and virtues of just such a lifestyle of *otium* for the upper classes within the context of a city. This is the antithesis of the modern phenomenon. Further, there is little evidence[11] for them building luxurious 'suburban' *villae* immediately outside the city walls, along the coast or elsewhere in the city's *territorium* to enjoy the pleasures of 'rural' or seaside life during the Earlier Roman Period. It was the working non-elite population of the region that was relegated to live in the non-urbanized 'burbs' around the city during the periods in question.

ACKNOWLEDGMENTS

Figures 1, 2, 4 and 8 were drawn by Loris Gasparotto (Cartographer, Department of Geography, Brock University) and David Rupp. The comments and suggestions of Metaxia Tsipopoulou, Michael Wedde, Cherie J. Lenzen and John R. Leonard have improved the line of argument and polished the manner of delivery. The remaining shortcomings are those alone of the author, as always.

surrounding Alexandria in Egypt may represent a similar pattern of 'suburban sprawl' to handle population growth.

11. The presence of a mosaic floor southeast of Anarita may indicate the existence of a *villa rustica* there of unknown date (D. Michaelides personal communication). A portion of another *villa* with a bath was excavated at Agios Leontis near Akhelia (Karageorghis 1981: 43). It dates, however, to the Late Roman Period when Nea Paphos was no longer the *metropolis* of the island and the arc of suburban settlements had ceased to be inhabited.

BIBLIOGRAPHY

Bagnall, R.S.
1976   *The Administration of the Ptolemaic Possessions Outside of Egypt* (Leiden: Columbia Studies in the Classical Tradition).
Bekker-Nielsen, T.
1994   'Centres and Road Networks in Hellenistic Cyprus', in *Centre and Periphery in the Hellenistic World* (ed. P. Bilde, T. Engberg-Pedersen, L. Hannestad, J. Zahle and K. Randsborg; Aarhus: Studies in Hellenistic Civilization): 176-91.
1995   'The Road Network', in *Ancient Akamas. I. Settlement and Environment* (ed. J. Fejfer; Aarhus: University Press): 87-132.
Boatwright, M.T.
1983   'Further Thoughts on Hadrianic Athens', *Hesperia* 52: 173-76.
Boyd, T.D.
1981   'Halieis: A Fourth Planned City in Classical Greece', *Town Planning Review* 52: 143-56.
Castagnoli, F.
1971   *Orthogonal Town Planning in Antiquity* (Cambridge, MA: MIT).
Christou, D.
1994   'Chronique des fouilles et decouvertes archeologiques à Chypre en 1993', *BCH* 118: 647-93.
Cohen, G.M.
1983   'Colonization and Population Transfer in the Hellenistic World', in *Egypt and the Hellenistic World* (ed. E. van T. Dack, P. van Dessel and W. van Gucht; Leuven: Studia Hellenistica): 63-74.
Daszewski, W.A.
1985   'Research at Nea Paphos, 1965–1984', in *Archaeology of Cyprus 1960–1985* (ed. V. Karageorghis; Nicosia: Leventis Foundation): 277-91.
1987   'Nicocles and Ptolemy—Remarks on the Early History of Nea Paphos', RDAC: 171-75.
Duncan-Jones, R.P.
1963   'City Population in Roman Africa', *JRS* 53: 85-90.
Fejfer, J., and P.P. Hayes
1995   'Ancient Akamas and the Abandonment of Sites in 7th Century AD Cyprus', in *Visitors, Immigrants, and Invaders in Cyprus* (ed. P. Wallace; Albany: Institute of Cypriot Studies, SUNY–Albany): 62-69.
Fejfer, J., and H.E. Mathiesen
1995   'Previous Archaeological Work in the Akamas', in *Ancient Akamas. I. Settlement and Environment* (ed. J. Fejfer; Aarhus: University Press): 54-62.
Hauben, H.
1987   'Cyprus and the Ptolemaic Navy', RDAC: 213-26.
Karageorghis, V.
1981   'Minor Excavations: Akhelia', RDAC 1980: 43.

Kelley, K.B.
  1976   'Dendritic Central-Place Systems and the Regional Organization of
              Navajo Trading Posts', in *Regional Analysis*. I. *Economic Systems* (ed.
              C. Smith; New York: Academic Press): 219-54.

Leonard, J.R.
  1995   'Evidence for Roman Ports, Harbours and Anchorages in Cyprus', in
              Proceedings of the International Symposium on Cyprus and the Sea
              (ed. V. Karageorghis and D. Michaelides; Nicosia: University of
              Cyprus/Cyprus Ports Authority): 227-46.

Leonard, J.R., and R.L. Hohlfelder
  1993   'Paphos Harbour, Past and Present: The 1991–1992 Underwater
              Survey', RDAC: 365-79.

Lund, J.
  1993   'Pottery of the Classical, Hellenistic and Roman Periods', in *The Land
              of the Paphian Aphrodite: The Canadian Palaipaphos Survey Project*.
              II. *Artifact and Ecofact Studies* (ed. L.W. Sorensen and D.W. Rupp;
              Goteborg: Studies In Mediterranean Archaeology 104: 2): 79-115.

MacDonald, W.L.
  1986   *The Architecture of the Roman Empire*. II. *An Urban Appraisal* (New
              Haven: Yale University Press).

Maier, F.-G., and V. Karageorghis
  1984   *Paphos: History and Archaeology* (Nicosia: Levantis Foundation).

Meiggs, R.
  1973   *Roman Ostia* (Oxford: Clarendon Press).

Metraux, G.P.R.
  1978   *Western Greek Land-Use and City Planning in the Archaic Period*
              (New York: Garland).

Mitford, T.B.
  1939   'Milestones in Western Cyprus', *JRS* 29: 184-98.
  1980   'Roman Cyprus', in *Aufstieg und Niedergang der römischen Welt*,
              II.7.2 (ed. H. Temporini and W. Hasse; Berlin: de Gruyter): 1285-385.

Mlynarczyk, J.
  1982   'Remarks on the Town Plan of Hellenistic Nea Paphos', in
              Proceedings of the 2nd International Congress of Cypriote Studies
              (ed. Th. Papadopoullou and S. Hatzistylli; Nicosia: Etaireia Kypriakon
              Spoudon): 317-25.
  1985a   'Remarks on the Classical Settlement on the Site of Nea Paphos',
              Archaeologia Cypria 1: 69-78.
  1985b   'Remarks on the Temple of Aphrodite Paphia in Nea Paphos in the
              Hellenistic Period', RDAC: 286-92.
  1990   *Nea Paphos in the Hellenistic Period: Nea Paphos*, III (Warsaw:
              Wydawnictwa Geologiczne).

Morris, I.
  1991   'The Early Polis as City and State', in *City and Country in the Ancient
              World* (ed. J. Rich and A. Wallace-Hadrill; London: Routledge): 22-
              57.

Nicolaou, K.
1966   'The Topography of Nea Paphos', in *Melanges offerts a Kazimierz Michalowski* (ed. M.-L. Bernhard; Warsaw: Panstwowe Wydawnictwo Naukowe): 561-601.

Oliver, J. H.
1953   'The Ruling Power. A Study of the Roman Empire in the Second Century after Christ through the Roman Oration of Aelius Aristides', *Transactions of the American Philosophical Society* 43: 873-908.

Peristianis, I.K.
1910   *General History of the Island of Cyprus* (Lefkosia: n.p. [Greek]).

Rupp, D.W.
1981   'The Canadian Palaipaphos Survey Project: Preliminary Report of the 1979 Season', RDAC: 147-56.

1987a   '*Vive le roi*: The Emergence of the State in Iron Age Cyprus', in *Western Cyprus: Connections. An Archaeological Symposium* (ed. D.W. Rupp; Goteborg: Studies in Mediterranean Archaeology): 147-68.

1987b   The Canadian Palaipaphos Survey Project: The Canadian Palaipaphos Survey Project: An Overview of the 1986 Field Season', *Echos du monde classique/Classical Views* 6: 217-24.

Rupp, D.W., L.W. Sørensen, R.H. King and W.A. Fox
1984   'The Canadian Palaipaphos (Cyprus) Survey Project: Second Preliminary Report, 1980–1982', *JFA* 11: 133-59.

Rupp, D.W., L.W. Sørensen, R.H. King, T.E. Gregory, J. Lund and S.T. Stewart
1986   'Canadian Palaipaphos (Cyprus) Survey Project: Third Preliminary Report, 1983–1985', *AcAr* 67: 27-45.

Rupp, D.W., J.T. Clarke, C. D'Annibale and S.T. Stewart
1992   'The Canadian Palaipaphos Survey Project: 1991 Field Season', RDAC: 285-317.

Rupp, D.W., J.T. Clarke, C. D'Annibale, P.W. Croft and R.H. King
1993   'The Western Cyprus Project: 1992 Field Season', RDAC: 381-412.

Salmon, E.T.
1969   *Roman Colonization under the Republic* (London: Thames & Hudson).

Shear, Jr., T.L.
1981   'Athens: From City-State to Provincial Town', *Hesperia* 50: 356-78.

Smith, C.A.
1976   'Introduction: The Regional Approach to Economic Systems', in *Regional Analysis*. I. *Economic Systems* (ed. C.A. Smith; New York: Academic Press): 1-63.

Stambaugh, J.E.
1988   *The Ancient Roman City* (Baltimore: Johns Hopkins University Press).

Ward-Perkins, J.B.
1981   *Roman Imperial Architecture* (Harmondsworth: Penguin Books).

PALACE-CENTERED POLITIES IN EASTERN CRETE: NEOPALATIAL PETRAS AND ITS NEIGHBORS

Metaxia Tsipopoulou

Topography is a constant determinative factor in the Cretan cultural landscape. Mountain ranges compartmentalize the island into semi-autonomous units, their size proportional to the extent of fertile land shoe-horned between the foothills. The plains of central Crete, incomparably smaller than the huge Near Eastern expanses, led to a concentration of power and resources of the Minoan redistributive economy to a small number of major centers, commonly labelled 'palaces'. The term was coined by the father of Minoan archaeology, Sir Arthur Evans, in a decidedly Victorian spirit, at the beginning of this century while excavating a large architectural complex on the Kephala Hill at Knossos near Herakleion, in Central Crete: the 'Palace of Minos'. A few years later Italian archaeologists initiated work at the second major such structure, Phaistos in South-Central Crete, in the middle of the largest and most fertile plain of the island, the Mesara. The French School of Archaeology, at about the same time, began investigations at Malia, a site near the northern coast some 35 km east of Herakleion, and situated on the third large plain, that of Pediada.

The term 'palace' remains vaguely defined, yet the phenomenon dominates Minoan archaeology. If scholars are not preoccupied with analysing the palatial system, they seek signs of prepalatial forerunners or attempt to reconstruct a politico–economic framework for life after the fall of the palaces. A Minoan palace is understood as a central administrative organism to which flows the produce of the surrounding lands for storage and redistribution. This requires substantial warehousing and detailed documentation by a bureaucratic system, expressed, in the Minoan case, by seals, sealings and various forms of texts on clay and perishable materials. In other words, similar to an Eastern palatial economy, but on a smaller scale, as dictated by the topography and natural resources of a medium-sized island with an underdeveloped transportation system due to a rugged terrain.

A further legacy of the earliest phase of Minoan archaeology is constituted by its chronological system. Uncovering a hitherto unknown civilization, Evans, in his attempts to understand the sequence of the finds, looked to Egypt for a framework: the Old, Middle and New Kingdom became the Early, Middle and Late Minoan Periods. Today it is clear that the terminology, based on the pottery, is ill adapted both to the architectural phases (even at Knossos) and to the development of other Minoan arts, such as stone vases and seal stones, as well as being highly Knossocentric. An attempt by Nicolaos Platon to introduce a system based on the major construction phases of the palaces, Pre-, Proto-, Neo- and Post-palatial, has not gained universal approval. The present parallel use of both systems illustrates the problems faced by Minoan archaeology. In addition, the absolute chronology is challenged by scientific dating for the eruption that destroyed the site of Akrotiri on Thera, leading to a difference of almost 200 years with the subjective dates proposed by synchronisms with Egypt.

As the discipline developed, other categories of structures were uncovered, but the reference remained the palaces. These sites, termed 'villas' by Evans, and burdened with an equally vague definition, were found to share, with their larger counterparts, specific architectural features, and elements of an administrative function. In addition to the palaces of Knossos, Malia and Phaistos, as further palatial structures of varying sizes were excavated at Gournia and Zakros in Eastern Crete, and further 'villas' came to light, the basic relatedness remained evident, yet the differences were underlined to the extent of creating two mutually exclusive categories. All further finds were classified as either the one or the other, although the definitional aspects of the terminology had been ignored.

The most recent candidates for inclusion among the palaces, Khania, Arkhanes and Galatas, all three in Western and Central Crete, to which fieldwork conducted in 1984–95 added a further location, Petras near Siteia at the opposite end of the island, have pointed out the short-comings of the traditional framework, which consisted of the safety provided by four palaces, the initial three (Knossos, Phaistos and Malia) to which was added Zakros. The currently available database invites Minoan archaeologists to pursue a better definition of the 'palace'/'villa' dichotomy, and thus an improved understanding of Minoan civilization.

Petras

Petras (fig. 1) is situated on the southern edge of a small plain formed by the recent silting in of a marine bay, a process aided by the tectonic shifting to which the island has been subjected. The northern edge is today dominated by the township of Siteia. The main Minoan settlement occupies a 50 m high hill behind the gaggle of holiday flats forming the present-day village. The three adjacent hills have seen Minoan activity at various periods. The site of Petras was first visited by Evans in 1896, while R.C. Bosanquet conducted excavations there in 1900 (Bosanquet 1900–1901: 282-85). Two days sufficed to convince him that further work was unpromising due to extensive damage. Bosanquet continued further east, where he excavated Palaikastro. Nonetheless the Siteia Bay was noted for its advantageous location as gateway towards the East, a view vaguely reiterated by Platon while investigating an important sanctuary at nearby Piskokephalo in the early 1950s. In the 1960s, Platon went on to discover the palace of Zakros. Petras remained outside the archaeological discourse until 1985.

The continuous work of 11 field seasons has uncovered an important Neopalatial administrative unit surrounded by a township, of which two large two-storey houses have been investigated. Traces of earlier occupation of the main hill, as well as continuity into the Post-palatial Period, underlines the importance of the location through time. Three surveys have offered an increased understanding of the human settlement patterns in the Siteia Bay area, leading to an extensive reconsideration of earlier research.

Archaeological evidence, along with geomorphological data, helps us to define a certain unified territory or sphere of influence, in which we believe Petras was the central settlement, with the other sites in some way subordinate to it and perhaps dependent on it, even if the probable inter-site relationships are as yet not completely clear. The geographic boundaries of this territory are: in the west the area of Chamaizi, in the south the region of Praisos, and in the east the mountains that divide the Siteia Bay from the area of Palaikastro (Tsipopoulou and Papacostopoulou in press).

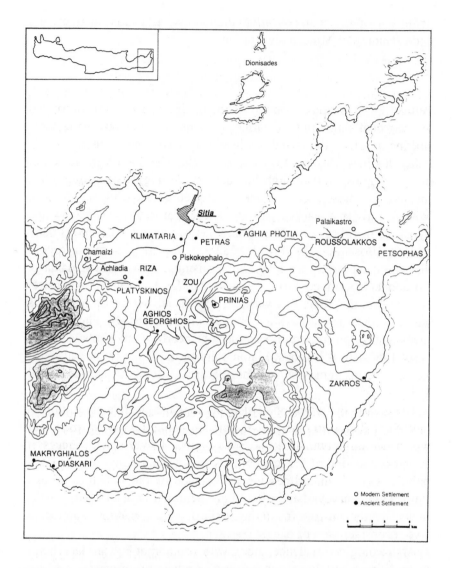

Figure 1. Map of eastern Crete showing the location of Petras and other ancient and
          modern settlements.

The Bay of Siteia was in Minoan times substantially larger, since the
coastline cut far into the present plain: it met the Stomion river at the
low hills of Anemomylia and Katrinia. Small plains exist between
Trypitos and Analoukas around Ayia Photia, and between the foothills
on either side of the Stomion, at Achladia–Riza, at Ayios Georgios
and at Zou. The foothills themselves added olives, carobs and almonds

to the economic base. In addition, honey and wine have traditionally been produced in the area.

The region became archaeologically known through the work of Platon, who excavated a number of installations called 'villas', at Klimataria (Platon 1952a: 636-39, 1953: 288-91, 1954: 361-63), Zou (Platon 1955: 288-93, 1956: 232-39), Achladia-Riza (Platon 1952b: 646-48, 1959: 210-17), and Ayios Georgios (Platon 1960: 294-300), as well as the sanctuary at Piskokephalo (Platon 1952c: 631-36). Later, Costis Davaras investigated the peak sanctuary at Prinias (Davaras 1971: 197-200, 1977: 651, 1976: 246, 1988: 45-54). Additionally, the plain of Ayia Photia survey has revealed the existence of no less than six small isolated farmhouses, owing their location to the agricultural exploitation of the surrounding area (Tsipopoulou 1989: 27-31, 99). Such a settlement pattern is virtually identical or equivalent to the traditional system of *metochia* of Crete, the small isolated farmhouses built out among the fields as temporary living quarters and storage of tools and produce. The respective sizes and architectural elaboration of these three different types of installations, combined with simple geographical considerations, suggest a hierarchical relationship.

Several models concerning the political and administrative organization of Neopalatial Crete have been proposed, though there are two main models of interpretation: the first supporting the supremacy of Knossos over the whole island and the second, accepting the division of Crete into smaller or larger independent polities (Soles 1991: 73-76). The 'peer polities' theory proposed by John Cherry (1986: 21, fig. 2.2) is very useful, but the recent research at Petras and the area of the Siteia Bay has changed the general picture, and as far as Eastern Crete is concerned, further division is needed. Indeed it is difficult to visualize it as a unified area centered on the palace of Zakros. In accepting Cherry's suggestion that the Gulf of Mirabello formed part of the polity of Malia, the eastern end of the island could have been further subdivided into three more territories: (1) the Bay of Siteia with Petras as the center, (2) the far eastern Zakros–Palaikastro area centered on Zakros, (3) the southern coast with the central place situated at Makrygialos or Diaskari.

The houses of the settlement of Petras have been compared (Tsipopoulou and Papacostopoulou in press) to the so-called 'villas' of the Siteia hinterlands in order to gain an understanding of their function and relationship to Petras, as illustrated by the architectural features and the objects uncovered in the various rooms and spaces. The formal comparison between the two houses excavated in the township and the 'villas' shows that the differences are neither many nor substantial in respect to architectural size, detail and artifact assemblages. One aspect which underlines the different purpose of these two categories of houses is the slightly larger storage capacity, and the attendant higher number of storage vessels (pithoi), exhibited by the 'villas'. Furthermore, except for Klimataria, which location suggests a special-purpose installation in connection with the main settlement, intensive survey activity in the immediate area indicates that the 'villas' are not isolated structures, but belong to larger settlement complexes. The 'villa' at Ayios Georgios is really three buildings and not, as originally thought, a single unit. They stand on a low hill surrounded by a settlement on the slopes. At Zou the situation is similar, with the 'villa', even though not at the summit of the hill for topographical reasons, raised above the settlement. Achladia–Riza presents a different pattern: the main structure is placed lower down on the slope, with traces of lesser buildings further up towards the plateau of a very large hill. Their prominent position within each habitation, and their architectural treatment, suggest that these 'villas' constitute the central entity in the intra-settlement hierarchy, thus enjoying a position comparable, although on a smaller scale, to that of the main unit at Petras, with the following caveat: Petras suggests an urban context not present at 'villa' sites.

The more recent campaigns at Petras have demonstrated that the large building on the middle plateau of Hill 1 should be termed a 'palace', despite the substantial difference in scale evidenced by a comparison with the better-known centers. The customary criteria for a designation as palace are (1) architectural: central court, storage space, stoa, drainage system, monumental staircase, light well, lustral basin, pier-and-door partition, plaster benches; (2) structural: ashlar masonry, orthostats, flagstone floors, plaster floors, painted plaster, mason's marks, mortises; (3) functional: administration, concentration and redistribution of produce, storage and transformation of raw materials, religious activities.

These features are present in the larger 'villas' of central Crete, yet always with significant gaps in the list, and never in a quality and size on par with the palaces. Petras offers evidence for all the above, except the lustral basin (with the light well uncertain or unnecessary), and clearly documented cultic areas. The smaller scale alters the framework within which the palace phenomenon of Minoan Crete must be discussed: the situation is clearly more complex than what was previously believed.

Description of the Palatial Building
Some 2000 square m of the 7000 constituting the plateau are covered by the central administrative building, excavated between 1987 and 1995. To the east and the north, the plateau is delimited by a substantial Protopalatial wall with a massive bastion-like projection.

The state plan reveals a four-part structuring of the built-up space (see fig. 2). Typically for a palace, the major feature, and organizing principle, is the central court, orientated, as it should be, roughly north to south. At 18 × 6.6 m in its earlier phase, it is small by comparison to the other palaces; nor is it enclosed by wings on each side: a single wing rises to the west, a (on the local scale) monumental staircase accesses the court from the north, and to the east there runs a corridor, or covered walkway. Slightly displaced towards the east, the North Magazines replaces a north wing, a solution imposed by the terrain, at this point one storey lower. The situation to the south of the court remains unclear, with no physical traces but for a staircase rising westward from a pier-and-door partition with flagstone floor beyond the southern limit, as it is known today.

A second phase, securely dated to Late Minoan IB, reduced the court to some 10 × 4.5 m through a single-course stoa foundation for alternating columns and pillars. The monumental stairway had ceased to function and was covered by an external court running in the shape of an 'L' along the east and north sides and above the older court. In this same phase, additional storage space was added at the foot of the stairway, forming an extension to the magazines.

On the basis of the excavated remains, it would appear that the eastern edge of the plateau was, in Neopalatial times, an open space, forming an external court contained only by the Protopalatial retaining wall. All activity in this area is either earlier, such as the Early Minoan IIB house cut into the northern edge and the scattered bedrock basins and mortars, or later, the Byzantine graves. The most imposing feature is the rock cut drainage channel, partially covered with slabs, running west to east for some 7 m. It is intimately associated with the earlier central court, which, by definition, antedates the Late Minoan IB Period.

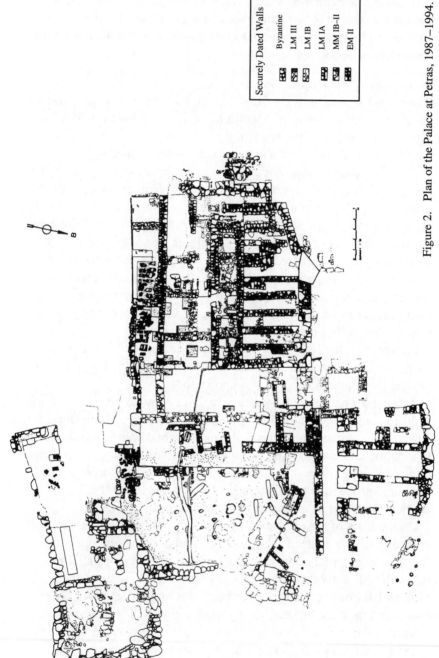

Securely Dated Walls

Byzantine
LM III
LM IB
LM IA
MM IB–II
EM II

Figure 2.   Plan of the Palace at Petras, 1987–1994.

The west wing is divided into two unequal halves by an east to west corridor, running 16 m to the west façade. The northern part is dominated by ten narrow parallel spaces, each 6 × 1.10 m behind the north façade. Since they are blind at both ends, their interpretation remains problematic. The entire area was covered by a thick Late Minoan IB destruction horizon, upon which there now stand remains of Late Minoan III buildings. The pattern of narrow dividing walls is broken by a short wall of double thickness between the sixth and seventh spaces. In the opening thus formed, we have slowly uncovered a thick Late Minoan IA destruction horizon, producing well over a thousand small finds from a 6 m square surface. A similar context was uncovered at the head of the monumental stairway leading to and from the central court.

The north façade and the south wall of the narrow parallel spaces form part of the backbone of the structure, a series of six east to west walls which divide the building into five separate areas: the narrow parallel spaces, a succession of Protopalatial units covered by the Late Minoan IB destruction level, the corridor and two series of rooms in the southern part. The first series was subjected to substantial change over time, with the final phase providing the only certain image: its use as a supplementary storage area is illustrative of a general increase in the need for magazine space in the Late Minoan IB Period. This phenomenon may be connected to the destruction of the 'villas', which Platon dated to the end of the Late Minoa IA period. Pithoi were also placed in the reduced central court. Again, a IB destruction horizon was excavated, characterized by impressive traces of fire.

The second series of rooms forming the southern edge on the plan is among the most carefully built of the palace. Access is gained through ashlar door jambs from the east, leading onto a floor paved with stone slabs set in a red clay bed.[1] Although devoid of finds *in situ*, this room exhibited emphatic signs of burning. The fill contained numerous fragments of ashlar blocks, many with mason's marks, fallen from the upper floor. The west wall was built on top of the paved floor which continued into the gypsum-and-plaster paving of the adjacent room. An 'L'-shaped plaster bench, the greater part along the south orthostat wall, constitutes a unique feature at Petras. The

---

1.   Although this room exhibits clear traces of a violent fire, the red color of the clay bed is not due to rubification since it is uniform over the full thickness of the floor.

orthostats continue into the third room, in which was found remnants of a plaster offering table. Again, an earlier state is modified by a later wall. In the final phase the room with the plaster bench, that is, the area between the two later walls, was filled in, while the eastern room with ashlar door jambs and the corner room remained in use.

At the opposite end of the eastern side of the plateau lie the North Magazines. They form a separate unit, 20 × 13 m, some 3 m lower than the central court. They consist of five separate rectangular rooms, the western-most serving as entrance and stairwell for the staircase leading to the upper floor, as well as access to a 15 m long corridor running east to west. The latter communicates with the other four rooms. Each doorway is formed by massive piers, each of which contains an 86 × 86 × 80 cm ashlar block, sufficient to carry one or two upper storeys. The north wall follows the terrain, arching southwards along the edge of the plateau. The magazines were found with 36 shattered pithoi on the rock cut floor. Total capacity at ground floor level would have attained some 60 pithoi.

Connected to the palatial building is an industrial area on a higher plateau to the south of the main complex. The finds included half-finished stone vases, raw material and a fragment of a potter's wheel. The some 40 m of terrain between the palace and the workshop appear to have constituted a garden as no architectural remains were uncovered (cf. Shaw 1993, who argues for a garden at Phaistos).

Finally, there are administrative data. A diskoid label, inscribed on both sides with the Hieroglyphic Script, came to light in the North Magazines, the sole instance known to date of this writing system in an archival context contemporaneous with a Late Minoan IB destruction. The surface level above the narrow parallel spaces in the north-western part of the complex produced two Linear A tablets. In addition, 12 Linear A signs were incised on a pithos rim found in the central court. House 2 in the township contained a clay lump with three incised signs and a sherd with two painted signs of Linear A. However, it must be stressed that these documents do not prove, in the absence of concrete evidence, that is, of roundels and seal-impressions, that a permanent archive existed at Petras (Tsipopoulou and Hallager 1996).

Petras as a Palatial Center
The architectural plan, the details in the construction and the find contexts argue in favor of reading Petras as a palatial center, despite

the lack of strong evidence for archiving. The existence of such a complex here finds its *raison d'être* in its geographical location. Petras overlooks a large maritime bay, offering safe anchorage not far from the mouth of a river that, although not navigable, would have provided a natural transport axis along its banks. The presence of three so-called 'villas' with surrounding settlement (Ayios Georgios, Zou, Achladia–Riza), one isolated 'villa' (Klimataria) at the river mouth, one sanctuary (Piskokephalo) in its immediate vicinity and thereby very close to Petras, a peak sanctuary (Prinias) and several farmsteads or small agglomerations (Analoukas, Ayia Photia plain, Siteia Airport, Achladia–Platyskoinos), all within a clearly circumscribed geographical region, offers a natural and cultural *mise en scène* for the following hypothetical reconstruction: (1) Petras constituted the main administrative unit, centered on a small palace and surrounded by a substantial settlement; (2) the so-called 'villas' functioned as subordinate entities, the functional extension of the palace into the outlying settlements of the hinterland, channelling produce towards the center and distributing the goods filtering down through the system; (3) the farmsteads or minor agglomerations housed the population closer to the fields and orchards, or to economic niches; and (4) the two sanctuaries formed part of the religious network covering the territory.

Conclusion

The spectrum of architectural forms offered by the various excavated 'palaces' and 'villas' indicates that neither building type can be defined by reference to a single archetypical site. Each site constitutes an individual solution to a specific context and to regional requirements and possibilities. Nonetheless, there clearly exists a 'palace model', respected to a substantial degree (despite differences of scale) by each structure that functions as an administrative center within a given geographical region. The designs of the 'villas', on the other hand, do not adhere to a 'villa model', but rather mimic aspects of the 'palace model', each in its own manner according to its topographical and systemic position. A 'villa model' does not appear to have ever existed, not withstanding the 'villa' typology generated by John McEnroe (1982: 18-19). This would reflect a less strict functional definition of the 'villa' in relationship to the 'palace', the architectural expression of each 'villa' being conditioned by the function the structure is to serve according to its position within the hierarchy. A 'palace' serves a global purpose within the administrative system, whereas a 'villa' is tailored to an economic niche.

Platon initially suggested that the 'villas' of Eastern Crete answered directly to Knossos as the seats of local chieftains, although it should be noted that he conceived of them as isolated structures, despite evidence to the contrary uncovered by his own excavations (Platon 1970: 186). At this time no known palatial center existed east of Gournia. The discovery of Zakros provided such an administrative focus, to which Platon naturally attached the East Cretan 'villas'.

By assigning, as is done here, the 'villas' and farmsteads around the Bay of Siteia to the control of Petras, Zakros is by no means diminished. Sites such as Ano Zakros (Platon 1971) and Chiromandres (Tzedakis *et al.* 1990) represent the second, 'villa' level of the hierarchy, while Azokeramos, Xirokampos–Katsounaki and Sfaka constitute smaller agglomerations. At Traostalos, Anthropolithous, Vigla and Sfaka there are peak sanctuaries (cf. Rutkowski 1986: 8, 73, 93, 95, 98, 245). Thus, Zakros is surrounded by the same subordinate entities as Petras, again clearly circumscribed by natural boundaries. Two dissimilarities must be noted: the difference in size and relevant database, and the presence of Palaikastro. Architecturally, Zakros forms a larger unit than Petras, although the agricultural base is smaller. The higher profit margin which enabled the construction of a larger palace must have been generated by the geographical position, the main exit towards the Middle East, a role amply documented by exotic, non-Cretan finds.

Until Palaikastro produces palatial architecture, it must be seen as subordinate to Zakros (within the present model). Yet, an unpublished 'villa' near Vaï (cf. Tiré and van Effenterre 1978: 105; de Santerre 1951: 143-46), and peak sanctuaries at Petsophas (Rutkowski 1991, with bibliography) and Modi (cf. Rutkowski 1986: 11, 80, 93, 95, 97) could go some way to reconstruct a palatial center at Palaikastro. The present framework would prefer to see the site as an important town. In the Late Minoan III Period, when the palaces at Zakros and Petras had come to an abrupt end, Palaikastro became the most significant settlement in all Eastern Crete. The phenomenon of non-palatial centers in Postpalatial Eastern Crete is not restricted to Palaikastro: a similar situation may be observed in the Mochlos–Myrsini–Tourloti area, where Mochlos constitutes the sole East Cretan site other than

Palaikastro to produce Late Minoan II pottery (in very small amounts), a sign of continuity after the destruction, followed by a Late Minoan IIIA1 reoccupation (Tsipopoulou 1995).

A further administrative unit is postulated for the Makrygialos–Diaskari region, but the area is not well investigated and the finds hitherto made have not seen their final publications. Davaras (1985) excavated a 'villa' at Makrygialos that he believes exhibits palatial architectural features and indications of a cultic function. It is surrounded by a settlement that remains uninvestigated. Nearby Diaskari, a major coastal site, was largely destroyed by developers. Eastward from Diaskari the author discovered in the 1986 survey that there are a number of small installations, always in connection with agricultural niches of restricted extent. Data relative to settlement patterns in Neopalatial Eastern Crete would then suggest the existence of three economic and political units centered on Petras, Zakros and Makrygialos–Diaskari, comprising a palatial unit, settlements headed by a 'villa', small outlying agglomerations, or even isolated farmsteads, and one or more sanctuaries, often near a mountain peak. It remains to be determined what relationships these centers entertained with each other, and the role of the major central Cretan palaces in the eastern province of the island, particularly Knossos, to which one hypothesis would assign supremacy over the whole of Crete.

ACKNOWLEDGMENTS

The project on Minoan occupation of the Siteia Bay area in Eastern Crete has been conducted since 1984, when excavation at Ayia Photia began. I wish to express my gratitude to the Greek Ministry of Culture for the necessary permits and financial support for excavation and expropriation at Ayia Photia and Petras, and particularly to the Institute for Aegean Prehistory, New York, and Mr Malcolm Wiener for the constant financial and moral support, which enable me to preserve the sites and continue my research. To all those who in various ways are helping me in carrying out the work I am most grateful. For the preparation of this publication and help with the English translation I am indebted to Dr Michael Wedde.

BIBLIOGRAPHY

Bosanquet, R.C.
1900–1901 'Excavations at Petras', BSA 8: 282-85.

Cherry, J.
  1986   'Polities and Palaces: Some Problems in Minoan State Formation', in
             Peer Polity, Interaction and Socio-Political Change (ed. C. Renfrew
             and J. Cherry; Cambridge: Cambridge University Press): 19-45.
Davaras, C.
  1971   'Archaeological Investigations in Siteia, Summer 1971', *Amaltheia* 2:
             197-200 (Greek).
  1976   *Guide to Cretan Antiquities* (Park Ridge, NJ: Noyes).
  1977   'Prinias (1972)', *Arch. Deltion* 27B (1972): 651 (Greek).
  1985   'Architectural Features of the LMIB Villa at Makrygialos', in *Acts of
             the Fifth International Cretological Congress* (ed. T. Detorakis;
             Herakleion: n.p. [Greek]): 77-92.
  1988   'A Minoan Beetle-Rhyton from Prinias Siteias', BSA 83: 45-54.
De Santerre, H. Gallet
  1951   'Recherches archéologiques dans la région d'Itanos', *RevArch* 38:
             134-46.
McEnroe, J.
  1982   'A Typology of Minoan Neopalatial Houses', *AJA* 86: 3-19.
Platon, N.
  1952a   'A Minoan Villa in Siteia', *Praktika*: 636-39 (Greek).
  1952b   'A Middle Minoan I House at Riza, Achladia', *Praktika*: 646-48
             (Greek).
  1952c   'A Sanctuary at Piskokephalo, Siteia', *Praktika*: 631-36 (Greek).
  1953   'Continuation of the Excavation of the Minoan Villa in Siteia',
             Praktika: 288-91 (Greek).
  1954   'Excavation of the Minoan Villa in Siteia', *Praktika*: 361-63 (Greek).
  1955   'A Minoan Farmhouse at Zou, Siteia', *Praktika*: 288-93 (Greek).
  1956   'Excavation of the Minoan Villa at Zou, Siteia', *Praktika*: 232-39
             (Greek).
  1959   'Excavation at Achladia, Siteia', *Praktika*: 210-17 (Greek).
  1960   'A Minoan Farmhouse at Prophitis Ilias, Tourtouloi', *Praktika*: 294-
             300 (Greek).
  1970   'Minoan Civilization', in *History of the Greek Nation* (Athens:
             Ekdotiki Athinon): 166-211.
  1971   *Zakros: The Discovery of a Lost Palace of Ancient Crete* (New York:
             Athens Archaeological Society).
Rutkowski, B.
  1986   *The Cult Places of the Aegean* (New Haven: Yale University Press).
  1991   *Petsophas, a Cretan Peak Sanctuary* (Warsaw: Perl).
Shaw, M.C.
  1993   'The Aegean Garden', *AJA* 97: 661-85.
Soles, J.S.
  1991   'The Gournia Palace', *AJA* 95: 17-78.
Tiré, C., and H. van Effenterre,
  1978   *Guide des fouilles françaises en Crète* (Paris: Ecole Française
             d'Athènes).
Tsipopoulou, M.
  1989   *Archaeological Survey at Aghia Photia, Siteia* (Partille: SIMA).

1995   'Late Minoan III Siteia. Patterns of Settlement and Land Use', in *Achladia: Scavi e ricerche della Missione Greco–Italiana in Creta Orientale (1991–1993). Incunabula Graeca Vol. 97. Istituto per gli Studi Micenei ed Egeo-Anatolici* (ed. M. Tsipopoulou and L. Vagnetti; Rome: Gruppo Editoriale Internazionale): 177-92.

Tsipopoulou, M., and E. Hallager

1996   'Inscriptions with Hieroglyphs and Linear A from Petras, Siteia', *SMEA* 37: 7-46.

Tsipopoulou, M., and A. Papacostopoulou

in press   ' "Villas" and Villages in the Hinterland of Petras, Siteia', in *The Function of the Minoan 'Villa'* (ed. R. Hägg).

Tzedakis, I., S. Chryssoulaki, S. Voutsaki and Y. Venieri

1990   'Les routes minoennes: le poste de Chiromandres et le contrôle des communications', *BCH* 114: 43-65.

A VIEW FROM THE OUTSKIRTS:
REALIGNMENTS FROM MODERN TO POSTMODERN
IN THE ARCHAEOLOGICAL STUDY OF URBANISM

D. Bruce MacKay

The world in which we live appears to be affected more and more, whether we like it or not, by a postmodern perspective. The modernist paradigm that has dominated fields of study from architecture and art to anthropology and archaeology through most of this century does not have as much authority as it did, and indeed is found by many to be more problematic than helpful. This modernist perspective can be characterized in very broad terms by such ideas as: the physical world can be manipulated and controlled for the better; problems of health and hunger can be solved through increased efficiency and application of scientific solutions; once people are liberated from the constraints of parochial political agendas, a true view of our common humanity will emerge to erase differences of race and creed and result in one peaceful and happy human family; a properly planned and constructed city can be the most effective and efficient way of organizing human beings so that they will reach their greatest productive potential.

It is obvious, however, that the optimism expressed by such modernist notions has not been realized in each and every case. Instead of a paradise, we live in a world threatened by environmental degradation. Instead of universal health and well-being and despite the best efforts of medical science, we are faced with continued ill-health and outbreaks of new virulent diseases. Instead of peace for all, we find increased violence and continued animosity between groups of people who appear to be more concerned about the loss of age-old identities than developing bonds of common humanity with their neighbours. And the city is less a well-organized home for happy and productive people than it is a battleground where disparities between rich and

poor and competition between various interests and political agendas
are played out in situations of increasing stress and fear. Views such
as these, and the critique of the modernist perspective which they
imply, are, in very broad terms, typical of the postmodernist perspective (see Watson and Gibson 1995).

The broad parameters of this shifting paradigmatic focus that are
characterized above describe the general social and intellectual context
in which the archaeological study of urbanism is practised. It is the
context in which questions about the human past are asked, the context
in which research proposals are written and grants given, and the
context in which research is published. It is not surprising then, that
the general shift from a modernist to a postmodernist perspective is
reflected in the fields of archaeology and urban studies. Some scholars
continue to ask questions and define research agendas more in the
framework of modernist positivistic science. Others reflect the trend
toward postmodernism, and, although they may not define themselves
or their work explicitly as postmodernist, the general concerns of
postmodernism, such as those characterized above, can be found in
their work.

In archaeology, the terms processual and postprocessual usually
frame discourse about the shift from modernism to postmodernism.
These terms and the archaeological discussion they reflect have a
much narrower focus than the broad parameters sketched above. In
general, however, a modernist approach to archaeology tends to
emphasize controlled and accurate presentation and description of
data, quantification, monocausal and nomothetic universal explanations
for changes in cultural systems, and in processual archaeology in particular a hypothetico-deductive and positivistic approach to theorizing
(Bell 1992: 144). Alternately, a postmodernist approach to archaeology tends to focus less on the data itself in favor of an emphasis on the
importance of interpretation, a plurality of explanatory approaches, a
plurality of voices and points of view reflected in the archaeological
data and the important role of the archaeologist in the interpretive
process. Postprocessual archaeologists tend to emphasize 'unique par-
ticularities' and stress the coincidental nature of similarities rather
than the universal (Bell 1992: 144; and see e.g. Hodder 1986).

Our approach to the papers of the University of Lethbridge conference on urbanism will be to use the framework outlined above in a
heuristic way, to reflect on how they fall into the broad categories of

modernist and postmodernist approaches to urbanism. While none of the papers was framed explicitly in the language of the modern/ postmodern or processual/postprocessual discussion, the two styles of questioning and explanation, modernist and postmodernist, are evident. It should be noted, however, that while some of the participants might not agree with the categorization of their work as modernist or postmodernist, the aim here is not to emphasize or entrench polarities, but merely to illustrate that broader intellectual patterns are evident in the conference papers. Indeed, disagreement might also be interpreted as indicative of the uncertainty and fluidity that accompanies such a paradigmatic shift in societal, intellectual and archaeological focus. In any case, the grouping suggested here does not imply any of the inflammatory political rhetoric that often accompanies the use of these labels nor a typecasting of the conference participants themselves. It is merely offered as one reading, from the outskirts so to speak, of the conference papers set in a broader societal context.

Modernist Approaches to Urbanism

A modernist approach to urbanism is evident in the papers by Sweet, Redford, Daviau, B. Routledge, Fortin, A. Rosen, Tsipopoulou and Dever.

Some of these papers explore the modernist notion of urbanism as a strategy employed by a power- and authority-wielding elite who impose order and efficiency on an otherwise disordered, inefficient and chaotic population. Ronald Sweet, for example, argues that the development of writing in fourth-millennium BCE Uruk was an innovation which enabled an elite to organize, administer and control a large population. This reflects a view of the city as an adaptation that a central authority imposed to create efficiency, order and control, which resulted from the development of an innovation that most benefited those elites who held power. Michèle Daviau views the city in similar terms. She argues that urbanism was an administration strategy which controlled aspects of the physical organization of a site, its architecture, and presumably its inhabitants as well. The authority of centralized control is represented, in the case of Iron Age Tell Jawa, by a fortification system, gate complex and a variety of building types, including domestic dwellings and large orthogonal structures. The result of the imposition of externally organized power was that the city functioned as a central place in the administrative and bureaucratic structures of the state. Bruce Routledge also investigates the city, in this case from the Iron Age in Moab, as a consequence of the imposition of political authority. The resulting urban organization, evidenced in part by the Mesha inscription, was not defined by a particular size or organizational structure, but by its role in a spatial hierarchy that provided a location for the processes of domination and control. Michel Fortin, as well, sees the growth of small settlements in the Syrian hinterland, such as fourth-millennium BCE Khabour, as a result of the imposition of the economic demands imposed by major urban centers such as Mari. The smaller communities represent the low end of the spatial hierarchy suggested by Routledge. Arlene Rosen also examines the results of the manipulative practices of urban elites. She suggests that, in the Early Bronze Age Levant, development of specialized farming techniques, control of the revenues from cash crops and storage of subsistence grains, together with control of the fertility cult, enabled the managerial classes to organize the large populations and social complexity, and to entice farmers to participate in the systems that are typical of urbanization and that support the urban elites.

Metaxia Tsipopoulou's paper exhibits a modernist concern for function. Her analysis assumes that a particular architectural model, the palatial center, reflects its function as an aspect of administrative authority. However, she suggests that the determining factor in the particular manifestation of authority and control, such as that found at Petras, Crete, is the natural environment and topography of the area. The focus on the influence of an agency apart from human intentionality is characteristic of a modernist approach.

So too, Donald Redford's analysis of the 'problem' of urbanism in Egypt reflects a modernist understanding of the city. He notes that the Egyptians did not view the 'city' as we do. This is demonstrated by the lack of lexographic evidence for urban centers that reflect the strong centralization of a ruling elite and a concentration of ruled workers. Urbanism in the Egyptian case does not fit with certain notions of what a city is; a city, in this case, already defined in modernist terms.

William Dever's paper on Iron Age Israel describes a state managed by an elite who create hierarchy and impose structures in order to meet successfully the added stresses that result from increasing population. This is a modernist notion. Ancient Israel meets the defining

criteria for a state, including the presence of urban centers typified by
social complexity and elite managers.

The broad context of a shifting perspective from modernist to
postmodernist which can be seen in the conference papers is explicit in
Dever's paper, particularly in his discussion of the 'revisionist historians' and his dismissal of 'postmodernist piffle'. Quite apart from the
content or merit of his argument with the 'revisionists', Dever's point
is that archaeology is best able to carry out the postmodernist program of giving back a voice to the people of the past. Yet in this
paper, Dever describes the city and the state as one measurable phase
in the recurring oscillation between rural and urban adaptions that
typify the evolutionary development of the region. Ancient Israelite
cities are thus indicators of the social complexity that characterizes a
state such as Israel and indeed are dependent on the centralized
authority that informs urbanization. This is a modernist model because
it minimizes the role of the vast majority of the city's population who
were not in positions of power and does not consider their influence in
any of the developments or processes associated with the emergence of
urbanism and the state. However, if we are to recover the voices of
these people from the past and to realize the promise Dever envisions
for archaeology, the modernist model of urbanism will have to be
tempered with postmodernist styles of explanation.

Postmodernist Approaches to Urbanism

Elements of postmodernist perspectives on urbanism are evident in the
papers by Aufrecht, Ben Zvi, Mirau, Herr, S. Rosen, C. Routledge,
Rupp and Banning.

As do authors of some papers with a modernist approach, some
conference participants addressed the relationship between the city and
elite members of a city's population. Walter Aufrecht, for example,
considers the role of the alphabet in Iron Age Levantine urbanism. He
argues that although writing and literacy remained tied to power, the
invention of the alphabet gave power to all of those who could learn
and use its simple system. Writing was not simply the province of the
ruling and administrative elites. Furthermore, this system was developed and became popular not in a rural setting but in an urban context. The implication is therefore that urbanism was not simply the
result of an order imposed by those in power but was, in part, a result

of the ability of a city's citizens to look out for their own interests through their own ability to read and write. This, in the discourse of postmodernism, is an example of empowerment. Ehud Ben Zvi, on the other hand, explores another aspect of the relationship between power and writing, in particular the interconnection between the authority of the literati and the authority of the literature that they produced. In his view, the social, economic and political circumstances of the literati in Persian Period Jerusalem were instrumental in the production of the work they created to legitimate their positions of authority and power within the city and the state. Although the focus is not on empowerment, it is postmodern in the way it exposes a situation in which those in power legitimated their position and their agenda with the literature they produced.

Larry Herr's description of urban features at Iron Age Tell el-'Umeiri is modernist in the sense that it aims to describe accurately the features excavated at the site that indicate urbanism. But the suggestion that urbanizing strategies, represented in part at Tell el-'Umeiri by the fortification system, were more a local adaption than part of a regular stage in a linear evolutionary process or a system imposed on the inhabitant of the city by controlling elites, is a postmodernist kind of explanation.

The paper by Carolyn Routledge expresses another aspect of a postmodernist perspective, that is, that the organization of the city is not solely dependent on efficiency or optimum organizational structures. She points out that New Kingdom Akhetaten (Amarna) was organized, in part, because of the religious ideology current at the time, an ideology that imposed a particular organizational principle on space. In other words, religious ideas can be the dominating organizing force in the city. Edward Banning argues a similar point. His approach to fourth-millennium BCE Sumer is postmodern since it examines evidence for social inequality and social complexity based on the recognition that urbanism does not result in homogeneity or in a reduction of differences. Indeed, it appears that the concentration of power in the hands of a few resulted in inequalities that were reflected in increasing differentiation between households. As well, his exploration of site size as an indication of how processes of urbanization affect peripheral zones of a region and the point that supposed efficiency may not be the sole explanation for the resulting pattern of spatial organization is a postmodernist approach. In other words, the observed pattern may not simply be the result of a rational drive toward greater efficiency.

David Rupp's analysis of the marginal zones around Nea Paphos, Cyprus, is of the postmodernist type because it shows that the urban sprawl strategy adopted by the area's inhabitants in the Hellenistic and Earlier Roman Period was the antithesis of a modern approach to urban sprawl. He demonstrates that the modernist paradigm of urban efficiency represented by a productive city center surrounded by a suburban margin of residences for workers and managers at ease is not necessarily the only method of urban organization.

The role of technology in urbanism is explored in the papers by Neil Mirau and Steven Rosen. Mirau argues that the development of urbanism in the Iron Age Levant was neither monocausal nor the result of the emergence of iron working, a development that, in the modernist paradigm, would have led to greater efficiency and hence urbanism. Rosen also argues that in the Early Bronze Age Levant, evidence for the general processes of change in the area of craft specialization, which resulted in or accompanied the development of cities, is more complex than a modernist monocausal explanation would imply.

Conclusion

This view from the outskirts suggests that the voices of those who inhabited the ancient Near East are, as they gain more attention, being recognized in a multiplicity of stories associated with the emergence of urbanism. The general shift in paradigm has led to a greater awareness that the city is not simply an organizational tool of a powerful elite which resulted from the application of authority to produce maximum efficiency. Authority was certainly a factor, but not the only one, and the closer attention being given to the influence of authorities on the majority of the inhabitants of an ancient city is resulting in an increasing awareness of the ways in which the elites and managerial classes manipulated those who had little or no power. Indeed, what is clear from the conference papers is an emerging awareness that there was no single factor behind the emergence of urbanism. The archaeological evidence shows, as is expected from a postmodernist perspective on urbanism (Watson and Gibson 1995), that there were a multiplicity of possibilities, a variety of struggles in both marginal and mainstream levels of complex society, and that the city's inhabitants in the past, as today, were not passive and inactive recipients of the agenda of the elites, but were capable of and active in formulating strategies to adapt in the changing circumstances that are a fact of life in an urban setting.

BIBLIOGRAPHY

Bell, J.A.
  1992   'Universalization in Archaeology', in *Metaarchaeology: Reflections by Archaeologists and Philosophers* (ed. L. Embree; Dordrecht: Kluwer): 143-63.
Hodder, I.
  1986   *Reading the Past: Current Approaches to Interpretation in Archaeology* (Cambridge: Cambridge University Press).
Watson, S., and K. Gibson (eds.)
  1995   *Postmodern Cities and Spaces* (Oxford: Basil Blackwell).

INDEX OF AUTHORS

Abu-es-Soof, B. 22, 25, 26
Abujaber, R.S. 156
al-'Adami, K. 25
Adams, R. McC. 17-19, 21, 28, 35, 37, 38, 50, 52, 63, 66, 180, 181, 187
Aharoni, Y. 109
Ahlström, G. 139, 202, 203
Akkermans, P. 51, 52
Albertz, R. 120
Albright, W. 176, 182
Alexander, R.T. 68
Algaze, G. 64, 66
Alt, A. 176
Amiran, R. 85, 87, 96
Andels, T.H. 67
Assmann, J. 231, 232
Aufrecht, W.E. 13, 122, 137, 282
Avigad, N. 120, 122

Badawy, A. 214, 223, 225, 229, 230, 232
Bagnall, R.S. 241
Baines, J. 195
Banning, E.B. 20, 21, 282, 283
Barkay, G. 184
Barnes, I.L. 52
Barstad, H.M. 194
Barucq, A. 230
Baslez, M.-F. 122
Baumgarten, J.J. 157, 160
Bayman, J.M. 50
Beale, T.W. 66, 67
Beard, M. 195
Beaudry, M. 124, 157, 160
Beit Arieh, I. 87
Bekker-Nielsen, T. 240, 251, 255, 256
Bell, J.A. 279
Ben Zvi, E. 197-99, 203, 205, 282

Ben-Tor, A. 158, 179
Bennett, C.-M. 137, 145
Betts, A.V.G. 83
Beyer, D. 59
Bielinski, P. 61
Bienkowski, P. 132, 134
Bietak, M. 211, 212, 214, 221, 223-28, 230
Biran, A. 178
Birot, M. 65
Blackburn, M. 56
Blenkinsopp, J. 197, 198
Boatwright, M.T. 238
Boling, R.G. 156, 168
Boorn, G.P.F. van den 211, 217
Boraas, R.S. 156
Bordreuil, P. 119, 120
Bosanquet, R.C. 263
Bottéro, J. 65
Bounni, A. 53
Boyd, T.D. 237
Braun, E. 85
Breniquet, C. 25, 26
Bright, J. 176
Brill, R.H. 52
Broshi, M. 184, 194-96
Brumfiel, E.M. 82-84
Buccellati, G. 51, 61
Budd, P. 101, 104, 110, 111
Buia, D. 61
Bunimovitz, S. 109, 111
Burke, M.L. 68
Butzer, K. 212
Byrd, B.F. 21

Cannadine, D. 231
Carneiro, R.L. 172, 174, 175
Carroll, R.P. 200

Carter, C.E. 194-98
Castagnoli, F. 237
Chabot, J. 64
Chambon, A. 158
Champion, T.C. 213
Charpin, D.F. 52, 65
Chatonnet, F.B. 122
Chernykh, E. 52
Cherry, J. 267
Childe, V.G. 17, 50, 63, 82, 83, 180, 181, 187
Christaller, W. 19-21
Christou, D. 255
Chryssoulaki, S. 274
Claessen, H.J.M. 173
Clark, G. 132, 136
Clark, V. 132
Clines, D.J.A. 200
Clough, R.E. 103
Cobb, C. 82
Cohen, G.M. 254
Cohen, R. 172
Collombier, A.-M. 122
Cooper, L. 54
Coote, R.B. 173, 175
Costin, C.L. 82, 83
Courty, M.A. 63-65
Cowgill, G.L. 213
Crawford, H. 64, 65, 68
Cross, F.M. 117, 118, 120, 122
Cross, J. 82
Crumley, C.L. 82
Cryer, F.H. 194
Curvers, H. 57

Dajani, R.W. 146
Dalley, S. 65
Damerow, P. 36, 40, 41, 45
Daszewski, W.A. 249-52
Daumas, F. 230
Davaras, C. 267, 275
Daviau, P.M.M. 158, 161, 162, 167, 280
Davies, G.I. 122
Davies, N. de G. 216
Davies, P.R. 175, 177, 179, 187, 194, 197, 198, 201
Davis, D. 110, 188

Dayton, J. 100
Dearman, J.A. 138, 139, 163
Delougaz, P. 27
Demsky, A. 117, 120, 121
Dennett, D.C. 119
Dever, W.G. 108, 109, 116-18, 120, 124, 176, 179, 182, 184-86, 201, 210, 280-82
Diakonoff, I.M. 27, 66
Digard, F. 31
Dirks, R. 94
Donbaz, V. 43
Dossin, G.J. 65
Dothan, T. 107, 109
Dreyer, H.J. 124
Duncan-Jones, R.P. 239
Durand, J.-M. 52, 65

Earle, T. 52, 82, 83
Edelman, D.V. 177
Effenterre, H. van 274
Eighmey, J. 132, 136
Eisenberg, E. 85
Englund, R.K. 36-41, 45
Erman, A. 211-13, 217
Esse, D.L. 84, 92, 94, 95
Evans, G. 124
Evans, R.K. 84
Eyre, C.J. 195

Fairman, H. 222, 223, 228
Falconer, S.E. 17, 20, 69, 131, 180
Faulkner, R.O. 211
Fejfer, J. 255
Finet, A. 52, 64, 65
Finkelstein, I. 109, 111, 152, 153, 157, 175, 182, 184, 185, 194, 196
Firchow, O. 214
Fisher, J.R. 146
Fitzmyer, J.A. 122
Flanagan, J.W. 172, 173, 175, 176
Flannery, K.V. 67, 172
Folk, R. 101, 111
Forbes, R.J. 100, 111
Forest, J.-D. 23, 25
Fortin, M. 21, 53, 54, 56, 61, 280
Foster, B.R. 66
Fox, R. 131

Fox, V. 201
Franken, H.J. 156, 158
Frick, F.S. 124, 172, 173, 175
Fried, M.H. 52, 172, 173, 175
Friedman, J. 172
Fritz, V. 109, 124, 173, 184

Gadd, C.J. 65
Gardiner, A.H. 211, 212, 217, 227, 228
Geertz, C. 130, 231
Gelb, I.J. 27, 43
Geraty, L. 132, 146
Geus, C. de 172
Geyer, B. 64
Gibson, K. 279, 284
Gilead, I. 88
Glass, J. 87
Gledhill, J. 66
Glueck, N. 156
Goedicke, H. 212, 214, 216, 217
Gomàa, F. 214
Goodway, M. 52
Goody, J. 121, 195
Gophna, R. 85, 96
Gottwald, N.K. 172
Graeve, M.-C. de 52
Grapow, H. 211-13, 217
Green, M.W. 39, 40, 44-47
Greenberg, R. 158
Greenfield, J.C. 117
Greenstein, E.L. 117

Haas, J. 52, 172
Habachi, L. 216
Hallager, E. 272
Hallo, W.W. 104
Halpern, B. 179
Halstead, P. 67
Hanson, J. 21, 25
Harding, G.L. 146
Harris, W.V. 195
Hassan, F.A. 215
Hauben, H. 251, 252, 255
Hauptmann, A. 87
Hayes, J.H. 203
Hayes, P.P. 255
Healey, J.F. 117

Helck, W. 216
Henrickson, E. 17
Herr, L.G. 122, 125, 132, 137, 145, 146, 158, 188, 282, 283
Herzog, Z. 124, 158-60, 162, 165, 185
Hill, H.D. 27
Hill, J.N. 21
Hillier, B. 21, 25
Hodder, I. 101, 104, 179, 184, 279
Hoffman, M.A. 210, 216
Hoftijzer, J. 124
Hoglund, K. 196, 198
Hohlfelder, R.L. 251
Hole, F. 62
Holladay, J.S. 159, 184, 185
Homäs-Fredrique, D. 134, 158
Hours, F. 85
Hübner, U. 122
Hunt, R.C. 66, 68
Huot, J.L. 50

Ibach, R. 132, 156, 158
Ibrahim, M. 145, 146
Ilan, O. 87, 117
Isserlin, B.S.J. 122, 146

Jackson, K.P. 163
Jacobs, L. 132
Jacobsen, T. 18, 28
Jamieson-Drake, D.W. 177
Janssen, J. 228
Japhet, S. 199
Jawad, A.J. 50
Joel, E.C. 52
Joffe, A.H. 97
Johnson, D. 69
Johnson, G.A. 17, 18, 21, 82, 83
Jones, B.A. 205
Jones, G. 68
Jongeling, K. 124
Joukowsky, M.S. 103

Kapolony, P. 211
Karageorghis, V. 256, 258
Kaufman, S.A. 122
Kelley, K.B. 240
Kelly-Buccellati, M. 51, 52
Kelso, J.L. 158

Kemp, B. 221-25, 228-30, 232
Kempinski, A. 82, 92
Kense, F. 100
Khoury, P.S. 173
Kipp, R.S. 52, 66
Kitchen, K. 213, 223, 226, 228
Klengel, H. 52
Kletter, R. 156
Knauf, E.A. 138
Kohl, P.L. 66
Kolb, F. 180
Kostiner, J. 173
Koucky, F. 132
Kowalewski, S. 17
Kramer, C. 67
Kubba, S.A.A. 23, 25
Kühne, H. 62, 157, 160
Kuhrt, A. 231
Kupper, J. 52, 65, 68

LaBianca, O.S. 109, 132, 138, 146
Lackenbacker, S. 52
Lafort, B. 52
Lampl, P. 50
Larsen, M. 66
Lebeau, M. 65
Lemaire, A. 117, 124, 130, 132, 138
Lemche, N.P. 172, 175-78, 182, 185,
    187, 194
Lenski, G. 196
Lenski, J. 196
Leonard, J.R. 249, 251, 254, 258
Levy, T.E. 116
Lewis, M. 200
Lewy, J. 52
Liebowitz, H. 101, 111
Lipinski, E. 138
Lloyd, S. 27
Longacre, W.A. 21
Lund, J. 247
Lurton Burke, M. 65

MacDonald, B. 157, 237, 238
Maddin, R. 100, 101, 103-105, 107,
    110, 111
Maier, F.-G. 256
Maisels, C. 131
Mallowan, M.E.L. 52, 65

Manzanilla, L. 50
Marder, O. 85
Margeraud, J.-C. 24
Margueron, J. 64, 65
Martin, G.T. 217
Mathiesen, H.E. 255
Mattingly, G. 132
Maxwell-Hyslop, K. 100
Mazar, A. 109, 152, 158, 179, 184
Mazzoni, S. 161
McCorriston, J. 64, 67
McCowan, C.C. 168
McEnroe, J. 273
McGovern, P.E. 145, 156
McGuire, R.H. 52
McKenzie, S.L. 203
McNutt, P.M. 99, 100, 104, 107, 108
Meeks, D. 213
Meiggs, R. 238
Metraux, G.P.R. 237
Meyerhof, E. 85
Milevski, I. 85
Millard, A.R. 117, 121-23
Miller, J.M. 132, 138, 157, 203
Miller, R. 107
Mirau, N.A. 13, 125, 282, 284
Miroschedji, P. de 92
Mitford, T.B. 242, 256
Mlynarczyk, J. 249, 252, 256, 257
Monchambert, J.-Y. de 62, 64
Moorey, P.R.S. 52
Morris, I. 237
Morton, W. 136
Muhly, J.D. 52, 99-101, 103-107, 110,
    111

Na'aman, N. 124, 175
Najjar, M. 156
Nassaney, M.S. 84
Naveh, J. 116, 117, 119, 120, 178
Negueruela, I. 137
Neufeld, E. 124
Newsom, C.A. 206
Niccacci, A. 138, 139
Nicolaou, K. 249, 251, 254
Niditch, S. 117
Nissen, H.J. 17, 18, 36-41, 44-47, 50
Nolan, P. 196

North, D.C. 66
Noth, M. 176

O'Connor, D. 210, 211, 213, 215,
    222-25, 228, 230, 232
O'Shea, J. 67
Oates, D. 51, 68
Oates, J. 22, 51, 63, 64, 68
Olávarri, E. 134
Oliver, J.H. 258
Olivier, J.P.J. 158, 159
Olszewski, D. 132, 136
Oppenheim, A.L. 66
Orthmann, W. 51
Orton, C. 184
Ozbal, H. 52
Ozgen, E. 107

Palmieri, A.M. 52
Parker, S.T. 132
Payayre, D. 51, 52
Paynter, R. 52
Peet, T.E. 213
Peristianis, I.K. 255
Peters, F.E. 123
Piccirillo, M. 146
Platon, N. 267, 274
Polanyi, K. 66
Portugali, Y. 96
Posener-Krieger, P. 213
Posnansky, M. 52
Postgate, J.N. 27, 43
Potts, T.F. 66
Powell, M.A. 27, 67, 122
Price, B. 52, 87
Provan, I.W. 175
Puech, E. 137
Pusch, E. 223

Rad, G. von 176
Rapoport, A. 25
Rathje, W.L. 28
Ray, J. 195
Redford, D.B. 212, 214, 216, 231, 257,
    280, 281
Redman, C.L. 63, 82, 130, 156, 159
Reed, W. 137
Reifenberg, A. 120

Reimer, S. 61
Renfrew, C. 66, 82, 83, 172
Renger, J. 28, 66
Ricke, H. 213
Rida, N. 132, 136
Röllig, W. 62
Roscoe, P. 132
Rosen, A.M. 88, 93-95
Rosen, S.A. 83, 85, 96, 280-82, 284
Rouillard-Bonraisin, H. 124
Routledge, B. 61, 132, 134, 136, 138,
    188, 280, 281
Routledge, C. 61, 134, 282, 283
Rova, E. 64
Rowlands, M.J. 68, 82, 172
Runnels, C.N. 67
Rupp, D.W. 239, 247, 258, 282, 284
Rutkowski, B. 274
Rykwert, J. 231

Saghié, M. 59
Sahlins, M.D. 83, 173
Salmon, E.T. 237
Santerre, H. Gallet de 274
Sass, B. 117, 120, 122
Savage, S.H. 17, 20, 69, 131
Sayre, E.V. 52
Schartz, G.M. 21
Schortman, E.M. 52, 66
Schulderrein, J. 132, 136
Schwartz, G.M. 51, 52, 57, 63-65
Sebbane, M. 87
Seger, J.D. 158
Seitz, C.R. 194
Sertok, K. 52
Service, E.R. 52, 87, 172, 173, 175,
    181
Sethe, K. 211, 216, 217
Shaw, M.C. 272
Shear, T.L. Jr 238
Shennan, S. 82, 83
Shiloh, Y. 137, 158, 160, 168, 184,
    194
Skalnik, P. 173
Smelik, K.A.D. 138, 139
Smith, C.A. 240
Smith, R.B. 204
Smith, R.H. 101, 103-105, 110

Smith, W.S. 223
Snell, D.C. 67
Snodgrass, A.M. 105
Soles, J.S. 267
Spiegel-Roy, P. 94
Stadelmann, R. 223, 229
Stager, L.E. 92, 94, 106, 109, 111, 185
Stambaugh, J.E. 238, 258
Stange, G. le 52
Stanley, R.S. 68
Stech, T. 101, 103-105, 107, 110, 111
Stech-Wheeler, T. 100, 103, 110
Stein, G. 51, 52, 62
Steinbrenner, L. 26
Steindorff, G. 214
Stone, E.C. 17, 28, 31
Sweet, R.F.G. 280

Tainter, J.A. 172-74
Tapper, R. 173
Taylor, T. 101, 104, 110, 111
Thalmann, J.-P. 50
Thirgood, J.V. 107
Thomas, R. 195
Thompson, H.O. 146, 156
Thompson, T.L. 175-78, 182, 185,
    187, 188, 201
Timm, S. 122, 132
Tiré, C. 274
Torrence, R. 84
Tosi, M. 82-84
Trigger, B. 210, 212
Trümpelmann, L. 66
Tsipopoulou, M. 267, 272, 275, 280,
    281
Tushingham, A.D. 136, 139
Tylecote, R.F. 102, 103
Tzedakis, I. 274

Ucko, P.J. 50
Uehlinger, C. 118, 120
Uphill, E. 224, 226, 227, 229, 232
Ussishkin, D. 158, 185

Valbelle, D. 50, 211, 217
Vandiver, P.B. 52
Venieri, Y. 274
Vercoutter, J. 214

Voannäs, F. 52
Voutsaki, S. 274

Wahida, G. 25
el-Wailly, F. 22, 25, 26
Waldbaum, J.C. 99, 105, 106
Ward, W.A. 103
Ward-Perkins, J.B. 238
Watson, P.J. 67
Watson, S. 279, 284
Wattenmaker, P. 62, 63
Webb, M.C. 52, 173
Weinstein, J.M. 109
Weippert, H. 179, 184
Weisberger, G. 87
Weiss, H. 51, 52, 63-65, 67
Wenke, R. 210
Wente, E. 217
Wertime, T.A. 100-102, 106, 110
Wesemael, B. van 212
Westendorf, W. 212, 217
Wheatley, P. 131, 231
Wheeler, T. 100, 103, 105
Whitelam, K.W. 173, 175-78, 187
Whiting, R. 51, 52
Wilentz, S. 231
Wilkinson, T.J. 51
Williamson, H.G.M. 199
Wilson, J.A. 210, 221
Wimmer, D. 158, 168
Winnett, F.V. 137, 158
Worschech, U. 132, 135, 136
Wright, H.T. 17, 69, 96, 100, 107, 158,
    173, 176

Yekutieli, Y. 85
Yener, K.A. 52
Yoffee, N. 43, 52, 67, 213
Younker, R.W. 109, 132, 138, 146, 156

Zaccagnini, C. 82
Zagarell, A. 67
Zayadine, F. 137
Zeder, M.A. 67, 69
Zertal, A. 152
Zimmerman, F. 124
Zohary, D. 94
Zorn, J.R. 194, 195, 203

JOURNAL FOR THE STUDY OF THE OLD TESTAMENT
SUPPLEMENT SERIES

102 M. Goulder, *The Prayers of David (Psalms 51–72): Studies in the Psalter, II*

103 B.G. Wood, *The Sociology of Pottery in Ancient Palestine: The Ceramic Industry and the Diffusion of Ceramic Style in the Bronze and Iron Ages*

104 P.R. Raabe, *Psalm Structures: A Study of Psalms with Refrains*

105 P. Bovati, *Re-Establishing Justice: Legal Terms, Concepts and Procedures in the Hebrew Bible*

106 P.P. Jenson, *Graded Holiness: A Key to the Priestly Conception of the World*

107 C. van Houten, *The Alien in Israelite Law*

108 P.M. McNutt, *The Forging of Israel: Iron Technology, Symbolism and Tradition in Ancient Society*

109 D. Jamieson-Drake, *Scribes and Schools in Monarchic Judah: A Socio-Archaeological Approach*

110 N.P. Lemche, *The Canaanites and their Land: The Tradition of the Canaanites*

111 J.G. Taylor, *Yahweh and the Sun: The Biblical and Archaeological Evidence for Sun Worship in Ancient Israel*

112 L.G. Perdue, *Wisdom in Revolt: Metaphorical Theology in the Book of Job*

113 R. Westbrook, *Property and the Family in Biblical Law*

114 D. Cohn-Sherbok (ed.), *A Traditional Quest: Essays in Honour of Louis Jacobs*

115 V. Hurowitz, *I Have Built You an Exalted House: Temple Building in the Bible in Light of Mesopotamian and Northwest Semitic Writings*

116 D.M. Gunn (ed.), *Narrative and Novella in Samuel: Studies by Hugo Gressmann and Other Scholars, 1906–1923* (trans. D.E. Orton)

117 P.R. Davies (ed.), *Second Temple Studies. I. Persian Period*

118 R.J. Tournay, *Seeing and Hearing God with the Psalms: The Prophetic Liturgy of the Second Temple in Jerusalem*

119 D.J.A. Clines & T.C. Eskenazi (eds.), *Telling Queen Michal's Story: An Experiment in Comparative Interpretation*

120 R.H. Lowery, *The Reforming Kings: Cult and Society in First Temple Judah*

121 D.V. Edelman, *King Saul in the Historiography of Judah*

122 L. Alexander (ed.), *Images of Empire*

123 E. Bloch-Smith, *Judahite Burial Practices and Beliefs about the Dead*

124 B. Halpern & D.W. Hobson (eds.), *Law and Ideology in Monarchic Israel*

125 G.A. Anderson & S.M. Olyan (eds.), *Priesthood and Cult in Ancient Israel*

126 J.W. Rogerson, *W.M.L. de Wette, Founder of Modern Biblical Criticism: An Intellectual Biography*

127 D.V. Edelman (ed.), *The Fabric of History: Text, Artifact and Israel's Past*

128 T.P. McCreesh, *Biblical Sound and Sense: Poetic Sound Patterns in Proverbs 10–29*

129   Z. Stefanovic, *The Aramaic of Daniel in the Light of Old Aramaic*

130   M. Butterworth, *Structure and the Book of Zechariah*

131   L. Holden, *Forms of Deformity*

132   M.D. Carroll R., *Contexts for Amos: Prophetic Poetics in Latin American Perspective*

133   R. Syrén, *The Forsaken Firstborn: A Study of a Recurrent Motif in the Patriarchal Narratives*

134   G. Mitchell, *Together in the Land: A Reading of the Book of Joshua*

135   G.F. Davies, *Israel in Egypt: Reading Exodus 1–2*

136   P. Morris & D. Sawyer (eds.), *A Walk in the Garden: Biblical, Iconographical and Literary Images of Eden*

137   H.G. Reventlow & Y. Hoffman (eds.), *Justice and Righteousness: Biblical Themes and their Influence*

138   R.P. Carroll (ed.), *Text as Pretext: Essays in Honour of Robert Davidson*

139   J.W. Watts, *Psalm and Story: Inset Hymns in Hebrew Narrative*

140   W. Houston, *Purity and Monotheism: Clean and Unclean Animals in Biblical Law*

141   G.C. Chirichigno, *Debt-Slavery in Israel and the Ancient Near East*

142   F.H. Cryer, *Divination in Ancient Israel and its Near Eastern Environment: A Socio-Historical Investigation*

143   D.J.A. Clines & J.C. Exum (eds.), *The New Literary Criticism and the Hebrew Bible*

144   P.R. Davies & D.J.A. Clines (eds.), *Language, Imagery and Structure in the Prophetic Writings*

145   C.S. Shaw, *The Speeches of Micah: A Rhetorical-Historical Analysis*

146   G.W. Ahlström, *The History of Ancient Palestine from the Palaeolithic Period to Alexander's Conquest* (ed. D. Edelman, with a contribution by G.O. Rollefson)

147   T.W. Cartledge, *Vows in the Hebrew Bible and the Ancient Near East*

148   P.R. Davies, *In Search of 'Ancient Israel'*

149   E. Ulrich, J.W. Wright, R.P. Carroll & P.R. Davies (eds.), *Priests, Prophets and Scribes: Essays on the Formation and Heritage of Second Temple Judaism in Honour of Joseph Blenkinsopp*

150   J.E. Tollington, *Tradition and Innovation in Haggai and Zechariah 1–8*

151   J.P. Weinberg, *The Citizen-Temple Community*

152   A.G. Auld (ed.), *Understanding Poets and Prophets: Essays in Honour of George Wishart Anderson*

153   D.K. Berry, *The Psalms and their Readers: Interpretive Strategies for Psalm 18*

154   M. Brettler & M. Fishbane (eds.), *Minhah le-Nahum: Biblical and Other Studies Presented to Nahum M. Sarna in Honour of his 70th Birthday*

155   J.A. Fager, *Land Tenure and the Biblical Jubilee: Uncovering Hebrew Ethics through the Sociology of Knowledge*

156   J.W. Kleinig, *The Lord's Song: The Basis, Function and Significance of Choral Music in Chronicles*

157   G.R. Clark, *The Word Ḥesed in the Hebrew Bible*

158   M. Douglas, *In the Wilderness: The Doctrine of Defilement in the Book of Numbers*

159   J.C. McCann (ed.), *The Shape and Shaping of the Psalter*

160   W. Riley, *King and Cultus in Chronicles: Worship and the Reinterpretation of History*

161   G.W. Coats, *The Moses Tradition*

162   H.A. McKay & D.J.A. Clines (eds.), *Of Prophet's Visions and the Wisdom of Sages: Essays in Honour of R. Norman Whybray on his Seventieth Birthday*

163   J.C. Exum, *Fragmented Women: Feminist (Sub)versions of Biblical Narratives*

164   L. Eslinger, *House of God or House of David: The Rhetoric of 2 Samuel 7*

166   D.R.G. Beattie & M.J. McNamara (eds.), *The Aramaic Bible: Targums in their Historical Context*

167   R.F. Person, *Second Zechariah and the Deuteronomic School*

168   R.N. Whybray, *The Composition of the Book of Proverbs*

169   B. Dicou, *Edom, Israel's Brother and Antagonist: The Role of Edom in Biblical Prophecy and Story*

170   W.G.E. Watson, *Traditional Techniques in Classical Hebrew Verse*

171   H.G. Reventlow, Y. Hoffman & B. Uffenheimer (eds.), *Politics and Theopolitics in the Bible and Postbiblical Literature*

172   V. Fritz, *An Introduction to Biblical Archaeology*

173   M.P. Graham, W.P. Brown & J.K. Kuan (eds.), *History and Interpretation: Essays in Honour of John H. Hayes*

174   J.M. Sprinkle, *'The Book of the Covenant': A Literary Approach*

175   T.C. Eskenazi & K.H. Richards (eds.), *Second Temple Studies. II. Temple and Community in the Persian Period*

176   G. Brin, *Studies in Biblical Law: From the Hebrew Bible to the Dead Sea Scrolls*

177   D.A. Dawson, *Text-Linguistics and Biblical Hebrew*

178   M.R. Hauge, *Between Sheol and Temple: Motif Structure and Function in the I-Psalms*

179   J.G. McConville & J.G. Millar, *Time and Place in Deuteronomy*

180   R. Schultz, *The Search for Quotation: Verbal Parallels in the Prophets*

181   B.M. Levinson (ed.), *Theory and Method in Biblical and Cuneiform Law: Revision, Interpolation and Development*

182   S.L. McKenzie & M.P. Graham (eds.), *The History of Israel's Traditions: The Heritage of Martin Noth*

183   J. Day (ed.), *Lectures on the Religion of the Semites (Second and Third Series) by William Robertson Smith*

184   J.C. Reeves & J. Kampen (eds.), *Pursuing the Text: Studies in Honour of Ben Zion Wacholder on the Occasion of his Seventieth Birthday*

185   S.D. Kunin, *The Logic of Incest: A Structuralist Analysis of Hebrew Mythology*

186   L. Day, *Three Faces of a Queen: Characterization in the Books of Esther*

187   C.V. Dorothy, *The Books of Esther: Structure, Genre and Textual Integrity*

188   R.H. O'Connell, *Concentricity and Continuity: The Literary Structure of Isaiah*

189   W. Johnstone (ed.), *William Robertson Smith: Essays in Reassessment*

190   S.W. Holloway & L.K. Handy (eds.), *The Pitcher is Broken: Memorial Essays for Gösta W. Ahlström*

191   M. Sæbø, *On the Way to Canon: Creative Tradition History in the Old Testament*

192   H.G. Reventlow & W. Farmer (eds.), *Biblical Studies and the Shifting of Paradigms, 1850–1914*

193   B. Schramm, *The Opponents of Third Isaiah: Reconstructing the Cultic History of the Restoration*

194   E.K. Holt, *Prophesying the Past: The Use of Israel's History in the Book of Hosea*

195   J. Davies, G. Harvey & W.G.E. Watson (eds.), *Words Remembered, Texts Renewed: Essays in Honour of John F.A. Sawyer*

196   J.S. Kaminsky, *Corporate Responsibility in the Hebrew Bible*

197   W.M. Schniedewind, *The Word of God in Transition: From Prophet to Exegete in the Second Temple Period*

198   T.J. Meadowcroft, *Aramaic Daniel and Greek Daniel: A Literary Comparison*

199   J.H. Eaton, *Psalms of the Way and the Kingdom: A Conference with the Commentators*

200   M.D. Carroll R., D.J.A. Clines & P.R. Davies (eds.), *The Bible in Human Society: Essays in Honour of John Rogerson*

201   J.W. Rogerson, *The Bible and Criticism in Victorian Britain: Profiles of F.D. Maurice and William Robertson Smith*

202   N. Stahl, *Law and Liminality in the Bible*

203   J.M. Munro, *Spikenard and Saffron: The Imagery of the Song of Songs*

204   P.R. Davies, *Whose Bible Is It Anyway?*

205   D.J.A. Clines, *Interested Parties: The Ideology of Writers and Readers of the Hebrew Bible*

206   M. Müller, *The First Bible of the Church: A Plea for the Septuagint*

207   J.W. Rogerson, M. Davies & M.D. Carroll R. (eds.), *The Bible in Ethics: The Second Sheffield Colloquium*

208   B.J. Stratton, *Out of Eden: Reading, Rhetoric, and Ideology in Genesis 2–3*

209   P. Dutcher-Walls, *Narrative Art, Political Rhetoric: The Case of Athaliah and Joash*

210   J. Berlinerblau, *The Vow and the 'Popular Religious Groups' of Ancient Israel: A Philological and Sociological Inquiry*

211   B.E. Kelly, *Retribution and Eschatology in Chronicles*

212   Y. Sherwood, *The Prostitute and the Prophet: Hosea's Marriage in Literary-Theoretical Perspective*

213   Y.A. Hoffman, *A Blemished Perfection: The Book of Job in Context*

214   R.F. Melugin & M.A. Sweeney (eds.), *New Visions of Isaiah*

215   J.C. Exum, *Plotted, Shot and Painted: Cultural Representations of Biblical Women*

216   J.E. McKinlay, *Gendering Wisdom the Host: Biblical Invitations to Eat and Drink*

217   J.F.D. Creach, *Yahweh as Refuge and the Editing of the Hebrew Psalter*

218   G. Glazov, *The Bridling of the Tongue and the Opening of the Mouth in Biblical Prophecy*

219   G. Morris, *Prophecy, Poetry and Hosea*

220   R.F. Person, Jr, *In Conversation with Jonah: Conversation Analysis, Literary Criticism, and the Book of Jonah*

221   G. Keys, *The Wages of Sin: A Reappraisal of the 'Succession Narrative'*

222   R.N. Whybray, *Reading the Psalms as a Book*

223   S.B. Noegel, *Janus Parallelism in the Book of Job*

224   P.J. Kissling, *Reliable Characters in the Primary History: Profiles of Moses, Joshua, Elijah and Elisha*

225   R.D. Weiss & D.M. Carr (eds.), *A Gift of God in Due Season: Essays on Scripture and Community in Honor of James A. Sanders*

226   L.L. Rowlett, *Joshua and the Rhetoric of Violence: A New Historicist Analysis*

227   J.F.A. Sawyer (ed.), *Reading Leviticus: Responses to Mary Douglas*

228   V. Fritz and P.R. Davies (eds.), *The Origins of the Ancient Israelite States*

229   S.B. Reid (ed.), *Prophets and Paradigms: Essays in Honor of Gene M. Tucker*

230   K.J. Cathcart and M.J. Maher (eds.), *Targumic and Cognate Studies: Essays in Honour of Martin McNamara*

231   W.W. Fields, *Sodom and Gomorrah: History and Motif in Biblical Narrative*

232   T. Binger, *Asherah: Goddesses in Ugarit, Israel and the Old Testament*

233   M.D. Goulder, *The Psalms of Asaph and the Pentateuch: Studies in the Psalter, III*

234   K. Stone, *Sex, Honor, and Power in the Deuteronomistic History*

235   J.W. Watts and P.R. House (eds.), *Forming Prophetic Literature: Essays on Isaiah and the Twelve in Honor of John D.W. Watts*

236   T.M. Bolin, *Freedom beyond Forgiveness: The Book of Jonah Re-Examined*

237   N.A. Silberman and D. Small (eds.), *The Archaeology of Israel: Constructing the Past, Interpreting the Present*

238   M.P. Graham, K.G. Hoglund and S.L. McKenzie (eds.), *The Chronicler as Historian*

239   M.S. Smith, *The Pilgrimage Pattern in Exodus* (with contributions by Elizabeth M. Bloch-Smith)

240   E.E. Carpenter (ed.), *A Biblical Itinerary: In Search of Method, Form and Content. Essays in Honor of George W. Coats*

241   R.K. Gnuse, *No Other Gods: Emergent Monotheism in Israel*

242   K.L. Noll, *The Faces of David*

243   H.G. Reventlow, *Eschatology in the Bible and in Jewish and Christian Tradition*

244   W.E. Aufrecht, N.A. Mirau & S.W. Gauley (eds.), *Aspects of Urbanism in Antiquity: From Mesopotamia to Crete*